高等学校本科英语教改新教材

文学里的生态
——英美生态文学赏读
（第二版）

南宫梅芳 ◇主编
韩启群 吴俊龙 ◇副主编
罗 灿 魏 文 朱红梅 武田田 ◇编 者

ECOLOGY IN LITERATURE
Selected Readings of British and
American Eco-Literature

北京大学出版社
PEKING UNIVERSITY PRESS

图书在版编目(CIP)数据

文学里的生态：英美生态文学赏读 / 南宫梅芳主编 . 2 版 . -- 北京：北京大学出版社，2025.1. -- （高等学校本科英语教改新教材）. -- ISBN 978-7-301-35614-2

Ⅰ. H319.39

中国国家版本馆 CIP 数据核字第 2024BS1543 号

书　　名	文学里的生态——英美生态文学赏读（第二版） WENXUE LI DE SHENGTAI——YINGMEI SHENGTAI WENXUE SHANGDU（DI-ER BAN）
著作责任者	南宫梅芳　主编
责任编辑	李　颖
标准书号	ISBN 978-7-301-35614-2
出版发行	北京大学出版社
地　　址	北京市海淀区成府路 205 号　100871
网　　址	http://www.pup.cn　新浪官方微博：@北京大学出版社
电子邮箱	编辑部 pupwaiwen@pup.cn　总编室 zpup@pup.cn
电　　话	邮购部 010-62752015　发行部 010-62750672　编辑部 010-62754382
印　刷　者	河北博文科技印务有限公司
经　销　者	新华书店
	787 毫米 ×1092 毫米　16 开本　15 印张　499 千字 2015 年 8 月第 1 版 2025 年 1 月第 2 版　2025 年 1 月第 1 次印刷
定　　价	69.00 元

未经许可，不得以任何方式复制或抄袭本书之部分或全部内容。
版权所有，侵权必究
举报电话：010-62752024　电子邮箱：fd@pup.cn
图书如有印装质量问题，请与出版部联系，电话：010-62756370

第二版前言

21世纪是生态文明的世纪。面对日益严峻的环境问题，党的二十大报告站在人与自然和谐共生的高度谋划发展，提出要增强人民群众的获得感、幸福感、安全感，最终实现人类与大自然的共赢。这一规划承载着厚重的中国天人合一文化底蕴及丰富的人与自然相处之道。

中国文学自古以来赞美自然，崇尚顺其自然，表现出向内寻求、内外兼修的追求。英美文学则受西方传统二元论的影响，体现出较强的人与自然相对立的倾向。21世纪以来，全球生态文学和生态批评在关切环境危机、消解二元论、强调自然与人交互、和谐相处的进路上迅猛发展。气候、能源、海洋、生物灭绝、人工智能等问题也越来越成为文学创作、文学研究、理论发展的热点主题。同时，生态批评在其发展过程中也不断借鉴人类世、新物质主义和后人类主义等概念和学术思潮，激发出若干新的理论和研究增长点，研究内涵更加丰富，视野更为开阔。

本版立足生态文学和生态批评发展史，在内容上立足生态文学和生态批评发展前沿，新增第五编"反思自然——21世纪英美生态文学"，增补了6位作家，通过相关作家作品的选读和导读，以文本为出发点，介绍相关生态批评的理论，以期读者在生态思想发展史的宏观视野中深入思考当代问题。同时，为了适应教学研究需要，更新全书推荐阅读书目，供教学和研究参考。

本教材自第一版出版以来备受读者关爱，并在北京林业大学的支持下，录制和建设了"英美文学里的生态"慕课（已在中国大学慕课平台上线）。第二版的修订和撰写再次得到了外语学院领导和老师，尤其是史宝辉教授的鼎力支持，在此一并致谢。同时，第二版邀请了兄弟院校专家学者的参与，编者阵容更加强大。我们在选材、新编和修订的过程中倾注了很多心血，以此答谢各位读者的厚爱，也敬请批评指正。

南宫梅芳
2023年7月

第一版前言

像其他人文学科一样,文学致力于回答人类存在的基本问题,生态文学则更专注于讨论人与自然的关系,将人与自然的关系作为人类认识自身的一个重要参照。人类既是大自然的一分子,又似乎常常超然于大自然之外。所以在研究人与自然的关系之前,我们首先要回答一些问题:大自然是什么?它是隐忍的大地母亲,还是没有思考能力的草木虫鱼?是人类赖以生存的环境和伙伴,还是会出其不意给人类带来灾难的神秘力量?人类与其他生命之间的关系是一个有着等级区分的金字塔,还是一个互相牵制、众生平等的生命圈?这些都是我们进行生态批评,研究生态文学的过程中常常会遇到的问题。

那么什么是生态批评?什么是生态文学?简单来说,生态文学是一种反映生态环境与人类社会发展的关系的文学。"ecology"(生态)一词第一次在英文中出现是在 1873 年[①],"生态批评"一词第一次在英文中出现已经到了 1978 年[②],但真正意义上的生态批评则出现在将近二十年后,于 20 世纪 90 年代开始逐渐萌芽并蓬勃发展起来。美国学者彻丽尔·格罗特费尔蒂(Cheryll Glotfelty)在 1996 年出版的《生态批评读本》(*The Ecocriticism Reader*)一书的序言中提到,生态批评是"对文学及其周围世界关系的研究"(the study of the relationship between literature and the physical world)[③]。这个说法大大扩展了以往文学批评的圈子,将文学批评从性别研究、心理批评、社会伦理等纯粹的人文语境中解放出来,将环境语境作为文学研究的一个新领域。我国较早关注生态文学的厦门大学中文系教授王诺先生提出,"生态文学是以生态整体主义为思想基础,以生态系统整体利益为最高价值的考察和表现自然与人之关系和探寻生态危机之社会根源的文学。生态责任、文明批判、生态理想和生态预警是其突出特点"[④]。

那么,如何对传统文学进行生态批评?如何具体进行生态文学研究?20 世纪以来文学理论的蓬勃发展为文学批评和研究打开了更加宽广的领域和多元化的视角,而从生态的角度出发研究人与自然的关系更进一步拓展了文学批评的视野。生态文学和生态批评的发展几乎与全球化的快速发展并行,关注生态问题的专家学者从各个领域、各个角度、各个层面对生态文学进行探讨和研究,所以生态文学和生态批评从一开始就具有多角度、多层面的跨学科特点,它与西方马克思主义相结合,从经济、社会、文化的角度对生态文学中的问题进行反思;它与心理分析的阐释方法相结合,对生态文学中所反映的人与自然的关系进行深层心理分析;它与女性主义相结合,将女性与自然在自然和社会中的不平等地位结合起来,挖掘女性与自然受压迫的深层社会和文化根源……当然,无论是对生态文学史的挖掘、具体作家作品的思想探寻,还是生态文学文本的分析阐述,究其根本还是回答自然是什么,人类社会

---

① White, Lynn. "The Historical Roots of Our Ecological Crisis." *JASA*. 21 (June 1969): 42—47.
② 美国批评家威廉·鲁克尔特(William Rueckert)在其撰写的一篇评论文章《文学和生态学:生态批评的实验》中提到了生态批评一词。
③ Glotfelty, Cheryll and Harold Fromm, *The Ecocriticism Reader*. The University of Georgia Press, 1996: xviii.
④ 王诺:《欧美生态文学》,北京大学出版社,2003 年,第 11 页。

与非人类社会的相互关系怎样,人与自然的关系与历史、文化、种族、阶级等之间的关系怎样这些问题。

当代著名文学评论家艾布拉姆斯(M. H. Abrams)在《镜与灯——浪漫主义文论及批评传统》一书的第一章中列出了一个坐标,提出了文学批评的四个基本要素和角度,即世界、作品、作家和读者。笔者认为从生态批评的角度进行文学研究大体上也可以从上述四个维度进入,进而研究人与自然的关系:(1)研究某一生态文学作家的生态思想。文学作品中不仅蕴含着作家自身的人格和生活经历等,也反映了作家的生态思想和他试图揭示人与自然关系的创作思路。(2)研究生态文学作品与社会现实的关系。生态文学作品与其他文学作品一样,反映了一定的社会现实,也受到当时社会现实的影响和局限,对生态文学作品与社会现实之间关系的深层挖掘是了解生态危机产生根源的途径之一。(3)研究生态文学作品本身的特殊性。生态文学作品具有自己特殊的主题、叙事手法、语言特色等,在细读的基础上对生态文学作品的文本进行研究,可以挖掘其如何有效地利用语言和叙事来反映生态现状,揭露生态问题,表达生态思想。(4)研究读者对生态文学的接受。文学对读者的影响力是毋庸置疑的,生态文学在揭露生态问题,警醒读者反思生态危机方面也起着不可替代的作用。同时,读者的接受对于生态文学的创作也有着能动的影响力,一部成功的生态文学作品一定有着与读者的互动。

除此之外,生态文学和生态批评与传统文学批评相比具有明显的跨学科性。生态文学和生态批评的出现回答了我们在关切自然的基础上所提出的生态需要和生态危机等相关问题,它是我们对自然环境的人文解读。同时,人类对于自然世界理解的深度和广度与自然科学的发展息息相关。生态文学作家中不乏研究生物、海洋、森林等自然环境的科学家。生态文学和生态批评的出现,也许会是一个将自然和人文领域的研究成果相融合的契机。

在这部《文学里的生态——英美生态文学赏读》中,我们首先追溯了英美文学的源头——古希腊罗马文化和《圣经》文学,从那里找寻生态文化的萌芽。接着从生态批评的视角重新阅读了英美文学中关于探讨人与自然关系的经典文本,最后呈现的是在生态批评影响下产生的当代英美文学的佳作。

英美文学作品中呈现出的人类对大自然的态度是一个渐进的过程,人类与大自然的关系具有伴随着悲欢的复杂传统。在古希腊罗马文学中,人类面对大自然,崇拜之心油然而生:大自然赋予了人休养生息的场所,也是人类探索宇宙和生存奥秘的出发点,在古代人类看来,与其说掌管宇宙的是神,不如说是大自然的神秘力量。春夏秋冬、草木山河都有着像神祇一样难以理解的生命力和控制力,是人类命运的主宰。在神和大自然的面前,人类不敢僭越,即便如俄狄浦斯王这样的伟大人物也难逃命运和神秘力量的安排。

在中世纪英美文学中,基督教的影响将人从对自然力的膜拜中解脱出来,人不再纠缠于不可知的自然神,而是将自己的命运托付给了唯一一位全知全能的主。在漫长的中世纪,人的痛苦不再来自与大自然邪恶力量的对抗,而是如何才能使自己更加完美,以图在天堂与基督相遇。《圣经》的创世神话大大提高了人的地位,人不再是要屈从于诸神所代言的自然力的最卑微最弱势的群体,而是上帝按照自己的形象所创造的最完美的造物,为神管理这地的管家。

从文艺复兴以来一直到启蒙时代的英美文学中我们可以看出,随着科学技术的突飞猛进,人的自信不仅因为与上帝形似而提升,而且因为具有像神一样的思辨能力而膨胀。人是"宇宙的精华、万物的灵长",大自然则成为被控制和被利用的他者。但即便在这样的人类中心主义的洪流中,依然有不少的写作在探讨如何维系人与自然关系的平衡,从而寻求生命的真谛。

浪漫主义诗人是伟大的,他们不仅让普通人和普通事件登上文学的大雅之堂,成为浪漫主义诗歌的主角,而且对人与自然的关系给予了最深切的关注。他们医治时代的良药是接近自然:越接近自然,就越接近上帝,越能达到神、人、自然的完美状态。或许可以说,在19世纪的经典文学作品中,浪漫是主旋律,这个主旋律不仅存在于浪漫主义诗歌,也存在于很多现实主义小说之中。在这些作品中,自然是一片净土,是那些敏锐的思想家们逃离喧嚣纷扰的人的社会,忘却人类文明高速发展所带来的诸多问题的地方,是诗人和小说家们休憩心灵的港湾。

20世纪科学技术的大发展使人类越来越远离对自然、神和生命的原初的敬畏,以致最终滑进人类中心主义的窠臼,成为导致环境危机的主因。亚里士多德在《诗学》第九章中说"历史记录的是已经发生的事情,而艺术(文学)描述的是将要发生的事情",也就是说,文学具有预言甚至创造的力量。这一力量尤其见于《寂静的春天》。1962年,蕾切尔·卡森(Rachel Carson)的一部《寂静的春天》(*Silent Spring*)拉开了现代生态文学发展的序幕。开篇第一句先把我们带回往昔美好的繁荣的农场、成林的果园、云朵般的繁花、绿色的原野——"从前,在美国中部有一个城镇,这里的一切生物看来与其周围环境生活得很和谐。"然而"有一天,第一批居民来到这儿建房舍、挖井筑仓,情况发生了变化"①。生态危机的矛头直指人类。卡森的作品犹如一记惊雷,不但促动政府采取行动保护环境,也引发现当代更多有识之士的思考与行动。20世纪60年代以来,致力于揭示生态现实的文学作品越来越多。作家们对自然的探索、研究的角度和层面趋向多元化,自然不仅局限于静态的、供人休养生息的草木山水,还包括与人类密切相关的各种动物,复杂生动的生态系统成为真正意义上的"大自然"。保护环境不仅是保护山川草木,也要关注动物的生存和权利。自然不是人类的主人,也不是人类的敌人,而是手足挚友,是人类文明发展的见证。

最后,本书既然主要定位为教材,还要谈谈教材的使用。如前所述,英美生态文学作为英语文学中的一个现象,贯穿在英美文学史中,本教材的特点是选读与文学史相结合,让读者既能对生态文学的发展演变有一个历时性认识,同时又注重对具体文本的阅读、分析和阐释。从教学角度上说,我们不希望把它上成"精读课"或"泛读课",而是要带领学生去思考,锻炼学生的思辨能力,因此,这门课程是一个以内容型(content-based)教学为主,兼顾语言技能培养的课程,即通过对生态文学作品的学习,启迪学生关于人类与自然、社会与生态、文明与环境问题的思考,同时通过听课、阅读、思考、研究、口述、讨论、写作等活动进行全方位的语言能力训练。

这类课程一般是32学时,而教材中的内容共有28篇选读,平均每学时要上完1篇选读,如果按传统的精讲办法进行教学显然是不可能完成的任务。因此,教师可以采取重点讲部分选文,由学生自己完成其他选文的办法,可以通过微课、视频课等新技术手段加强学生的课外学习,也可以尝试小组项目、课堂演示、翻转课堂等新的教育理念和教学方法,以期达到最佳教学效果。

---

① Carson, Rachel. *Silent Spring*. Houghton Mifflin Company, 1962. 译文采用吕瑞兰、李长生译《寂静的春天》,上海译文出版社,2008年。

不论采用何种教学方法,都可以从以下两个维度使用本教材:

1. 理解英美生态文学发展史。采用文学史教学的方式,按照教材的编写顺序为学生讲解和分析英美生态文学从古代到现代的发展脉络,让学生感受英美文学所表现出的有关人与自然关系的变迁。本教材共分为四编,从古代开始,经过近现代,最后落于当代。在每一编开头都有对相应历史时期英、美文学中所体现的生态思想的概述,使读者对该历史时期的自然或生态文学先有一个提纲挈领的感受。在此基础上,为了更深入地了解该历史时期的文学所反映的生态观,教师可以从每一时期的作家作品中选取有代表性的进行阅读和分析,结合对思考题的讨论让学生通过具体作家作品观照生态文学的发展,得到更加具体和深入的认识,实现对英美生态文学史以面带点、由点及面的理解。

2. 作家作品中的生态思想分析。侧重文学作品分析,教师可以从教材中选取有代表性的作家作品进行讲解。由于本教材的编写基本按照历时的框架,对英美文学史已经有所了解的同学可直接进入作家作品,先阅读选篇,选篇后有"注释"帮助读者克服语言和文化障碍;细读作品后可以尝试回答选篇后所给出的思考题。在思考题的设计上,我们是将具体细节题与主题大意题目相结合,既通过细节类题目帮助读者理解语言层面的含义,又通过主题大意类题目引导读者思考文本所反映的深层的生态意义。之后,学生可以阅读"作品导读"和"背景介绍"部分,对自己的理解和阐释或印证,或补充。最后,对相关作家作品感兴趣的同学还可以参考"推荐阅读"部分的参考书目进行扩展阅读和研究。

在生态危机日趋严峻的情况下,国内外进入生态文学领域的学者不断增加,为本科生和研究生开设生态文学课程的学校也越来越多,这部《文学里的生态》正是为了适应这一需要应运而生的。本教材虽无法将英美文学中的所有生态元素一一呈现,将所有的生态文学作家一一介绍,但是希望尽力帮助读者在赏读生态文学作品的过程中回顾和反思英美文学中所呈现的人与自然关系的传统,理解当代生态文学的风貌,思考人类当下所面临的生态问题。考虑到生态文学选读不仅可以在英语系开设,也可以供其他专业的学生选修课之用,或供英美文学爱好者赏读和学习,这部教材除选读外用中文编写,注释也尽量详尽,希望既能满足在校学生学习的需要,也可以成为英美文学和生态文学爱好者的读本。

南宫梅芳

2015 年 3 月

Preface

I have been working in the field of literature and environment—or "eco-literature"—for nearly thirty years, since entering a Ph. D. program at Brown University in the United States in 1984. Soon after I started working on my doctorate, I encountered in the Brown library a recently published collection of articles by the prominent American conservationist John Muir, one of the founders of the Sierra Club (the largest American environmental organization) and Yosemite National Park in California. I took this book titled *Wilderness Essays* home and immersed myself in Muir's ecstatic essays about hiking and climbing and observing wildlife in the rugged Sierra Nevada mountains, "the range of light," as he called it. Reading this book changed the way I thought about literature: It inspired me to begin thinking about the role of literature in helping human beings to explore and explain our relationship with the planet on which we live. It helped me to realize that there are beautiful pieces of writing by authors who may not (yet) belong to the ordinary "canon" of accepted writers, the writers whose works are regularly taught in literature departments at universities and included in formal examinations concerned with "classic works of the literary tradition." Muir's writing—in *Wilderness Essays* and other books—also helped me appreciate the powerful potential of environmental literature and other socially engaged modes of writing to have a real impact on important social change.

After spending so many years studying and teaching environmental literature by writers throughout the world, I started to have a slightly different view of the field. For many years, my goal was always to "expand the canon," to discover new authors whose works had not yet been folded into the official literary tradition. I wrote my Ph. D. thesis on canonical Henry David Thoreau and (at that time) non-canonical Annie Dillard, Edward Abbey, Wendell Berry, and Barry Lopez. I have for many years written articles and book chapters on a strange combination of canonical and non-canonical authors ranging from William Faulkner to Terry Tempest Williams, from Robinson Jeffers to Rick Bass. Recently, though, I have taken special pleasure in seeing how the field of "ecocriticism" (ecological literary criticism) has begun not only to reach out toward non-canonical authors and texts, but to turn back toward the canon, scrutinizing familiar works of great literature by writers such as William Shakespeare and Tao Yuanming from environmental perspectives (see, for instance, Professor Lu Shuyuan's 2012 book *The Specter of Tao Yuanming*). This new book, *Ecology in Literature: Selected Readings of British & American Eco-Literature*, offers a fascinating combination of traditional, canonical works of Western literature (going all the way back to The Holy Bible) and works by prominent "environmental writers" whose works may be familiar to ecocritics but not entirely familiar to all teachers of literature, despite the efforts by scholars like me to make Edward Abbey, Wendell Berry, Rachel Carson, Gary Snyder, and other writers like them routine subjects in literature classes. The effect of combining canonical and non-canonical literature in a book like this is, I think, to acknowledge the literary beauty and social importance of the environmental writers I've just mentioned, while also acknowledging the environmental relevance of writers such as Mary Shelley, Joseph Conrad, Emily Dickinson, and Kazuo Ishiguro. It is exciting and delightful for me to see the striking combination of writers included in this anthology.

The field of ecocriticism (the study of environmental implications in literature and other texts, including film and music) has expanded greatly in the past three decades. Much of this work has been encouraged by the organization called "The Association for the Study of Literature and Environment" (website: www.asle.org), which has members all over the world, including university students. China has become one of the world centers for ecocriticism (*shengtai piping*), publishing many important books and articles in the field every year, hosting significant international conferences, and giving students the opportunity to earn M.A. and Ph.D. degrees in English, Comparative Literature, and Chinese departments with a special focus on environmental literature, ecoaesthetic theory, and/or environmental literature. This field of study is both intellectually interesting and socially significant. If we (human beings) are going to work toward greater balance between our technological power and our ability to live in harmony with the planet, we must ask serious questions about who we are as a species, what we need in order to live meaningful lives, and what our responsibilities toward other species and toward future generations of human beings might be. Literature and other art forms help us to ask these fundamental questions about human nature and about our relationships with each other and with the more-than-human world. This anthology is an extremely useful tool in facilitating these crucial explorations.

Scott Slovic
Professor of Literature and Environment
University of Idaho, USA

目 录

第一编
认识自然——古代西方的生态观

背景介绍 ········· 1
忒奥克里托斯（Theocritus） ········· 3
维吉尔（Virgil） ········· 7

第二编
浪漫自然——生态视域中的英国经典文学

背景介绍 ········· 13
《贝奥武夫》（*Beowulf*） ········· 15
杰弗雷·乔叟（Geoffrey Chaucer） ········· 22
威廉·莎士比亚（William Shakespeare） ········· 31
约翰·弥尔顿（John Milton） ········· 47
玛丽·雪莱（Mary Shelley） ········· 55
威廉·华兹华斯（William Wordsworth） ········· 65
托马斯·哈代（Thomas Hardy） ········· 70
威廉·巴特勒·叶芝（William Butler Yeats） ········· 83

第三编
探索自然——生态视域中的美国经典文学

背景介绍 ········· 89
亨利·大卫·梭罗（Henry David Thoreau） ········· 91
拉尔夫·沃尔多·爱默生（Ralph Waldo Emerson） ········· 100
艾米莉·狄金森（Emily Dickinson） ········· 106
罗伯特·弗罗斯特（Robert Frost） ········· 111
杰克·伦敦（Jack London） ········· 117
薇拉·凯瑟（Willa Cather） ········· 124

第四编
融入自然——当代英美生态文学

背景介绍 131
蕾切尔·卡森(Rachel Carson) 135
奥尔多·利奥波德(Aldo Leopold) 143
爱德华·艾比(Edward Abbey) 148
加里·斯耐德(Gary Snyder) 152
温德尔·贝里(Wendell Berry) 159
多丽丝·莱辛(Doris Lessing) 166

第五编
反思自然——21世纪英美生态文学

背景介绍 173
罗伯特·麦克法兰(Robert Macfarlane) 177
伊恩·麦克尤恩(Ian McEwan) 183
石黑一雄(Kazuo Ishiguro) 197
杰夫·范德米尔(Jeff VanderMeer) 204
科马克·麦卡锡(Cormac McCarthy) 213
露易丝·格丽克(Louise Glück) 219

第一版后记 224

第一编　认识自然——古代西方的生态观

背景介绍

　　人类是大自然的一部分,而大自然是人类生存和发展不可或缺的外部环境。早在人类文明诞生以前的漫长岁月里,人类就和其他生物一样,从大自然获取资源来维系自身的生存和发展。当人类进入文明社会以后,在不同的文明阶段,对大自然也产生了不尽相同的认识。在古希腊古罗马文明时期,由于生产力水平和意识水平的局限,人类对大自然更多的是崇敬和敬畏。在古希腊古罗马文学作品中所体现出来的人类的自然观念中,虽然也有如荷马的《奥德赛》式的征服自然的豪情,但更多的则是对大自然力量的谦卑的歌颂,以及对回归古朴大自然的情怀的抒发。这两种思想感情在本章所选取的两位诗人忒奥克里托斯(Theocritus)和维吉尔(Virgil)的作品中有充分的体现。

　　在古代,人类对大自然的理解基本局限于宗教的角度,打雷、下雨、干旱、洪水等大自然现象都被人类用宗教的形式予以解读。因此人类文明中出现了神的形象,人们对诸神的崇拜其实就是对大自然的崇敬。人类的一切活动必须遵循一定的法则——自然规律,否则就会惹怒神灵,遭到惩罚。在维吉尔的作品《农事诗》中,诗人在每一章的开头都向和农业有关的神灵进行庄严的祷告。在维吉尔看来,人类的农业生产活动是一种和大自然的互动和交流,作物的播种、耕作、丰收的过程实际上是人类利用自然规律向大自然索取资源的过程。农作物的丰收实质上是大自然对人类的恩赐。人类应该对大自然怀有感恩和敬畏之情。人类绝对不是至高无上的,并不能为所欲为。这种对神(或者说自然规律)的敬畏和尊崇的思想与后世所膜拜的征服、改造、统治大自然的人类中心主义的思想形成了鲜明的对比。

　　当然,在古人眼中,大自然不仅仅是高高在上、喜怒无常的主宰者,它同时也是一种美好的精神寄托。在忒奥克里托斯的《田园诗》以及他后来的模仿者维吉尔的《牧歌》中,两位诗人都向读者展示了完全理想化的、远离现实的田园世界。在这个世界里,牧羊人放声歌唱,歌颂爱情和友情,过着恬静惬意的田园生活。但我们知道,这种世外桃源般的生活在现实中是不存在的,作品所表现的仅仅是诗人对现实的不满和对美好生活的向往;或者更准确地说,对"回归"大自然的向往。因为从人类发展的历程来看,人类本来就是来自丛林,起源于大自然的。但随着"文明"的产生和发展,人类逐渐脱离了大自然,建立起了属于自己的居住环境——城市。然而对现实生活的诸多不满又让人们对那种虚幻的、无忧无虑的生活充满了向往。此时,与城市文明生活相对的田园生活,便成了人们逃避现实的精神寄托。

忒奥克里托斯(Theocritus)

【作者简介】

忒奥克里托斯(前305?—前250),古希腊诗人,以田园诗闻名于世。后人对于他的了解大部分来源于他的代表作《田园诗》(*Idylls*)。他被认为是西方田园诗的创始人,因为他开创了一种新的诗歌模式,并成为后世诸如维吉尔等诗人的模仿对象。以下诗行节选自《田园诗》第十二篇。

XII

Art come, dear youth? Two days and nights away!
(Who burn with love, grow aged in a day.)
As much as apples sweet the damson[1] crude
Excel; the blooming spring the winter rude;
In fleece the sheep her lamb; the maiden in sweetness
The thrice-wed dame; the fawn the calf in fleetness;
The nightingale in song all feathered kind—
So much thy longed-for presence cheers my mind.
To thee I hasten, as to shady beech,
The traveller, when from the heaven's reach
The sun fierce blazes. May our love be strong,
To all hereafter times the theme of song!
Two men each other loved to that degree,
That either friend did in the other see
A dearer than himself. They loved of old
Both golden natures in an age of gold.

O father Zeus! Ageless immortals all!
Two hundred ages hence may one recall,
Down-coming to the irremeable[2] river,
This to my mind, and this good news deliver:
E'en now from east to west, from north to south,
Your mutual friendship lives in every mouth,
This, as they please, th' Olympians will decide:
Of thee, by blooming virtue beautified,

My glowing song shall only truth disclose;
With falsehood's pustules I'll not shame my nose.
If thou dost sometime grieve me, sweet the pleasure
Of reconcilement, joy in double measure
To find thou never didst intend the pain,
And feel myself from all doubt free again.

And ye Megarians[3], at Nesaea dwelling,
Expert at rowing, mariners excelling,
Be happy ever! For with honors due
Th' Athenian Diocles[4], to friendship true
Ye celebrate. With the first blush of spring
The youth surround his tomb; there who shall bring
The sweetest kiss. Whose lip is Purest found,

Back to his mother goes with garlands crowned.
Nice touch the arbiter must have indeed,
And must, methinks, the blue-eyed Ganymede[5]
Invoke with many prayers-a mouth to own
True to the touch of lips, as Lydian stone[6]
To proof of gold-which test will instant show
The pure or base as money changers know.

注释

1. damson：乌荆子李树，欧亚野李树。一种欧亚李树，因其果子可食用，远古时代就有人栽培，也作 bullace plum。

2. irremeable：(古)一去不复返的，无法恢复原状的。

3. Megarians：Megara(墨伽拉)是古希腊 Attica(阿提卡)地区的一座港口城市，该城市以出口羊毛以及其他动物及动物制品而闻名当时。古希腊著名的数学家和哲学家欧几里得(Euclid)就出生在这个地区。

4. Athenian Diocles：Diocles 是一个被流放到 Megara 的雅典人，在一次战斗中为了拯救自己的朋友而付出了生命。

5. Ganymede：在希腊神话中，Ganymede 来自特洛伊。在荷马的笔下，他是凡间最俊美的男子，宙斯曾变作一只鹰将他带到奥林匹亚山上。从此 Ganymede 成为众神的斟酒人，并获得永生。

6. Lydian stone：即 touchstone，试金石。Lydia 是古代小亚细亚地区的一个王国，滨临爱琴海，位于今天土耳其的西北部，以其富庶和极其宏伟的首都萨第斯著称，它可能是最早使用铸币的国家(公元前7世纪)。该地区盛产的碧玄岩质地坚硬，被古代人用来测试金银

的真伪,因此有了"Lydian stone"的说法。

作品导读

  忒奥克里托斯出生于意大利西西里岛,他的《田园诗》描写的也是西西里岛上牧羊人质朴的生活。但他的许多作品却并不是真正走到乡村里去创作的,而是诗人在埃及亚历山大的宫廷里写出来的。诗人用充满诗意的语言,向读者描绘了一个完全理想化的、远离现实的田园世界,在这个世界里,读者可以了解到牧羊人们的爱情故事,可以见证人们在唱山歌、辩论等丰富的活动中尽情享受生活的美好,感受到那种恬静和惬意。

  但必须指出的是,作品中的田园生活并不是现实生活的真实写照,因为在诗人生活的时代,西西里山区的生存条件是非常恶劣的,人们的生活也远没有诗歌中描绘的那么惬意和舒适。诗歌中的田园世界几乎完全是诗人凭想象虚构出来的。诗人通过对这种乌托邦式的田园风光和乡村生活的诗意的描绘,表达了一种对城市文明生活的厌恶和对大自然的向往;或者更准确地说,对"回归"大自然的向往。因为从人类发展的历程来看,人类本来就是来自丛林,起源于大自然的。但随着"文明"的产生和发展,人类逐渐脱离了大自然,建立起了属于自己的居住环境——城市。在诗人所处的公元前3世纪,埃及的亚历山大城已经有了高度的发展,城里人口众多,商业十分繁荣。然而伴随着文明的发展,城市生活的问题也日益显现。人类虽然在物质生活上较以往更加富足,但精神生活方面却没有出现相应的进步,反而出现了诸如贪婪、偷窃、杀戮等问题。因此人们逐渐对现实生活产生种种不满。此时,与城市文明生活相对的田园生活,便成了人们逃避现实的精神寄托。因此,也许诗人并不熟悉真正的乡村生活,但他依然用诗歌语言虚构了一个理想化的田园世界,以此寄托自己的精神理想。诗歌中西西里岛上的人们生活得非常恬静悠闲,并且精神生活十分丰富。这种世外桃源般的生活模式正是诗人所幻想和渴望的。诗人对田园生活的美化和向往与当代生态主义思想所倡导的回归大自然、融入大自然的简单的生活观有诸多相似。

思考题

1. What kind of natural environment does the poet try to represent in this poem?
2. What kind of rural life do people in the poem have?
3. How does the poet describe the friendship between the speaker and his young friend?

推荐阅读

  Bing, Peter. "Theocritus' Epigrams on the Statues of Ancient Poets." *Antike und Abendland*, 1988.

  Davies, Malcolm. "Theocritus' Adoniazusae." *Greece & Rome*, 1995.

Fantuzzi, Marco. "Mythological paradigms in the bucolic poetry of Theocritus." *The Cambridge Classical Journal*, 1996.

Gutzwiller, Kathryn J. *Theocritus' Pastoral Analogies: The Formation of a Genre*. University of Wisconsin Press, 1991.

Segal, Charles. "Landscape into Myth: Theocritus' Bucolic Poetry." *Ramus*, 1975.

Segal, Charles. *Poetry and Myth in Ancient Pastoral: Essays on Theocritus and Virgil*. Princeton University Press, 2014.

维吉尔(Virgil)

【作者简介】

维吉尔(前 70—前 19),古罗马最伟大的诗人。维吉尔早年住在曼图亚(Mantua)附近安第斯(Andes)一个小村的农庄里,父亲是个富足的农民,这使得维吉尔受到了良好的教育。他 17 岁时赴罗马,向当时最优秀的老师学习修辞学和哲学,著有长诗《牧歌》(*Eclogues*)、《农事诗》(*Georgics*),史诗《埃涅阿斯纪》(*The Aeneid*)等。

维吉尔最重要的作品是史诗《埃涅阿斯纪》。全诗 12 卷,1 万余行,叙述英雄埃涅阿斯(Aeneas)在特洛伊城被希腊军队攻陷后离开故土,历尽艰辛,到达意大利建立新的邦国的故事(其后代奥古斯都建立罗马),以当地部落首领图尔努斯与埃涅阿斯决斗被杀结束。史诗借用神话传说歌颂罗马帝国,歌颂奥古斯都统治的历史必然性。其情节结构模仿了荷马史诗,但具体描写有自己的特色。全诗情节生动,故事性强,语言凝练。《埃涅阿斯纪》是欧洲文学史上第一部个人创作的史诗,自问世到现在,一直受到很高评价。

维吉尔第一部公开发表的诗集《牧歌》共收诗 10 首。维吉尔的牧歌主要是虚构一些牧人的生活和爱情,通过对话或对唱,抒发田园之乐,有时也涉及一些政治问题。维吉尔的第二部作品《农事诗》,写于公元前 37 年至前 30 年间,共 4 卷,每卷分别叙述一个农业问题:种谷、园艺、畜牧和养蜂。

以下诗行选自《牧歌》第十首。

X Gallus

This now, the very latest of my toils,
Vouchsafe me, Arethusa[1]! Needs must I
Sing a brief song to Gallus—brief, but yet
Such as Lycoris' self may fitly read.
Who would not sing for Gallus? So, when thou   5
Beneath Sicilian billows glidest on,
May Doris[2] blend no bitter wave with thine,
Begin! The love of Gallus be our theme,
And the shrewd pangs he suffered, while, hard by,
The flat-nosed she-goats browse the tender brush.   10
We sing not to deaf ears; no word of ours
But the woods echo it. What groves or lawns
Held you, ye Dryad[3]-maidens, when for love—

Love all unworthy of a loss so dear—
Gallus lay dying? For neither did the slopes   15
Of Pindus[4] or Parnassus[4] stay you then,
No, nor Aonian Aganippe[5]. Him
Even the laurels and the tamarisks wept;
For him, outstretched beneath a lonely rock,
Wept pine-clad Maenalus[6], and the flinty crags   20
Of cold Lycaeus[6]. The sheep too stood around—
Of us they feel no shame, poet divine;
Nor of the flock be thou ashamed: even fair
Adonis[7] by the rivers fed his sheep—
Came shepherd too, and swine-herd footing slow,   25
And, from the winter-acorns dripping-wet
Menalcas[8]. All with one accord exclaim:
"From whence this love of thine?" Apollo came;
"Gallus, art mad?" he cried, "thy bosom's care
Another love is following." There withal   30
Silvanus[9] came, with rural honours crowned;
The flowering fennels and tall lilies shook
Before him. Yea, and our own eyes beheld
Pan[10], god of Arcady, with blood-red juice
Of the elder-berry, and with vermilion, dyed.   35
"Wilt ever make an end?" quoth he, "behold
Love recks not aught of it: his heart no more
With tears is sated than with streams the grass,
Bees with the cytisus, or goats with leaves."
"Yet will ye sing, Arcadians, of my woes   40
Upon your mountains," sadly he replied—
Arcadians, that alone have skill to sing.
O then how softly would my ashes rest,
If of my love, one day, your flutes should tell!
And would that I, of your own fellowship,   45
Or dresser of the ripening grape had been,
Or guardian of the flock! For surely then,
Let Phyllis, or Amyntas[11], or who else,
Bewitch me-what if swart Amyntas be?
Dark is the violet, dark the hyacinth—   50
Among the willows, 'neath the limber vine,
Reclining would my love have lain with me,
Phyllis plucked garlands, or Amyntas sung.

Here are cool springs, soft mead and grove, Lycoris;
Here might our lives with time have worn away. 55
But me mad love of the stern war-god holds
Armed amid weapons and opposing foes.
Whilst thou- Ah! Might I but believe it not! —
Alone without me, and from home afar,
Look Times new Romanst upon Alpine snows and frozen Rhine. 60
Ah! May the frost not hurt thee, may the sharp
And jagged ice not wound thy tender feet!
I will depart, re-tune the songs I framed
In verse Chalcidian[12] to the oaten reed
Of the Sicilian swain. Resolved am I 65
In the woods, rather, with wild beasts to couch,
And bear my doom, and character my love
Upon the tender tree-trunks: they will grow,
And you, my love, grow with them. And meanwhile
I with the Nymphs will haunt Mount Maenalus, 70
Or hunt the keen wild boar. No frost so cold
But I will hem with hounds thy forest-glades,
Parthenius[13]. Even now, methinks, I range
O'errocks, through echoing groves, and joy to launch
Cydonian arrows from a Parthian bow[14]. 75
As if my madness could find healing thus,
Or that god soften at a mortal's grief!
Now neither Hamadryads[15], no, nor songs
Delight me more: ye woods, away with you!
No pangs of ours can change him; not though we 80
In the mid-frost should drink of Hebrus' stream,
And in wet winters face Sithonian[16] snows,
Or, when the bark of the tall elm-tree bole
Of drought is dying, should, under Cancer's Sign,
In Aethiopian deserts[17] drive our flocks. 85
Love conquers all things; yield we too to love!
These songs, Pierian Maids[18], shall it suffice
Your poet to have sung, the while he sat,
And of slim mallow wove a basket fine:
To Gallus ye will magnify their worth, 90
Gallus, for whom my love grows hour by hour,
As the green alder shoots in early Spring.
Come, let us rise: the shade is wont to be

>Baneful to singers; baneful is the shade
>Cast by the juniper, crops sicken too
>In shade. Now homeward, having fed your fill—
>Eve's star is rising-go, my she-goats, go.

 注释

1. Arethusa:她起初是一位仙女。有一次在沐浴时被河神 Alpheus 看见,Alpheus 对她一见钟情,但是 Arethusa 却不为所动。在河神 Alpheus 不断追求下,Arethusa 最后变为了一股清泉,流向 Ortygia 岛。但 Alpheus 却紧紧地跟随她,让自己的河水和 Arethusa 的水混合在一起。

2. Doris:古希腊山区。

3. Dryad:古希腊神话中的树仙。她们通常非常害羞,除非是有猎神阿尔忒弥斯(Artemis)的陪伴。

4. Pindus or Parnassus:都是希腊的山区,在古希腊神话中这里是缪斯女神们(Muses)居住的地方。

5. Aonian Aganippe:缪斯女神们所居住的 Parnassus 山中的圣泉之一。

6. Maenalus, Lycaeus:这两个都是阿卡狄亚(Arcadia)地区的山名。

7. Adonis:在希腊神话中是一位俊美少年。爱神阿佛洛狄忒(Aphrodite)和冥后珀耳塞福涅(Persephone)同时爱上他。最后宙斯出面化解了两人为他而起的争端:Adonis 和每位女神各相处三分之一年的时间,剩下的三分之一年由他自己决定。最终他决定每年三分之二的时间都和 Aphrodite 在一起。

8. Menalcas:牧人的名字。

9. Silvanus:古罗马神话中的山林之神。

10. Pan:古希腊神话中的荒野、畜牧、狩猎之神。他的身世并不明确,有的神话说他是宙斯的儿子,而也有神话说他是酒神狄俄尼索斯(Dionysus)或赫尔墨斯(Hermes)的儿子。

11. Phyllis 和 Amyntas:女子名。

12. Chalcidian:出自 Chalcis 一词。卡尔刻(Chalcis)是希腊地名,诗人欧福里翁(Euphorion)就来自该地区。欧福里翁(前 275—?),古希腊诗人与语法学家。他的作品在希腊语文学世界和公元前 1 世纪卡图卢斯时期的古罗马诗人中产生了很大影响。他的著作包括以神话为主要内容的小型史诗、抨击诗、警句诗以及学术论文等。这里指伽鲁斯(Gallus)模仿欧福里翁的诗句。

13. Parthenius:阿卡狄亚地区的山名。

14. Cydonian arrows 和 Parthian bow:安息(Parthia)是古代伊朗高原上的大国,季当(Cydonia)位于克里特岛。Cydonian arrows 和 Parthian bow 的说法是因为这两个地方都因为盛产弓箭而出名。

15. Hamadryads:希腊神话中的树仙,她们是一种特殊的树仙(Dryad),与特定的树木共生共亡。

16. Hebrus' stream 和 Sithonian snows:Hebrus 和 Sithonia 都是北方的地名,诗中用

来指代严寒的地方。

17. Aethiopian deserts：Aethiopia 在非洲，是当时所知的最南部的地区，诗中指代的是酷热的地方。

18. Pierian Maids：Pieria 是古希腊神话中缪斯女神们的圣泉所在的地方，诗泉（Pierian Spring）被认为是激发人们音乐和诗歌创作灵感的圣泉。

 作品导读

　　维吉尔的《牧歌》大约问世于公元前 37 年，诗集的问世让维吉尔闻名全国。牧歌这种田园诗歌形式，能在后世繁盛发展起来，部分要归功于维吉尔，它通常是诗人对在理想化的自然环境中的牧羊人和其他农人的淳朴恬静生活的描述。维吉尔的《牧歌》是对古希腊诗人忒奥克里托斯所首创的田园诗歌的摹仿，但同时又形成了自己的风格。《牧歌》以阿卡狄亚（Arcadia）山区理想化的田园环境为背景，通过流畅而精美的语言描写了牧人们的生活。他们或在阳光下歌唱他们的欢乐，或通过对大自然的景物的描述来悲叹爱情和死亡所带来的不幸。很多诗歌也暗含诗人想要表达的政治主题，有很大的现实意义。

　　《牧歌》由十首诗歌组成，本书选录的是其中的第十首。这首诗中的伽鲁斯（Gallus）也是现实中的人物。他是罗马一位优秀的将军，同时也是一名出色的诗人。在安东尼于阿克提姆海战失败后，伽鲁斯担任了罗马共和国的埃及总督，但最终却在政治斗争中遭遇失败。在这首诗里，伽鲁斯爱上了一名叫做吕柯丽斯（Lycoris）的女子，但她却随别人远走他方。情感上受到巨大打击的伽鲁斯只能对着自然界里的各种生命抒发自己的悲痛之情。牧人们也很同情他。最终他只能接受爱情残酷的现实。

　　在维吉尔的许多作品中，古朴的生态主义观点有较为明显的体现。在《牧歌》中，作者用生动的语言塑造了一个理想化的田园世界。在这个世界里，人类（以牧羊人为代表）和大自然（山川、动植物以及天神）并不是对立的。相反，人和自然和谐相处，并融为一体。人类并不是自然界的中心，不是其他生物的高高在上的统治者，而是和其他生物一样，是自然界不可分割的一部分。人类和自然界其他生物能够平等地进行情感上和思想上的交流。诗歌中，牧羊人总是把自己的喜怒哀乐向大自然诉说。此时，自然界就像人类的朋友，认真地聆听人类的情感表达，并且对人类的经历和遭遇感同身受。在这首诗中，一个人与自然和谐相处的理想世界生动形象地展现在读者的面前。当诗人为饱受恋爱折磨的伽鲁斯唱起哀歌时，自然界的一切都充满了灵性，像一个个知心朋友一样，能够感知伽鲁斯心中的悲伤。高山、动物、植物默默地聆听诗人的哀诉，并为之落泪；而自然界中的神灵则不断安慰伽鲁斯。此时人和自然界中的其他生物并不是征服与被征服的关系，毫无高低之分。相反，两者相互理解、相互关联、高度融合。因此维吉尔笔下《牧歌》的世界，是一个人和自然高度和谐、密不可分的理想化世界。这体现了维吉尔的生态整体主义的观点。

思考题

1. How do the animals, plants, shepherd as well as gods respond to Gallus' suffering? What do their responses imply?

2. What is the relationship between Gallus and the natural environment? Are human beings (Gallus) viewed as opposed to or superior to nature and other creatures?

3. How does the poet represent the peace, simplicity and harmony of the pastoral life?

推荐阅读

Hardie, Philip. "Virgil and Tragedy." *The Cambridge Companion to Virgil*, 1997.

Jenkyns, Richard. "Virgil and Arcadia." *The Journal of Roman Studies*, 1989.

Patterson, Annabel M. *Pastoral and Ideology: Virgil to Valéry*. Universtity of California Press, 1987.

Quint, David. *Epic and Empire: Politics and Generic Form from Virgil to Milton*. Princeton University Press, 1993.

Winterbottom, Michael. "Virgil and the Confiscations." *Greece & Rome*, 1976.

徐娜:"维吉尔史诗在文艺复兴时期的续写及伦理重估",《外国文学动态研究》,2023(02)。

杨宏芹:"'卡昂尼的鸽子'——试论维吉尔的先知诗人形象",《外国文学评论》,2021(04)。

第二编 浪漫自然——
生态视域中的英国经典文学

背景介绍

虽然作为文学理论的生态文学批评发展的时间并不长,但是在英国文学中对自然与人的关系的思考却古而有之。英国文学具有悠久的历史,从发展之初就在试图探讨人与自然的关系。从早期的史诗《贝奥武夫》、骑士文学《高文爵士与绿衣骑士》到乔叟的《坎特伯雷故事集》,都或多或少地反映了早期英国人民对自然的态度。被贝奥武夫打败的魔怪,有着超能力的绿衣骑士都可以看作是自然的象征,种种离奇的情节也可以视为人类早期文明和自然的矛盾与调和。在《坎特伯雷故事集》的开篇,诗人则用四月里的春色为朝圣者的出行进行了最好的铺垫,给读者留下深刻印象。

值得指出的是,乔叟、莎士比亚等文艺复兴时期的作家对自然的态度是复杂的、多层次和多角度的。人文主义"以人为本"的思想决定了这一时期的作家逐渐将人看作自然的主宰,人是"宇宙的精华、万物的灵长",理当统领万物。在《暴风雨》中,普洛斯彼罗呼风唤雨,驱使精灵爱丽儿为他服务,奴役野蛮人凯列班,无疑表现了人作为主体控制自然、利用自然的思想。然而同样是在《暴风雨》中,莎士比亚也意识到了人文主义的问题,批评了不择手段获得财富和权力的人类,试图在人与自然的和谐中寻求调和社会矛盾的精神与道德力量。

事实上,文艺复兴时期这种对自然的复杂看法以及长期以来形成的哲学上的二元论奠定了几百年来西方世界对自然的基本态度。人与自然是对立的,自然界被当成客观对象,人类往往用傲慢的眼光来看待自然。17世纪以来,随着人类文明,尤其是机器文明的不断进步,人们拥有了更大的力量、更便利的工具来了解自然、开发自然。这固然在很大程度上改善了人类的生活,但也造成了人与人、人与自然关系的异化,这促使人类开始对人类中心主义进行反思,批判工业化对自然美和诗意生存的破坏,预测科技发展可能给自然和人类带来的毁灭性灾难。从玛丽·雪莱的《弗兰肯斯坦》到浪漫主义诗歌及至20世纪的文学作品,英国的文学家们一直在科学和技术的浪潮中不断重新定位自然与人的关系,希望能够重返自然,从自然中寻求生命的真谛。《弗兰肯斯坦》既可以称得上是英国的第一部科幻小说,也可以视为第一部反乌托邦小说,书中的科学家弗兰肯斯坦不但没有成为怪物的主宰,反而被怪物所胁迫,他的朋友和恋人则付出了生命的代价。"这是有关科技摧毁整个人类之可能性的第一次文学描写"[①],也反映了自然是如何抵制人类征服她的欲望的。除了担心科学发展不尊重自然规律,扭曲自然进程带来严重后果,19世纪初的作家们对启蒙时代以来被忽视的自然本身也迸发出了新的热情。浪漫主义诗人徜徉于湖光山色中,自然是浪漫主义诗歌的永恒主题。华兹

---

① Krouber, Karl. *Romantic Fantasy and Science Fiction*. Yale UP, 1988, p.20.

华斯的《咏水仙》并不停留于描写水仙花本身,而是强调自然景色对人的内心世界的感染。柯尔律治的《古舟子咏》更是通过老水手的遭遇告诉世人,自然是富有神性的,是值得敬畏的。启蒙时代固然开启了人的心智,却又在另一方面破坏了自然对人类曾经具有的神秘感,使人们远离自然,无法再与自然水乳交融,和谐共生。浪漫主义诗人寄情山水并非简单地逃避现实,而是出于对工业文明和科学主义的厌恶。他们描写纯真的童年和乡下质朴的生活,把自然美与人性美结合在一起,重新赋予自然神性。

尽管浪漫主义时代的激情很快为维多利亚时代的理性所取代,作家对自然环境的恶化,自鸣得意的人类中心主义却可能有了更切实的体会。狄更斯笔下阴霾密布、肮脏凌乱的雾都伦敦令人印象深刻,这个代表了当时最发达的工业国家的大都市却无法为贫民提供最基本的卫生、健康的生活环境。在《弗洛斯河上的磨坊》里,乔治·爱略特对童年麦琪的描绘把自然之美和女性之美和谐统一起来,而在反映工业化对自然的破坏的时候,她也用类比的方式描绘了女性在男权世界中所受的压迫和精神上的扭曲。对于生活在世纪之交的哈代来说,工业化不仅摧毁了乡村经济,而且进一步打破了人与自然的和谐。苔丝在乡下总是安详自在,但她却不得不进城务工,最终落入工商业暴发户的陷阱。她好像自然的女儿,正如被破坏的自然一样,最终成为时代的牺牲品。

19世纪末、20世纪初,社会动荡不安,传统价值观支离破碎,文明的前途晦暗不明。在《黑暗的心》里,康拉德借马洛之眼目睹了非洲的惨状,借马洛之口描述了殖民者的残暴。在这个把人当做牲口使唤的世界,人类文明只是一个虚伪的幌子,它带来的不是甜美和光明,而是无边无际的黑暗,不仅带给自然不可恢复的创伤,也将深陷其中的人拉入万劫不复的深渊。出身矿工家庭的 D. H. 劳伦斯熟悉矿区恶劣的生活状况,亲眼目睹不断扩张的矿区如何对自然环境造成了不可逆转的破坏。他用饱含感情的语言描述美丽的自然,也哀叹和抗议由于工业发展造成的环境污染。这一时期具有生态意识和生态思想的作家远不止以上列举的这些。伍尔芙的双性同体思想中所包含的男女平等和谐的观点与生态女性主义者解构人与自然、男性与女性二元对立的努力有着内在的一致性。叶芝深切地体会到现代工业社会的悲哀,厌恶都市生活,因此产生了脱离现实,逃向仙境的倾向。他笔下的大自然纯洁美丽,魅惑着都市人远离尘嚣,返璞归真。

今天触目惊心的生态危机"起因不在生态系统自身,而在于我们的文化系统"[①]。解读文学作品可以帮助我们探讨"整个人类思想文化如何导致了生态危机、文学及文学研究能为缓解生态危机发挥什么作用"[②]。限于篇幅,本编只精选了代表不同时代的几位作家和作品,这些作家和他们的作品本已是经典中的经典,而当我们运用生态批评理论去解读其中的生态思想和生态意识时,不仅能够从新的角度阐释经典,赋予经典新的意义,而且能够帮助我们更清楚地理解我们的文化与自然的关系,对人类文明作出深层次的反思和批判,为构建生态文明做出贡献。

---

① 转引自王诺:《欧美生态文学》,北京大学出版社,2005年,第232页。
② 王诺:"总序:我们不是出路的一部分,就是问题的一部分",《英国生态文学》,学林出版社,2008年,第5页。

《贝奥武夫》(*Beowulf*)

【作品简介】

《贝奥武夫》(又译《贝奥武甫》)是现存古英语文献中最重要的英雄叙事长诗。这部头韵体史诗长 3182 行,其作者已不可考,初以口头形式传播,成文大约在 8 世纪前后,以威塞克斯(Wessex)方言写成。故事发生在公元 5 世纪晚期,这个时期来自北欧日耳曼部落的盎格鲁-撒克逊人(Anglo-Saxons)已开始向英格兰迁移并在此定居,他们传说着北欧斯堪的纳维亚(Scandinavia)的英雄贝奥武夫(Beowulf)的英勇事迹。虽然至今尚未确定历史上是否有贝奥武夫其人,但诗中提到的许多其他人物与事迹却得到了印证。

这部史诗分为两大部分。第一部分描叙丹麦国王荷罗斯加(King Hrothgar)建造了宏伟的希奥罗特大殿(Heorot),举办盛宴,不想招来了半人半魔的怪物格兰戴尔(Grendel),每晚出没捕食荷罗斯加的战士。恰巧瑞典南部济阿兹(Geats)国王的外甥贝奥武夫王子率部下来访,协助除害。贝奥武夫英勇善战,力大无比,在格斗中扭断格兰戴尔的手臂,迫使怪物逃回洞穴,重伤而死。随后,格兰戴尔的母亲前来为子复仇,贝奥武夫在其湖泊洞穴中把她杀死,载誉而归。第二部分描叙贝奥武夫返国,被拥为济阿兹国王,做了五十年贤明君主。最后贝奥武夫在晚年杀死喷火巨龙,自己也身受重创而逝,全诗以其葬礼和挽歌结束。

《贝奥武夫》中的英雄故事既体现了 6 世纪时期北欧和英格兰各王国部落之间的政治、社会关系,也是刻画了早期人类适应、征服、改造恶劣的自然条件的传奇记载。贝奥武夫所代表的超人的战斗力,与怪物和恶龙所代表的超自然力相对抗,客观地表现了人类在陌生环境中顽强求生的历程,是一部人类为了存活和发展与自然抗争的战斗史。

以下两章选自《贝奥武夫》[①]第十二节、第二十一节。

XII Grendel and Beowulf

'Neath the cloudy cliffs came from the moor then
Grendel going, God's anger bare he.
The monster intended some one of earthmen
In the hall-building grand to entrap and make way with:
He went under welkin¹ where well he knew of

[①] 《贝奥武夫》原文以威塞克斯方言写成,这里的选篇是现代英语译本,译者 Lesslie Hall,译本名为 *Beowulf, An Anglo-Saxon Epic Poem*(《贝奥武夫,一部盎格鲁-撒克逊史诗》,2005),版本选自古腾堡电子版本(网址 http://www.gutenberg.org/files/16328/16328-h/16328-h.htm)。

The wine-joyous building, brilliant with plating,
Gold-hall of earthmen. Not the earliest occasion
He the home and manor of Hrothgar[2] had sought:
Ne'er found he in life-days later nor earlier
Hardier hero, hall-thanes[3] more sturdy!

Then came to the building the warrior marching,
Bereft of his joyance. The door quickly opened
On fire-hinges fastened, when his fingers had touched it;
The fell one had flung then—his fury so bitter—
Open the entrance. Early thereafter
The foeman trod the shining hall-pavement,
Strode he angrily; from the eyes of him glimmered
A lustre unlovely likest to fire.

He beheld in the hall the heroes in numbers,
A circle of kinsmen sleeping together,
A throng of thanemen: then his thoughts were exultant,
He minded to sunder from each of the thanemen
The life from his body, horrible demon,
Ere morning came, since fate had allowed him
The prospect of plenty. Providence willed not
To permit him any more of men under heaven
To eat in the night-time. Higelac[4]'s kinsman
Great sorrow endured how the dire-mooded creature
In unlooked-for assaults were likely to bear him.
No thought had the monster of deferring the matter,
But on earliest occasion he quickly laid hold of
A soldier asleep, suddenly tore him,
Bit his bone-prison[5], the blood drank in currents,
Swallowed in mouthfuls: he soon had the dead man's
Feet and hands, too, eaten entirely.

Nearer he strode then, the stout-hearted warrior
Snatched as he slumbered, seizing with hand-grip,
Forward the foeman foined[6] with his hand;
Caught he quickly the cunning deviser,
On his elbow he rested. This early discovered
The master of malice, that in middle-earth's regions,
'Neath the whole of the heavens, no hand-grapple greater

In any man else had he ever encountered:
Fearful in spirit, faint-mooded waxed he,
Not off could betake him; death he was pondering,
Would fly to his covert, seek the devils' assembly:
His calling no more was the same he had followed
Long in his lifetime. The liege-kinsman[7] worthy
Of Higelac minded his speech of the evening,
Stood he up straight and stoutly did seize him.
His fingers crackled; the giant was outward,
The earl stepped farther. The famous one minded
To flee away farther, if he found an occasion,
And off and away, avoiding delay,
To fly to the fen-moors[8]; he fully was ware of
The strength of his grapple in the grip of the foeman.

'Twas an ill-taken journey that the injury-bringing,
Harrying harmer to Heorot[9] wandered:
The palace re-echoed; to all of the Danemen,
Dwellers in castles, to each of the bold ones,
Earlmen, was terror. Angry they both were,
Archwarders[10] raging. Rattled the building;
'Twas a marvellous wonder that the wine-hall withstood then
The bold-in-battle, bent not to earthward,
Excellent earth-hall; but within and without it
Was fastened so firmly in fetters of iron,
By the art of the armorer[11]. Off from the sill there
Bent mead-benches[12] many, as men have informed me,
Adorned with gold-work, where the grim ones did struggle.
The Scylding[13] wise men weened[14] ne'er before
That by might and main-strength a man under heaven
Might break it in pieces, bone-decked, resplendent,
Crush it by cunning, unless clutch of the fire
In smoke should consume it. The sound mounted upward
Novel enough; on the North Danes fastened
A terror of anguish, on all of the men there
Who heard from the wall the weeping and plaining[15],
The song of defeat from the foeman of heaven,
Heard him hymns of horror howl, and his sorrow
Hell-bound bewailing. He held him too firmly
Who was strongest of main-strength of men of that era.

XXI Hrothgar's Account of the Monsters

Hrothgar rejoined, helm[16] of the Scyldings:
"Ask not of joyance! Grief is renewed to
The folk of the Danemen. Dead is Æschere[17],
Yrmenlaf Times new Romans brother, older than he,
My true-hearted counsellor, trusty adviser,
Shoulder-companion, when fighting in battle
Our heads we protected, when troopers were clashing,
And heroes were dashing; such an earl should be ever,
An erst-worthy atheling[18], as Æschere proved him.

The flickering death-spirit became in Heorot
His hand-to-hand murderer; I can not tell whither
The cruel one turned in the carcass exulting,
By cramming discovered. The quarrel she wreaked then,
That last night igone Grendel thou killedst
In grewsomest manner, with grim-holding clutches,
Since too long he had lessened my liege-troop and wasted
My folk-men so foully. He fell in the battle
With forfeit of life, and another has followed,
A mighty crime-worker, her kinsman avenging,
And henceforth hath 'stablished her hatred unyielding,
As it well may appear to many a liegeman,
Who mourneth in spirit the treasure-bestower,
Her heavy heart-sorrow; the hand is now lifeless
Which availed you in every wish that you cherished.

Land-people heard I, liegemen, this saying,
Dwellers in halls, they had seen very often
A pair of such mighty march-striding creatures,
Far-dwelling spirits, holding the moorlands:
One of them wore, as well they might notice,
The image of woman, the other one wretched
In guise of a man wandered in exile,
Except he was huger than any of earthmen;
Earth-dwelling people entitled him Grendel
In days of yore: they know not their father,
Whe'r ill-going spirits any were borne him
Ever before. They guard the wolf-coverts,

Lands inaccessible, wind-beaten nesses,
Fearfullest fen-deeps, where a flood from the mountains
'Neath mists of the nesses netherward[19] rattles,
The stream under earth: not far is it henceward
Measured by mile-lengths that the mere-water standeth,
Which forests hang over, with frost-whiting covered,
A firm-rooted forest, the floods overshadow.

There ever at night one an ill-meaning portent
A fire-flood may see; 'mong children of men
None liveth so wise that wot[20] of the bottom;
Though harassed by hounds the heath-stepper[21] seek for,
Fly to the forest, firm-antlered he-deer,
Spurred from afar, his spirit he yieldeth,
His life on the shore, ere in he will venture
To cover his head. Uncanny the place is:
Thence upward ascendeth the surging of waters,
Wan to the welkin, when the wind is stirring
The weathers unpleasing, till the air groweth gloomy,
And the heavens lower. Now is help to be gotten
From thee and thee only! The abode thou know'st not,
The dangerous place where thou'rt able to meet with
The sin-laden hero: seek if thou darest!
For the feud I will fully fee thee with money,
With old-time treasure, as erstwhile I did thee,
With well-twisted jewels, if away thou shalt get thee."

注释

1. welkin:天空,苍穹。
2. Hrothgar:丹麦国王荷罗斯加。
3. thane:thaneman,有封号的贵族,爵士。
4. Higelac:海吉拉克国王,贝奥武夫所在的济阿兹国君主。
5. bone-prison:骨架,骨头围起的屏障。
6. foin:刺穿。
7. The liege-kinsman:君王的血脉,指的是贝奥武夫,他是国王的外甥。
8. the fen-moors:沼泽地,尤指苏格兰东部的沼泽地区。
9. Heorot:希奥罗特,荷罗斯加国王所建大殿的名字。
10. archwarders:大门的看守者们。

11. armorer:兵器制造者,军械修护者。
12. mead-bench:古日耳曼部落盛宴上的座椅。
13. Scylding:丹麦的,丹麦人。
14. ween:(古英语用法)expect,assume。
15. plaining:惨叫,哀嚎。
16. helm:舵手,领袖。
17. Æschere:丹麦国王荷罗斯加的亲信大臣,被前来复仇的格兰戴尔之母杀死。
18. erst-worthy atheling:一流的贵族。erst,first。
19. the nesses netherward:下面的海岬。
20. wot:知道(wit 的过去式)。
21. heath-stepper:踏着石楠走路者。

作品导读

　　史诗《贝奥武夫》里有两个世界:一个是人类世界,以丹麦国王的宏伟大殿为代表。在大殿里,君王、大臣、勇士们举办盛宴,畅谈豪饮。另一个是荒凉阴森的自然世界,居住着格兰戴尔母子这样的怪物,是自然界邪恶暴虐的化身。这两个世界并非相安无事,人类在大殿中的盛宴把怪物从自然中引来,怪物捕食武士,对抗于是开始。

　　节选的第十二节是贝奥武夫来到丹麦的夜晚,格兰戴尔又一次来到大殿捕食人类。他来自沼泽深处雾霭笼罩的悬崖底下('Neath the cloudy cliffs came from the moor then),走进这座刚结束王室欢宴的大殿,吞吃了一名武士。可是这次他没能安然脱身,力大无穷的贝奥武夫扭住了他,他的嚎叫声震动殿宇,让殿外所有的武士胆战心惊。在下一节中贝奥武夫扯断了怪物的一条胳膊,怪物重伤逃回沼泽,死在那里。他的母亲前来为他报仇,杀死了丹麦国王的重臣。在节选的第二十一节里,丹麦国王向贝奥武夫痛陈了怪物给丹麦造成的灾难,详细描述了这对怪物母子藏身的环境,那里野狼出没,人迹罕至,有着风吹雨打的海崖、令人生畏的深谷。山上冲下的激流汇聚成深潭,周围森林密绕,在这深潭底下就住着两个怪物。人类对这样的自然世界充满恐惧和敌意,就像格兰戴尔对人类的大殿和欢宴也充满敌意一样。人与怪物的冲突和对抗,从侧面反映了盎格鲁-撒克逊人在北欧和英格兰的艰苦环境中顽强求生的经历。

　　另一方面,半人半兽的格兰戴尔母子是野性与人性相结合的产物,而贝奥武夫则有着半人半神的希腊英雄的特性。事实上,从名字上看,Beowulf 本意是"北欧之狼",在贝奥武夫身上体现了野性、人性和神性的三种混合。这首长诗反映了神性对抗野性的胜利,人间英雄贝奥武夫战胜具有超自然能力的怪物母子,是人类战胜野蛮、征服荒野的理想和证明。

思考题

1. Why do you think Grendel enjoyed attacking the same palace for years?

2. How did Hrothgar think of Grendel and his mother?
3. What was the significance of Beowulf's helping the Danes fight?
4. What was the image of Nature reflected in the epic?
5. According to your understanding, how is this epic analyzed ecocritically?

推荐阅读

Battles, Paul. "Dying for a Drink: 'Sleeping after the Feast' Scenes in *Beowulf*, *Andreas*, and the Old English Poetic Tradition." *Modern Philology*, vol. 112, no. 3, 2015.

Bintley, Michael. "*Hrinde Bearwas*: The Trees at the Mere and the Root of All Evil in *Beowulf*." *The Journal of English and Germanic Philology*, vol. 119, no. 3, 2020.

Donaldson, E. Talbot. *Beowulf: A Prose Translation*. W. W. Norton & Company, 2001.

Hall, Catherine. "'The Evil Side of Heroic Life': Monsters and Heroes in *Beowulf* and *The Hobbit*." *Mythlore*, vol. 41, no. 1, 2022.

Hall, John Lesslie (trans.). *Beowulf* (The Standard Translation), http://www.gutenberg.org/files/16328/16328-h/16328-h.htm.(本书中的网址访问日期为2024年8月12日。)

Low, Matt. "'Heard Gripe Hruson' (the Hard Grip of the Earth): Ecopoetry and the Anglo-Saxon Elegy." *Mosaic (Winnipeg)*, vol. 42, No. 3, 2009.

Tolkien, J. R. R., *Beowulf and the Critics* (Medieval & Renaissance Texts & Studies, Vol. 248), edt. Drout Michael D. C. Tucson: Arizona State University, 2002.

李赋宁:"古英语史诗《贝奥武夫》",《外国文学》,1998(06)。

项东,王继辉:"《贝奥武夫》中的日耳曼英雄世界",《广西民族大学学报》(哲学社会科学版),2022,44(01)。

杰弗雷·乔叟(Geoffrey Chaucer)

【作者简介】

杰弗雷·乔叟(1340—1400),英国诗人,出身于一个富有的酒商家庭,十几岁起进入宫廷当差。乔叟因外交事务出使过许多国家和地区,到过比利时、法国、意大利等国,有机会遇见薄伽丘(Giovanni Boccaccio)与彼特拉克(Francesco Petrarch),这对他的文学创作产生了很大的影响。他熟悉拉丁、法、意等语言的文哲著作,译过法国的《玫瑰的传奇》(Roman de la Rose),写过《公爵夫人之书》(The Book of the Duchess)、《荣誉之家》(The House of Fame)、《禽鸟会议》(Parlement of Foules)等诗,其中以《特洛伊罗斯与克莉西德》(Troilus and Criseyde)最为出色。他的不朽传世之作是《坎特伯雷故事集》(The Canterbury Tales),虽未能按诗人的计划全部完成,只完成24则故事(17000行),但已成英国文学史上的一座丰碑。1400年乔叟逝世,他是第一位安葬在伦敦威斯敏斯特教堂"诗人角"的诗人。①

乔叟的创作大体上常被分为三个阶段:受法国文学影响阶段、受法国与意大利文学双重影响阶段、成熟的创作阶段。在前两个阶段,他受欧洲传统影响较大,将欧洲文学作为自己创作的样板。后期主要是他自己的创新,充分展示出乔叟自己的创作才华和讲故事的高超本领。

在乔叟生活的年代里,英语仍然是地位较低的市井语言,上层社会的通用语言是法语,文学创作的语言一般以拉丁语和法语为主,但是乔叟的《坎特伯雷故事集》却第一次将英语推上了文学创作的大雅之堂。乔叟用的英格兰南部的口语体文字后来发展成为英格兰的标准语,这与乔叟和《坎特伯雷故事集》的影响是分不开的。同时我们也可以看到,当时英格兰南部的方言已经发展到了一个比较成熟的阶段,能够胜任文学创作的复杂要求。总之,乔叟对英语的使用使他自己深深扎根于英国本土,使他能够在新兴英国的清新空气中尽情发挥自己的创新,"英国文学之父"这一称号对于乔叟来说是当之无愧的。

以下诗行选自《坎特伯雷故事集》中的"女尼的教士的故事"("The Nun's Priest's Tale")。

The Nun's Priest's Tale

...
A yard she had, enclosed all roundabout
With pales, and there was a dry ditch without[1],

---

① 乔叟是作为王室官员被葬在威斯敏斯特教堂的,但是此后葬在他身边的都是著名文学家了,这块墓地遂得名"诗人角"。

And in the yard a cock called Chanticleer.
In all the land, for crowing, he's no peer[2].
His voice was merrier than the organ gay
On Mass days, which in church begins to play;
More regular was his crowing in his lodge
Than is a clock or abbey horologe.
By instinct he's marked each ascension down
Of equinoctial[3] value in that town;
For when fifteen degrees had been ascended,
Then crew he so it might not be amended.
His comb was redder than a fine coral,
And battlemented like a castle wall.
His bill was black and just like jet it shone;
Like azure were his legs and toes, each one;
His spurs were whiter than the lily flower;
And plumage of the burnished gold his dower.
This noble cock had in his governance
Seven hens to give him pride and all pleasance,
Which were his sisters and his paramours
And wondrously like him as to colours,
Whereof the fairest hued upon her throat
Was called the winsome Mistress Pertelote.
Courteous she was, discreet and debonnaire[4],
Companionable, and she had been so fair

Since that same day when she was seven nights old,
That truly she had taken the heart to hold
Of Chanticleer, locked in her every limb;
He loved her so that all was well with him.
But such a joy it was to hear them sing,
Whenever the bright sun began to spring,
In sweet accord, "My love walks through the land."
For at that time, and as I understand,
The beasts and all the birds could speak and sing.

So it befell that, in a bright dawning,
As Chanticleer 'midst wives and sisters all
Sat on his perch, the which was in the hall,
And next him sat the winsome Pertelote,
This Chanticleer he groaned within his throat
Like man that in his dreams is troubled sore.

And when fair Pertelote thus heard him roar,
She was aghast and said: "O sweetheart dear,
What ails[5] you that you groan so? Do you hear?
You are a sleepy herald. Fie, for shame!"
And he replied to her thus: "Ah, madame,
I pray you that you take it not in grief:
By God, I dreamed I'd come to such mischief,
Just now, my heart yet jumps with sore affright.[6]
"Now God," cried he, "my vision read aright
And keep my body out of foul prison!
I dreamed, that while I wandered up and down
Within our yard, I saw there a strange beast
Was like a dog, and he'd have made a feast
Upon my body, and have had me dead.
His colour yellow was and somewhat red;
And tipped his tail was, as were both his ears,
With black, unlike the rest, as it appears;
His snout was small and gleaming was each eye.
Remembering how he looked, almost I die;
And all this caused my groaning, I confess."
...
A brant-fox, full of sly iniquity,[7]
That in the grove had lived two years, or three,
Now by a fine premeditated plot
That same night, breaking through the hedge, had got
Into the yard where Chanticleer the fair
Was wont[8], and all his wives too, to repair;
And in a bed of greenery still he lay
Till it was past the quarter of the day,
Waiting his chance on Chanticleer to fall,
As gladly do these killers one and all
Who lie in ambush for to murder men.
O murderer false, there lurking in your den!
O new Iscariot, O new Ganelon![9]
O false dissimulator, Greek Sinon[10]
That brought down Troy all utterly to sorrow!
O Chanticleer, accursed be that morrow
When you into that yard flew from the beams!
You were well warned, and fully, by your dreams

That this day should hold peril damnably.
But that which God foreknows, it needs must be,
So says the best opinion of the clerks.
Witness some cleric perfect for his works,
That in the schools there's a great altercation
In this regard, and much high disputation
That has involved a hundred thousand men.
But I can't sift it to the bran with pen,
As can the holy Doctor Augustine,[11]
Or Boethius[12], or Bishop Bradwardine,[13]
Whether the fact of God's great foreknowing
Makes it right needful that I do a thing
(By needful, I mean, of necessity);
Or else, if a free choice he granted me,
To do that same thing, or to do it not,
Though God foreknew[14] before the thing was wrought;
Or if His knowing constrains never at all,
Save by necessity conditional.

I have no part in matters so austere;
My tale is of a cock, as you shall hear,
That took the counsel of his wife, with sorrow,
To walk within the yard upon that morrow
After he'd had the dream whereof I told.
Now women's counsels oft are ill to hold;
A woman's counsel brought us first to woe,
And Adam caused from Paradise to go,
Wherein he was right merry and at ease.[15]
But since I know not whom it may displease
If woman's counsel I hold up to blame,
Pass over, I but said it in my game.
Read authors where such matters do appear,
And what they say of women, you may hear.
These are the cock's words, they are none of mine;
No harm in women can I e'er divine.

All in the sand, a-bathing merrily,
Lay Pertelote, with all her sisters by,
There in the sun; and Chanticleer so free
Sang merrier than a mermaid in the sea

(For Physiologus[16] says certainly
That they do sing, both well and merrily.)
And so befell that, as he cast his eye
Among the herbs and on a butterfly,
He saw this fox that lay there, crouching low.
Nothing of urge was in him, then, to crow;
But he cried "Cock-cock-cock" and did so start
As man who has a sudden fear at heart.
For naturally a beast desires to flee
From any enemy that he may see,
Though never yet he's clapped on such his eye.
When Chanticleer the fox did then espy,
He would have fled but that the fox anon[17]
Said: "Gentle sir, alas! Why be thus gone?
Are you afraid of me, who am your friend?
Now, surely, I were worse than any fiend
If I should do you harm or villainy.
I came not here upon your deeds to spy;
But, certainly, the cause of my coming
Was only just to listen to you sing.
For truly, you have quite as fine a voice
As angels have that Heaven's choirs rejoice;
Boethius to music could not bring
Such feeling, nor do others who can sing.
My lord your father (God his soul pray bless!)
And too your mother, of her gentleness,
Have been in my abode, to my great ease;
And truly, sir, right fain am I to please.
But since men speak of singing, I will say
(As I still have my eyesight day by day),
Save you, I never heard a man so sing
As did your father in the grey dawning;
Truly 'twas from the heart, his every song.
And that his voice might ever be more strong,
He took such pains that, with his either eye,
He had to blink, so loudly would he cry,
A-standing on his tiptoes therewithal[18],
Stretching his neck till it grew long and small.
And such discretion, too, by him was shown,
There was no man in any region known

That him in song or wisdom could surpass.
I have well read, in Dan Burnell the Ass[19],
Among his verses, how there was a cock,
Because a priest's son gave to him a knock
Upon the leg, while young and not yet wise,
He caused the boy to lose his benefice.
But, truly, there is no comparison
With the great wisdom and the discretion
Your father had, or with his subtlety.
Now sing, dear sir, for holy charity,
See if you can your father counterfeit."
This Chanticleer his wings began to beat,
As one that could no treason there espy,
So was he ravished by this flattery
Alas, you lords! Full many a flatterer
Is in your courts, and many a cozener,
That please your honours much more, by my fay,
Than he that truth and justice dares to say.
Go read the Ecclesiast[20] on flattery;
Beware, my lords, of all their treachery!
This Chanticleer stood high upon his toes,
Stretching his neck, and both his eyes did close,
And so did crow right loudly, for the nonce[21];
And Russel Fox, he started up at once,
And by the gorget grabbed our Chanticleer,
Flung him on back, and toward the wood did steer,
For there was no man who as yet pursued.

注释

1. without：在外面。
2. had no peer：没有人能够匹敌。peer：同等的人。
3. equinoctial：*adj.* 昼夜平分的；春分或秋分时的。
4. Courteous she was, discreet and debonnaire：She was courteous, discreet and debonnaire. 她品性温柔贤淑，举止优雅。
5. ail：*vi.* 有病痛，生病；感到不舒服。
6. my heart yet jumps with sore affright：我的心此刻还在因为惊吓而跳动。
7. sly iniquity：狡猾邪恶。sly：*adj.* 狡猾的。iniquity：*n.* 邪恶，不公正。
8. wont：习惯于。

9. O new Iscariot, O new Ganelon：又是一个加略人犹大来了，又是一个加纳伦！Iscariot：n. 背信者，叛徒；出卖耶稣的犹大之姓。Ganelon 是查理大帝十二圣骑士最后一个，他出卖了法国英雄、十二圣骑士之首罗兰。

10. Greek Sinon：引木马进特洛伊城（Troy）的希腊奸细西侬。

11. the holy Doctor Augustine：圣奥古斯丁（354—430），古罗马帝国时期基督教思想家，欧洲中世纪基督教神学、教父哲学的重要代表人物。

12. Boethius：波伊休斯（480—524 或 525），古罗马晚期的政治家、哲学家，著有《哲学的慰藉》(Consolations of Philosophy)。他对中世纪的逻辑学影响很大，具有神秘主义和禁欲主义的传统，在东哥特王国执政官任上因涉及叛变案件被处死。除《哲学的慰籍》外他还写过几何、音乐等作品。下文提到他的音乐。

13. Bishop Bradwardine：坎特伯雷大主教。

14. foreknew：原形为 foreknow：vt. 预知，先知。

15. A woman's counsel brought us first to woe, / And Adam caused from Paradise to go, / Wherein he was right merry and at ease：女人的话最初就带来了灾祸，使亚当失去了曾经舒适快意的乐园。这里指《圣经·创世记》中夏娃吃禁果的故事。

16. Physiologus：《菲西洛格斯》，是一部希腊文编写而成的训诫之书，约成书于 2 世纪，作者不可考，内容以道德或宗教的解释加之于各种动物、植物、矿物，后被译成多种文字。

17. anon：adv. 不久；立刻。

18. therewithal：adv. 于是；因此；随其；此外。

19. Dan Burnell the Ass：《驴哥波纳儿传》。12 世纪末一篇拉丁文讽刺长诗。

20. the Ecclesiast：the Ecclesiastes，《传道书》，《圣经·旧约》中的一卷，传为大卫的儿子所罗门所著，向当时耶路撒冷的居民宣讲教义，使他们敬畏上帝。

21. for the nonce：暂且；目前。

作品导读

正如我国老一辈文学评论家、诗人王佐良先生所说，从古英语文学进入到中古英语文学，是从一个刚强而单纯的英雄时代进入到一个远为复杂的新世纪，社会的面貌明朗起来，同后世相似的东西也多起来。乔叟便是这一新世纪的开创者之一。《坎特伯雷故事集》全诗用英雄双韵体（the heroic couplet）写成。一打开《坎特伯雷故事集》，我们就立刻呼吸到了英国春天的清新空气："当四月的甘霖渗透了三月枯竭的根须，沐濯了丝丝经络，触动了生机，使枝头涌现出花蕾……"（When April with his showers sweet with fruit / The drought of March has pierced unto the root / And bathed each vein with liquor that has power / To generate therein and sire the flower…）然后，诗人带着我们进入泰巴旅店，将朝圣客逐一介绍，宛如为我们展开一幅幅生动的肖像画：渴望爱情的骑士、世俗的修女、操着法国腔的上层人士、胆大风趣的巴斯妇人等等。乔叟的《故事集》中不仅人物呼之欲出，同时在细致观察的基础上，诗人用风趣幽默的语言，将当时的社会风貌也生动呈现在读者面前：餐桌上的规矩、爱狗的习惯、妇女的装扮等等。24 个故事五花八门，讲故事的人三教九流，全书的内容丰富多样，正如 17 世纪文学评论家德莱顿所赞的："这里像上帝那样无所不有。"

在这段选读中，主人公是一只漂亮的大公鸡腔得克立(Chanticleer)。一天凌晨，公鸡从噩梦中惊醒。他告诉自己最喜爱的母鸡坡德洛特，说梦见一只野兽潜伏在草丛里要伺机咬死他。坡德洛特嘲笑他胆小，劝他不必把梦放在心上。腔得克立举了很多例子说明人在遭恶运之前都曾在梦中得到预兆，但是他听从母鸡的话宽慰了自己一番。天亮了，他像平常一样与母鸡们觅食寻欢，突然发现躲在草丛里的狐狸。正要逃跑，狐狸叫住他，说自己是专门来欣赏公鸡的歌声的。一番奉承话说得公鸡心花怒放。他刚摆好姿势准备引吭高歌，狐狸冲上前咬住他的颈项，急步向窝奔去。这个故事的结局是：大公鸡设计骗狐狸张开嘴说话，乘机逃出狐口，飞到了树上。故事中公鸡腔得克立骄傲自大、目空一切，但又生性胆怯、疑神疑鬼。母鸡坡德洛特话语尖刻锋利，十分任性。通过富有个性的语言，作者活灵活现地展示了这一对性格迥异却又趣味相投的公鸡母鸡的身影。同时，故事也展示了作者驾驭语言的才能，《坎特伯雷故事集》的幽默讥讽的特色在此也得到了生动的体现。教士用学者的口吻讲话，或者搬弄华丽的辞藻，或者一本正经地引经据典，讲叙的却仅仅是一个关于公鸡、母鸡、狐狸的动物故事，传达的只是街头巷尾的琐闻。这种气势和内容的脱节，产生了一种幽默、滑稽的艺术效果。

乔叟的自然观代表了 14 世纪西方关于宇宙与人的位置、人的理性与天性（自然）的思考。他继承并吸收了古代和中世纪的传统，同时又展现了当时文艺复兴之前西方学者和文学家们丰富多样的理解。乔叟将人与自然的关系与他对人性的探寻融合在一起，他认为人与其他造物的不同就在于人类是有理性的，但同时人又是自然的一部分，要遵从自然的规律，与自然和谐融合。人性常常处于天性与理性的纠结之中，这种纠结无法得到圆满解决，而且常常在人与自然的关系中显示出来。公鸡腔得克立的故事中，乔叟借叙述者之口暗示人必须要保持理性，不慌乱，才能维持一个平衡的发展。

此外，在这个故事中，乔叟通过动物的声音和话语使读者看到了至少两个层面的关系：一个是人与动物，以被人驯化的腔得克立和野生动物——狐狸为代表；另一个则是女人与男人的关系。生态女性主义认为女人和动物的共同点是都受到压迫，女人受到男权的压迫，而动物则受到人类中心主义的贬抑。乔叟借叙述者之口说："妇人的话是害人的，妇人的话最初就闯下了祸，使亚当离开了舒适快意的乐园。"明显表现出来对女性的贬抑，对理性的歌颂。这一观点也代表了即将到来的新时代的主流思想。

思考题

1. What do you think the relationships among Chanticleer, Pertelote and the Fox symbolize in this moral story?

2. Does Chanticleer love Pertelote?

3. How do you compare the relationship between Chanticleer and Pertelote with that of Adam and Eve?

4. What does the story teller imply when she refers to Biblical story?

5. If Chanticleer and the Fox can be understood respectively as human and animal in nature, how do you understand their relationship?

推荐阅读

Alias, Simona. "An Eco-critical Approach to Chaucer. Representations of the Natural," dissertation, Università degli Studi di Trento, 2011.

Buell, Lawrence. *The Environmental Imagination*. Harvard University Press, 1995.

Greenblatt, Stephen. (General Editor), *The Norton Anthology of English Literature*, "The Middle Ages," 8th edition, Vol A, 2006.

Karla, Armbruster & Wallace, Kathleen R. ed. *Beyond Nature Writing. Expanding the Boundaries of Eco-criticism*. University of Virginia Press, 2001.

North, J. D. *Chaucer's Universe*. Clarendon Press, 1988.

杰弗雷·乔叟:《坎特伯雷故事集》,方重译,上海译文出版社,1983年。

王佐良:《英国诗史》,译林出版社,2008年。

威廉·莎士比亚(William Shakespeare)

【作者简介】

莎士比亚(1564—1616)是英国文艺复兴时期伟大的剧作家和诗人,是当时人文主义文学的集大成者,一生创作了38部戏剧,两首叙事长诗和154首十四行诗。莎士比亚戏剧的代表作包括悲剧《哈姆雷特》(*Hamlet*)、《奥赛罗》(*Othello*)、《李尔王》(*King Lear*)、《麦克白》(*MacBeth*),喜剧《仲夏夜之梦》(*A Midsummer Night's Dream*)、《威尼斯商人》(*The Merchant of Venice*)、《第十二夜》(*The Twelfth Night*)等和历史剧《亨利四世》(*Henry IV*)、《亨利五世》(*Henry V*)等。马克思称他和古希腊的埃斯库罗斯为"两个最伟大的天才戏剧家"。《暴风雨》(*The Tempest*)是莎士比亚创作生涯后期的代表作,既深刻剖析了当时的社会现实,也试图通过神话式的幻想,借助超自然的力量来解决理想与现实之间的矛盾,被称为剧作家"诗化的遗嘱"。以下选自《暴风雨》第五幕,也是全剧的最后一幕。

ACT V

SCENE I. Before PROSPERO'S cell[1].

Enter PROSPERO in his magic robes, and ARIEL

PROSPERO

Now does my project gather to a head[2]:
My charms crack not; my spirits obey; and time
Goes upright with his carriage[3]. How's the day?

ARIEL

On the sixth hour; at which time, my lord,
You said our work should cease.

PROSPERO

I did say so,
When first I raised the tempest. Say, my spirit,
How fares[4] the king and's followers?

ARIEL

Confined together
In the same fashion as you gave in charge,

Just as you left them; all prisoners, sir,
In the line-grove which weather-fends your cell;
They cannot budge till your release. The king,
His brother and yours, abide all three distracted
And the remainder mourning over them,
Brimful of sorrow and dismay; but chiefly
Him that you term'd, sir, The good old lord Gonzalo;
His tears run down his beard, like winter's drops
From eaves of reeds. Your charm so strongly works 'em
That if you now beheld them, your affections
Would become tender.
PROSPERO
Dost thou think so, spirit?
ARIEL
Mine would, sir, were I human.
PROSPERO
And mine shall.
Hast thou, which art but air, a touch, a feeling
Of their afflictions, and shall not myself,
One of their kind, that relish all as sharply,
Passion as they, be kindlier moved than thou art?
Though with their high wrongs I am struck to the quick[5],
Yet with my nobler reason 'gainst my fury
Do I take part: the rarer action is
In virtue than in vengeance: they being penitent,
The sole drift of my purpose doth extend
Not a frown further[6]. Go release them, Ariel:
My charms I'll break, their senses I'll restore,
And they shall be themselves.
ARIEL
I'll fetch them, sir.
Exit
PROSPERO
Ye elves of hills, brooks, standing lakes and groves,
And ye that on the sands with printless foot
Do chase the ebbing Neptune and do fly him
When he comes back; you demi-puppets that
By moonshine do the green sour ringlets make,
Whereof the ewe not bites, and you whose pastime
Is to make midnight mushrooms, that rejoice

To hear the solemn curfew; by whose aid,
Weak masters though ye be, I have bedimm'd
The noontide sun, call'd forth the mutinous winds,
And 'twixt the green sea and the azured vault
Set roaring war: to the dread rattling thunder
Have I given fire and rifted Jove's stout oak
With his own bolt; the strong-based promontory
Have I made shake and by the spurs pluck'd up
The pine and cedar: graves at my command
Have waked their sleepers, oped[7], and let'em forth
By my so potent art. But this rough magic
I here abjure, and, when I have required
Some heavenly music, which even now I do,
To work mine end upon their senses[8] that
This airy charm is for, I'll break my staff,
Bury it certain fathoms in the earth,
And deeper than did ever plummet sound[9]
I'll drown my book.

Solemn music

Re-enter ARIEL before; then ALONSO, with a frantic gesture, attended by GONZALO; SEBASTIAN and ANTONIO in like manner, attended by ADRIAN and FRANCISCO they all enter the circle which PROSPERO had made, and there stand charmed; which PROSPERO observing, speaks:

A solemn air and the best comforter
To an unsettled fancy cure thy brains,
Now useless, boil'd within thy skull! There stand,
For you are spell-stopp'd.
Holy Gonzalo, honourable man,
Mine eyes, even sociable to the show of thine[10],
Fall fellowly drops. The charm dissolves apace,
And as the morning steals upon the night,
Melting the darkness, so their rising senses
Begin to chase the ignorant fumes that mantle
Their clearer reason. O good Gonzalo,
My true preserver, and a loyal sir
To him you follow'st! I will pay thy graces
Home[11] both in word and deed. Most cruelly
Didst thou, Alonso, use me and my daughter:
Thy brother was a furtherer in the act.
Thou art pinch'd fort now, Sebastian. Flesh and blood,

You, brother mine, that entertain'd ambition,
Expell'd remorse and nature; who, with Sebastian,
Whose inward pinches therefore are most strong,
Would here have kill'd your king; I do forgive thee,
Unnatural[12] though thou art. Their understanding
Begins to swell, and the approaching tide
Will shortly fill the reasonable shore
That now lies foul and muddy. Not one of them
That yet looks on me, or would know me Ariel,
Fetch me the hat and rapier in my cell:
I will discase[13] me, and myself present
As I was sometime Milan: quickly, spirit;
Thou shalt ere long be free.
ARIEL sings and helps to attire him
Where the bee sucks, there suck I:
In a cowslip's bell I lie;
There I couch when owls do cry.
On the bat's back I do fly
After summer merrily.
Merrily, merrily shall I live now
Under the blossom that hangs on the bough.
PROSPERO
Why, that's my dainty Ariel! I shall miss thee:
But yet thou shalt have freedom: so, so, so.
To the king's ship, invisible as thou art:
There shalt thou find the mariners asleep
Under the hatches; the master and the boatswain
Being awake, enforce them to this place,
And presently, I prithee[14].
ARIEL
I drink the air before me[15], and return
Or ere your pulse twice beat.
Exit
GONZALO
All torment, trouble, wonder and amazement
Inhabits here: some heavenly power guide us
Out of this fearful country!
PROSPERO
Behold, sir king,
The wronged Duke of Milan, Prospero:

For more assurance that a living prince
Does now speak to thee, I embrace thy body;
And to thee and thy company I bid
A hearty welcome.

ALONSO

Whether thou be'st he or no,
Or some enchanted trifle to abuse me,
As late I have been, I not know: thy pulse
Beats as of flesh and blood; and, since I saw thee,
The affliction of my mind amends, with which,
I fear, a madness held me: this must crave,
And if this be at all, a most strange story.
Thy dukedom I resign and do entreat
Thou pardon me my wrongs. But how should Prospero
Be living and be here?

PROSPERO

First, noble friend,
Let me embrace thine age[16], whose honour cannot
Be measured or confined.

GONZALO

Whether this be
Or be not, I'll not swear.

PROSPERO

You do yet taste
Some subtilties[17] o'n the isle, that will not let you
Believe things certain. Welcome, my friends all!

Aside to SEBASTIAN and ANTONIO

But you, my brace of lords, were I so minded,
I here could pluck his highness' frown upon you
And justify you traitors: at this time
I will tell no tales[18].

SEBASTIAN

[Aside] The devil speaks in him.

PROSPERO

No.
For you, most wicked sir, whom to call brother
Would even infect my mouth, I do forgive
Thy rankest fault; all of them; and require
My dukedom of thee, which perforce, I know,
Thou must restore.

ALONSO

If thou be 'st Prospero, Give us particulars of thy preservation;

How thou hast met us here, who three hours since

Were wreck'd upon this shore; where I have lost—

How sharp the point of this remembrance is! —

My dear son Ferdinand.

PROSPERO

I am woe for't, sir.

ALONSO

Irreparable is the loss, and patience

Says it is past her cure[19].

PROSPERO

I rather think

You have not sought her help, of whose soft grace

For the like loss I have her sovereign aid

And rest myself content.

ALONSO

You the like loss!

PROSPERO

As great to me as late; and, supportable

To make the dear loss, have I means much weaker

Than you may call to comfort you, for I

Have lost my daughter.

ALONSO

A daughter?

O heavens, that they were living both in Naples,

The king and queen there[20]! that they were, I wish

Myself were mudded in that oozy bed

Where my son lies. When did you lose your daughter?

PROSPERO

In this last tempest. I perceive these lords

At this encounter do so much admire[21]

That they devour their reason[22] and scarce think

Their eyes do offices of truth, their words

Are natural breath: but, howsoe'er you have

Been justled[23] from your senses, know for certain

That I am Prospero and that very duke

Which was thrust forth of Milan, who most strangely

Upon this shore, where you were wreck'd, was landed,

To be the lord on't. No more yet of this;

For 'tis a chronicle of day by day,
Not a relation for a breakfast[24] nor
Befitting this first meeting. Welcome, sir;
This cell's my court: here have I few attendants
And subjects none abroad: pray you, look in.
My dukedom since you have given me again,
I will requite you with as good a thing;
At least bring forth a wonder, to content ye
As much as me my dukedom.
Here PROSPERO discovers FERDINAND and MIRANDA playing at chess
MIRANDA
Sweet lord, you play me false.
FERDINAND
No, my dear'st love,
I would not for the world[25].
MIRANDA
Yes, for a score of kingdoms you should wrangle,
And I would call it, fair play.
ALONSO
If this prove
A vision of the Island, one dear son
Shall I twice lose.
SEBASTIAN
A most high miracle!
FERDINAND
Though the seas threaten, they are merciful;
I have cursed them without cause.
Kneels
ALONSO
Now all the blessings
Of a glad father compass thee about!
Arise, and say how thou camest here.
MIRANDA
O, wonder!
How many goodly creatures are there here!
How beauteous mankind is! O brave new world,
That has such people in't!
PROSPERO
'Tis new to thee.
ALONSO

What is this maid with whom thou wast at play?
Your eld'st acquaintance cannot be three hours[26]:
Is she the goddess that hath sever'd us,
And brought us thus together?
FERDINAND
Sir, she is mortal;
But by immortal Providence she's mine:
I chose her when I could not ask my father
For his advice, nor thought I had one. She
Is daughter to this famous Duke of Milan,
Of whom so often I have heard renown,
But never saw before; of whom I have
Received a second life; and second father
This lady makes him to me.
ALONSO
I am hers[27]:
But, O, how oddly will it sound that I
Must ask my child forgiveness!
PROSPERO
There, sir, stop:
Let us not burthen our remembrance with
A heaviness that's gone.
GONZALO
I have inly wept,
Or should have spoke ere this. Look down, you god,
And on this couple drop a blessed crown!
For it is you that have chalk'd forth the way
Which brought us hither.
ALONSO
I say, Amen, Gonzalo!
GONZALO
as Milan[28] thrust from Milan, that his issue[29]
Should become kings of Naples? O, rejoice
Beyond a common joy, and set it down
With gold on lasting pillars: In one voyage
Did Claribel her husband find at Tunis,
And Ferdinand, her brother, found a wife
Where he himself was lost, Prospero his dukedom
In a poor isle and all of us ourselves
When no man was his own[30].

ALONSO

[*To FERDINAND and MIRANDA*] Give me your hands:

Let grief and sorrow still embrace his heart

That doth not wish you joy![31]

GONZALO

Be it so! Amen!

Re-enter ARIEL, with the Master and Boatswain amazedly following

O, look, sir, look, sir! here is more of us:

I prophesied, if a gallows were on land,

This fellow could not drown. Now, blasphemy[32],

That swear'st grace o'er board, not an oath on shore?

Hast thou no mouth by land? What is the news?

Boatswain

The best news is, that we have safely found

Our king and company; the next, our ship—

Which, but three glasses since, we gave out split[33]—

Is tight and yare and bravely rigg'd as when

We first put out to sea.

ARIEL

[*Aside to PROSPERO*] Sir, all this service

Have I done since I went.

PROSPERO

[*Aside to ARIEL*] My tricksy spirit!

ALONSO

These are not natural events; they strengthen

From strange to stranger[34]. Say, how came you hither?

Boatswain

If I did think, sir, I were well awake,

I'd strive to tell you. We were dead of sleep,

And—how we know not—all clapp'd under hatches;

Where but even now with strange and several noises

Of roaring, shrieking, howling, jingling chains,

And more diversity of sounds, all horrible,

We were awaked; straightway, at liberty;

Where we, in all her trim, freshly beheld

Our royal, good and gallant ship, our master

Capering to eye her: on a trice, so please you,

Even in a dream, were we divided from them

And were brought moping hither.

ARIEL

[*Aside to* PROSPERO] Wa't well done?
PROSPERO
[*Aside to* ARIEL] Bravely, my diligence. Thou shalt be free.
ALONSO
This is as strange a maze as e'er men trod
And there is in this business more than nature
Was ever conduct of: some oracle
Must rectify our knowledge.
PROSPERO
Sir, my liege,
Do not infest your mind with beating on
The strangeness of this business; at pick'd leisure
Which shall be shortly, single[35] I'll resolve you,
Which to you shall seem probable, of every
These happen'd accidents; till when, be cheerful
And think of each thing well.
Aside to ARIEL
Come hither, spirit:
Set Caliban and his companions free;
Untie the spell.
Exit ARIEL
How fares my gracious sir?
There are yet missing of your company
Some few odd lads that you remember not.
Re-enter ARIEL, *driving in* CALIBAN, STEPHANO *and* TRINCULO, *in their stolen apparel*
STEPHANO
Every man shift for all the rest, and
let no man take care for himself[36]; for all is
but fortune. Coragio[37], bully-monster, coragio!
TRINCULO
If these be true spies which I wear in my head[38],
here's a goodly sight.
CALIBAN
O Setebos, these be brave spirits indeed!
How fine my master is! I am afraid
He will chastise me.
SEBASTIAN
Ha, ha!
What things are these, my lord Antonio?

Will money buy 'em?
ANTONIO
Very like; one of them
Is a plain fish, and, no doubt, marketable.
PROSPERO
Mark but the badges of these men, my lords,
Then say if they be true. This mis-shapen knave,
His mother was a witch, and one so strong
That could control the moon, make flows and ebbs,
And deal in her command without her power.
These three have robb'd me; and this demi-devil—
For he's a bastard one—had plotted with them
To take my life. Two of these fellows you
Must know and own; this thing of darkness!
Acknowledge mine.
CALIBAN
I shall be pinch'd to death.
ALONSO
Is not this Stephano, my drunken butler?
SEBASTIAN
He is drunk now: where had he wine?
ALONSO
And Trinculo is reeling ripe[39]: where should they
Find this grand liquor that hath gilded 'em[40]?
How camest thou in this pickle[41]?
TRINCULO
I have been in such a pickle since I
saw you last that, I fear me, will never out of
my bones: I shall not fear fly-blowing[42].
SEBASTIAN
Why, how now, Stephano!
STEPHANO
O, touch me not; I am not Stephano, but a cramp.
PROSPERO
You Times new Romand be king o' the isle, sirrah?
STEPHANO
I should have been a sore one then.
ALONSO
This is a strange thing as e'er I look'd on.
Pointing to Caliban

PROSPERO

He is as disproportion'd in his manners

As in his shape. Go, sirrah, to my cell;

Take with you your companions; as you look

To have my pardon, trim it handsomely.

CALIBAN

Ay, that I will; and I'll be wise hereafter

And seek for grace. What a thrice-double ass

Was I, to take this drunkard for a god

And worship this dull fool!

PROSPERO

Go to; away!

ALONSO

Hence, and bestow your luggage where you found it.

SEBASTIAN

Or stole it, rather.

Exeunt CALIBAN, STEPHANO, and TRINCULO

PROSPERO

Sir, I invite your highness and your train

To my poor cell, where you shall take your rest

For this one night; which, part of it, I'll waste

With such discourse as, I not doubt, shall make it

Go quick away; the story of my life

And the particular accidents gone by

Since I came to this isle: and in the morn

I'll bring you to your ship and so to Naples,

Where I have hope to see the nuptial

Of these our dear-beloved solemnized;

And thence retire me to my Milan, where

Every third thought shall be my grave[43].

ALONSO

I long

To hear the story of your life, which must

Take the ear strangely[44].

PROSPERO

I'll deliver all;

And promise you calm seas, auspicious gales

And sail so expeditious that shall catch

Your royal fleet far off.

Aside to ARIEL

My Ariel, chick,

That is thy charge: then to the elements

Be free, and fare thou well! Please you, draw near.

Exeunt

EPILOGUE

SPOKEN BY PROSPERO

Now my charms are all o'er thrown,

And what strength I have's mine own,

Which is most faint: now, 'tis true,

I must be here confined by you,

Or sent to Naples. Let me not,

Since I have my dukedom got

And pardon'd the deceiver, dwell

In this bare island by your spell;

But release me from my bands

With the help of your good hands:

Gentle breath of yours my sails

Must fill, or else my project fails,

Which was to please. Now I want [45]

Spirits to enforce, art to enchant,

And my ending is despair,

Unless I be relieved by prayer,

Which pierces so that it assaults

Mercy itself and frees all faults.

As you from crimes would pardon'd be,

Let your indulgence set me free.

注释

1. 米兰大公普洛斯彼罗被觊觎王位的弟弟安东尼奥和那不勒斯国王阿隆佐陷害,被迫和女儿米兰达在孤岛上生活了十几年。普洛斯彼罗最后终于利用魔法的力量捉弄、惩罚了那些谋害他的人。在最后一幕中,他宽恕了众人,并放弃魔法,重新成为米兰的大公。

2. gather to a head:将告完成。

3. time/ Goes upright with his carriage:一切按部就班。

4. fare:情况。

5. I am struck to the quick:我感到痛心。

6. oped:即 opened。

7. the sole drift of my purpose doth extend/ Not a frown further:我唯一的目的也就达

到了,再无愁苦烦恼。

    8. To work mine end upon their senses:化导他们的心性,使我能得到我所希望的结果。

    9. deeper than did ever plummet sound:比探测锤所及之处还要深,即深不可测的海底。sound:探测深度。

    10. Mine eyes, even sociable to the show of thine:我的眼睛一看到你。

    11. I will pay thy graces/ Home both in word and deed:我要在语言上和行动上重重报答你。

    12. unnatural:刻薄。

    13. discase:显出本来面目。

    14. prithee:pray thee,此处是催促爱丽儿快一点。

    15. I drink the air before me:我乘风而去。

    16. embrace thine age:拥抱您老人家。

    17. subtilty:即 subtlety,此处指通过魔法显现出来的一些奇幻的现象。

    18. I will tell no tales:不打算揭发你们。

    19. patience/ Says it is past her cure:忍耐也失去了作用。

    20. that they were living both in Naples,/ The king and queen there:虚拟语气,要是他们活着,在那不勒斯当国王和王后该多好。

    21. admire:惊奇。

    22. devour their reason:惶惑不安。

    23. justle:即 jostle,挤,推。

    24. Not a relation for a breakfast:不是一顿饭的时间能说完的。

    25. I would not for the world:即使给我整个世界我也不愿欺骗你。

    26. Your eld'st acquaintance cannot be three hours:你们相识最多不过三小时。

    27. I am hers:我也是她的父亲。

    28. Milan:米兰的主人。

    29. issue:后裔。

    30. all of us ourselves/ When no man was his own:在每个人迷失了本性的时候,重新找回了自己。

    31. Let grief and sorrow still embrace his heart/ That doth not wish you joy!:谁不希望你们快乐,就让忧伤和悲哀永远占据他的心灵。

    32. blasphemy:亵渎神灵,骂骂咧咧的家伙,指水手长。

    33. our ship—/ Which, but three glasses since, we gave out split:三小时前我们以为已经撞碎了的船。

    34. they strengthen/ From strange to stranger:它们越来越奇怪了。

    35. single:简单地。

    36. Every man shift for all the rest, and/ let no man take care for himself:人人为别人考虑,不要为自己盘算。斯丹法诺醉酒后语无伦次,他应该是想说"人人替自己打算,不要考虑别人"。

    37. coragio:勇气。

38. If these be true spies which I wear in my head：要是装在我头上的眼睛不曾欺骗我。

39. reeling ripe：醉得天旋地转。

40. gilded：本意为镀金，装饰等，此处应指特林鸠罗等人喝醉后满脸通红的样子。

41. pickle：困境。此处指喝醉酒的模样。

42. I shall not fear fly-blowing：我身上的酒味恐怕可以熏得连苍蝇也不会在我身上产卵了。

43. Every third thought shall be my grave：在那里心满意足地等待长眠的一天。

44. Take the ear strangely：让我们的耳朵觉得不可思议。

45. want：缺乏。

作品导读

　　《暴风雨》是莎士比亚创作生涯后期的代表作，而且在第一对开本（First Folio，第一部莎士比亚剧本合集）中它被列为首篇，在莎剧中有着重要的地位。在猛烈的暴风雨中，曾经陷害过米兰大公普洛斯彼罗的王公贵族和他们的臣仆被迫登上了荒岛。这座荒岛正是侥幸活命的普洛斯彼罗和女儿米兰达生活的地方。在普洛斯彼罗的魔法的控制下，众人历经磨难，最终幡然悔悟，而普洛斯彼罗也慷慨仁慈地宽恕了他们。莎士比亚构思和创作这部作品之时，正值英国海外拓殖的早期，人们普遍对"新世界"充满了强烈的好奇心。"新世界"那辽阔美丽的土地，充满神秘色彩的土著人，未经开发的原始森林，甚至新的动植物品种都无疑为作家提供了写作的素材，也启发作家更加深入地探讨人文主义思想的精髓。文艺复兴后期，英国社会矛盾逐渐激化，面对理想与现实的差距，莎士比亚的戏剧一度比较低沉悲壮，然而在这之后，莎士比亚开始将目光投向大自然，运用浪漫的幻想，试图在人与自然的和谐中寻求调和社会矛盾的精神与道德力量。人文主义肯定个人的尊严价值和世俗欲望，对于冲破中世纪的精神桎梏有着重要的意义，但是对个人欲望的极力张扬也造成了人类的精神危机和人文主义自身的根本性危机。在《暴风雨》中，通过建立天地人神和谐共处的世界，莎士比亚表达了重建人类和谐乐园的理想。

　　《暴风雨》塑造了几类人物形象，有贪婪自私、损人利己的贵族，有相貌丑陋、野性难驯的自然人凯列班，也有成长于平静和谐的荒岛上，深受大自然熏陶，同时也接受父亲教导的米兰达。米兰达聪明灵秀，她和腓迪南的纯洁爱情帮助父亲化解了仇怨。通过米兰达的形象，莎士比亚似乎在暗示，大自然的浸润和滋养与人类文明的结合才能生成米兰达这样自然淳朴、和谐健康的美丽形象。大自然还具有修补破裂的人伦、人际关系的作用。在故事的最后，人们对自然、对人类自身都有了新的认识。腓迪南说："海水虽然似乎那么凶暴，然而却是仁慈的，我错怪了它们。"米兰达则由衷地感叹："神奇啊，这里有多少好看的人！人类是多么美丽！啊，新奇的世界，有这么出色的人物！"普洛斯彼罗宽恕了众人的罪行，罪人也表示了忏悔，和谐的社会秩序重新建立起来。普洛斯彼罗最后向爱丽儿的"旁白"以及"收场诗"都意味深长。他把自由还给爱丽儿，情愿放弃魔法，放弃岛上的统治权，只是请求大自然送他"吉利顺风"，助人们重返文明世界。在戏剧的结尾，人与自然、人与人相互依存、彼此作用，达到了天地人神和谐自由、共存共在的境界。

思考题

1. Make comments on Prospero from an eco-critical perspective.
2. What do you think of Caliban, the savage?
3. What is (are) the symbolic meaning(s) of the island where the story happens?
4. How do you interpret Prospero's magic power and his relation with his servant Ariel?
5. How do you interpret Prospero's epilogue?

推荐阅读

Boehrer, Bruce. *Shakespeare among the Animals: Nature and Society in the Drama of Early Modern England*. Palgrave Macmillan, 2002.

Borlik, Todd Andrew. *Ecocriticism and Early Modern English Literature: Green Pastures*. Routledge, 2011.

—. (ed). *Literature and Nature in the English Renaissance: An Ecocritical Anthology*. Cambridge University Press, 2019.

Brayton, Dan. *Shakespeare's Ocean: An Ecocritical Exploration*. University of Virginia Press, 2012.

Bruckner, Lynne and Daniel Brayton (eds). *Ecocritical Shakespeare*. Ashgate, 2011.

Egan, Gabriel. *Green Shakespeare: From Ecopolitics to Ecocriticism*. Routledge, 2006.

Estok, Simon C. *Ecocriticism and Shakespeare*. Palgrave Macmillan, 2011.

—. "Environmental Implications of the Writing ad Policing of the Early Modern Body: Dismemberment and Monstrosity in Shakespearean Drama." In *Shakespeare Review*, vol. 33 (1998).

Gruber, Elizabeth. *Renaissance Ecopolitics from Shakespeare to Bacon: Rethinking Cosmopolis*. Routledge, 2019.

Hallock, Thomas, IvoKamps, and Karen L. Raber, eds. *Early Modern Ecostudies: From Florentine Codex to Shakespeare*. Palgrave Macmillan, 2008.

Hamilton, Jennifer Mae. *This Contentious Storm: An Ecocritical and Performance History of King Lear*. Bloomsbury Academic, 2017.

Jones, Gwilym. *Shakespeare's Storms*. Manchester University Press, 2015.

MacFaul, Tom. *Shakespeare and the Natural World*. Cambridge University Press, 2015.

利奥·马克斯:《花园里的机器》,马海良、雷月梅译,北京大学出版社,2011年。

约翰·弥尔顿(John Milton)

【作者简介】

约翰·弥尔顿（1608—1674）是英国诗人、思想家和政论家，也是伟大的革命者，文艺复兴人文主义的继承者。弥尔顿出身清教家庭，自幼喜爱读书，在剑桥拿到硕士学位以后，他先是在家中潜心读书，后又在欧洲游历，受到欧洲人文主义者的很大影响。这一时期他创作的姊妹篇《快乐的人》(L'Allegro) 和《忧思的人》(IL Penseroso)对快乐和忧郁进行了哲理性思考，是他早期的代表作。1638年弥尔顿出版了悼念亡友的挽诗《利西达斯》(Lycidas)，寄托哀思，也表达了诗人对人生的感慨。这首诗被有些批评家誉为"英国挽诗的最高峰"。

英国内战爆发以后，弥尔顿很快中断旅行，回到英国为克伦威尔的革命政府服务，出任外文秘书一职，撰写了大量政论小册子，为人民的革命行动进行辩护，是政府的重要代言人。王政复辟结束了弥尔顿的政治生涯，此时他已经因为辛苦的工作而双目失明，但却仍然在非常困难的情况下口述了巨著《失乐园》(Paradise Lost)、《复乐园》(Paradise Regained)和《力士参孙》(Samson Agonistes)。

弥尔顿一直想要创作出能与古希腊、古罗马史诗相媲美的英语史诗，《失乐园》正是这样的作品。《失乐园》取材于圣经，用无韵诗体写成，弥尔顿还创造性地将拉丁文及其他语言的文法、词汇糅合在英语中，整首诗气势磅礴，雄浑庄严又富于变化，很好地诠释了诗歌崇高的主题。

以下选自《失乐园》第四部和第七部。

Book Four

... where the Fiend
Saw undelighted all delight, all kind
Of living Creatures new to sight and strange:
Two of far nobler shape erect and tall,
Godlike erect, with native Honour clad
In naked Majesty seemed Lords of all,
And worthy seemed, for in their looks Divine
The image of their glorious Maker shone,
Truth, wisdom, Sanctitude severe and pure,
Severe but in true filial freedom[1] placed;
Whence true authority in men; though both

Not equal, as their sex not equal seemed;
For contemplation he and valour formed,
For softness she and sweet attractive Grace,
He for God only, she for God in him[2]:   15
His fair large Front[3] and Eye sublime declar'd
Absolute rule; and Hyacinthine Locks[4]
Round from his parted forelock manly hung
Clustering, but not beneath his shoulders broad:
She as a veil down to the slender waist   20
Her unadorned golden tresses wore
Dishevelled[5], but in wanton ringlets wav'd
As the Vine curls her tendrils, which impli'd
Subjection, but requir'd with gentle sway[6],
And by her yielded, by him best received,   25
Yielded with coy submission, modest pride,
And sweet reluctant amorous delay.
Nor those mysterious parts[7] were then concealed,
Then was not guilty shame, dishonest[8] shame
Of natures works, honor dishonorable[9],   30
Sin-bred, how have ye[10] troubl'd all mankind
With shows instead, mere shows of seeming pure,
And banished from man's life his happiest life,
Simplicity and spotless innocence.
So passed they naked on, nor shunned the sight   35
Of God or Angel, for they thought no ill:
So hand in hand they passed, the lovliest pair
That ever since in loves embraces met,
Adam the goodliest man of men since borne
His Sons, the fairest of her Daughters Eve[11].   40
Under a tuft of shade that on a green
Stood whispering soft, by a fresh Fountain side
They sat them down, and after no more toil
Of their sweet Gardening labour[12] then suffic'd
To recommend[13] cool Zephyr[14] and made ease   45
More easy[15], wholesome thirst and appetite
More grateful, to their Supper Fruits they fell,
Nectarine Fruits which the compliant boughs
Yielded them, side-long as they sat recline[16]
On the soft downy Bank damasked[17] with flowers: 50
The savoury pulp they chew, and in the rind

Still as they thirsted scoop the brimming stream;
Nor gentle purpose[18], nor endearing smiles
Wanted[19], nor youthful dalliance[20] as beseems[21]
Fair couple, linked in happy nuptial League,   55
Alone as they. About them frisking played
All Beasts of th' Earth, since wild, and of all chase[22]
In Wood or Wilderness, Forrest or Den;
Sporting the Lion ramped[23], and in his paw
Dandl'd the Kid; Bears, Tygers, Ounces[24], Pards[25]   60
Gambolled before them, th' unwieldy Elephant
To make them mirth us'd all his might, and wreathed
His Lithe Proboscis[26]; close the Serpent sly
Insinuating, wove with Gordian twine[27]
His breaded train[28], and of his fatal guile   65
Gave proof unheeded; others on the grass
Couched, and now filled with pasture[29] gazing sat,
Or Bedward ruminating: for the Sun,
Declin'd, was hasting now with prone career[30]
To th' Times new Roman Ocean Isles[31], and in th' ascending Scale   70
Of Heav' the Stars that usher Evening rose[32]:
When *Satan* still in gaze, as first he stood,
Scarce thus at length failed speech recovered sad.

 注释

1. filial freedom：子女的自由意志。

2. He for God only, she for God in him：亚当是按照上帝的模样造的，夏娃则是用亚当的一部分造的。

3. Front：前额。

4. Hyacinthine Locks：浓密、颜色很深的头发。

5. Dishevelled：乱蓬蓬的。

6. sway：命令。

7. mysterious parts：生殖器官。

8. dishonest：不纯洁的。

9. honor dishonorable：文雅地将生殖器官遮盖起来其实是不雅的，因为这样做就承认了人类的堕落和伴随而来的羞耻感。

10. ye：指前面提到的 shame 和 honor。

11. *Adam* the goodliest man of men since borne/ His Sons, the fairest of her Daughters *Eve*：亚当和夏娃的身体是人类中最美的。

12. Gardening labor：在弥尔顿的想象中，亚当和夏娃需要在伊甸园做一些园艺工作。这在一定程度上反映了弥尔顿的清教思想。从诗人的描述看来，适当的工作和劳作后惬意的休憩可以增进亚当和夏娃的感情。

13. recommend：使变得有吸引力。

14. Zephyr：西风。

15. easy：舒适。

16. recline：即 reclining，斜倚。

17. damasked：用各种形态装饰的。

18. gentle purpose：温柔的情话。

19. Wanted：缺乏。

20. dalliance：调情。

21. beseem：(古)合适。

22. chase：本义为猎场，此处指动物生活的地方。

23. ramped：用后腿为支点跃立，扬起前爪的。

24. Ounces：猞猁。

25. Pards：即 leopards，猎豹。

26. lithe Proboscis：灵活的长鼻子。

27. Gordian twine：即 Gordian Knot，希腊神话中弗利基亚国的国王戈尔迪打的难解的结。按照神谕，只有入主亚洲的人才能解开，后马其顿国王亚历山大挥剑把它斩开。

28. breaded train：即 braided train，辫子形状的尾巴。

29. pasture：食物。

30. prone career：迅速的、向下的运动。

31. Ocean Isles：根据后文的提示，此处指的是北大西洋中东部的亚速尔群岛(Azores)。

32. the Stars that usher Evening rose：传报夜晚来临的星星升起了。

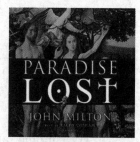

Book Seven

And God said, let the Waters generate
Reptile¹ with pawn abundant, living Soul:
And let Fowl fly above the Earth, with wings
Displayed² on the op'n Firmament of Heav'n.
And God created the great Whales, and each   5
Soul living, each that crept, which plenteously
The waters generated by their kinds³,
And every Bird of wing after his kind;
And saw that it was good, and bless'd them, saying,
Be fruitful, multiply, and in the Seas   10
And Lakes and running Streams the waters fill;
And let the Fowl be multiply'd on the Earth.
Forthwith the Sounds and Seas, each Creek and Bay

With Fry⁴ innumerable swarm, and Shoals
Of Fish that with their Finns and shining Scales   15
Glide under the green Wave, in Sculls⁵ that oft
Bank⁶ the mid Sea: part single or with mate
Graze the Sea weed their pasture, and through Groves
Of Coral stray, or sporting with quick glance
Show to the Sun their wav'd coats dropt with Gold⁷,   20
Or in their Pearly shells at ease, attend
Moist nutriment, or under Rocks their food
In jointed Amour⁸ watch: on smooth⁹ the Seal,
And bended Dolphins play: part huge of bulk
Wallowing unwieldy, enormous in their Gate¹⁰   25
Tempest¹¹ the Ocean: there Leviathan¹²
Hugest of living Creatures, on the Deep
Stretched like a Promontory sleeps or swims,
And seems a moving Land, and at his Gills¹³
Draws in, and at his Trunk spouts out a Sea.   30
Mean while the tepid¹⁴ Caves, and Fens and shores
Their Brood as numerous hatch, from the Egg that soon
Bursting with kindly¹⁵ rupture forth disclos'd
Their callow¹⁶ young, but feathered soon and fledge
They summ'd their Penns¹⁷, and soaring th' air sublime   35
With clang¹⁸ despis'd the ground¹⁹, under a cloud²⁰
In prospect; there the Eagle and the Stork
On Cliffs and Cedar tops their Eyries²¹ build:
Part²² loosely wing the Region, part more wise
In common, rang'd in figure wedge their way²³,   40
Intelligent of seasons, and set forth
Their Aery Caravan²⁴ high over Sea's
Flying, and over Lands with mutual wing²⁵
Easing their flight; so steers the prudent Crane
Her annual Voyage, borne on Winds; the Air   45
Floats²⁶, as they pass, fann'd with unnumber'd plumes:
From Branch to Branch the smaller Birds with song
Solac'd the Woods, and spread their painted wings
Till Ev'n, nor then the solemn Nightingale
Ceas'd warbling, but all night tun'd her soft lays: 50
Others on Silver Lakes and Rivers Bath'd
Their downy Breast; the Swan with Arched neck
Between her white wings mantling proudly, Rows

Her state²⁷ with Oary feet: yet oft they quit
The Dank²⁸, and rising on stiff Pennons²⁹, tower   55
The mid Aereal Sky: Others on ground
Walk'd firm; the crested Cock whose clarion sounds
The silent hours, and th' other³⁰ whose gay Train
Adorns him, colour'd with the Florid hue
Of Rainbows and Starry Eyes. The Waters thus   60
With Fish replenished, and the Air with Fowl,
Ev'ning and Morn solemniz'd the Fifth day.

注释

1. reptile：此处应包括爬行动物及一切鱼类。
2. displayed：展开。
3. by their kinds：按照它们的种类。
4. fry：小鱼。
5. Scull：一大群鱼。
6. Bank：筑成长堤。
7. dropt with Gold：带着金色斑点。
8. jointed Amour：此处可能指的是甲克纲动物在观察它们的食物。
9. smooth：平静的海面。
10. Gate：即 gait，姿态。
11. Tempest：把大洋掀起风波。
12. Leviathan：利维坦，传说中的海上巨怪，此处指的是鲸。
13. Gills：鱼鳃。
14. tepid：因为要孕育生命，因此洞穴、沼泽等都是微温的。
15. kindly：natural，卵自己裂开。
16. callow：初生无毛的幼鸟。
17. summ'd their Penns：长全了羽毛。
18. clang：鸟的啼叫。
19. despis'd the ground：俯瞰。
20. under a cloud：鸟在高空（云层之上）俯瞰云层下的地球。
21. Eyries：（筑于高山峭壁等处的）猛禽的巢。
22. Part：有些鸟。
23. rang'd in figure wedge their way：组成楔形的队列。
24. Caravan：旅行队。
25. mutual wing：并翼齐飞，交替领先以对抗风力。
26. the Air/Floats：(因为翅膀的扇动)空气荡漾波动。
27. State：指天鹅高贵的风姿。

28. Dank：水。
29. Pennons：翅膀。
30. th' other：此处指的是孔雀。

 作品导读

  《失乐园》取材于圣经，讲述了撒旦与上帝的斗争，以及亚当和夏娃在撒旦的引诱下偷吃禁果，被逐出伊甸园的故事。在很多生态批评家看来，受到基督教二元论的影响，达尔文之前的西方文学中没有环境概念或者是生态意识。但是细读弥尔顿的《失乐园》，读者却能够看到一种朴素的生态主义思想，这种思想比较集中地体现在弥尔顿对伊甸园的描写上。

  史诗中的伊甸园是一个阳光明媚、生机盎然的世界。人类的始祖亚当与夏娃亲密无间，幸福地生活在上帝为他们提供的乐园中。乐园中还生长着各种植物，亚当和夏娃需要做一些恰当的园艺工作，以使乐园更加美好。乐园中的动物自由自在地生活在人类身边，与人类和谐相处。当亚当和夏娃劳作后小憩的时候，他们能看到狮子在一旁玩耍，大象卷起了长鼻子，还有更多的动物则在悠闲地度过美好的黄昏。动物们既自得其乐，也愉悦了人类。

  在史诗的第七卷中，天使向亚当和夏娃谈起了创世的情景。必须承认，弥尔顿并不具备现代生态思想，他借天使之口说，上帝造人的目的就是让人统治地球、驯服动物，做伊甸园的统治者。不过仔细品味作品，我们会发现亚当和夏娃其实是自然生态中的一环，与伊甸园中的各种动植物平等相处，和谐共生。在描写上帝第五天的工作时，诗人提到了爬行动物、体型小巧的小鱼和体型庞大的鲸，以及仙鹤、夜莺、天鹅、雄鸡、孔雀等各种鸟类。弥尔顿熟悉自然、热爱自然，他指出，孕育生物的湿地是温暖的，还生动地描绘了雏鸟出生和成长的过程，聪明的鸟儿列队飞翔的景象。上帝在第六天还创造了狮子、豹子、大象、河马、鳄鱼、爬虫、蟒蛇、蜜蜂等陆地的动物。这些飞禽走兽都是上帝从最初的物质中创造出来的，人类也是如此，只不过是形态不同而已。人类与万物同源，与万物也是平等的，而万物的创造也与人类的存在、人类的需求没有直接关联，它们有着自己的内在价值，当然也给人类带来了美的感受与天真无邪的快乐。人类与动物都是伊甸园的生态环境中不可或缺的环节。

  弥尔顿对自然充满了崇敬之情，他的诗歌用一种具有生态意识的语言描述了世间万物和谐共处的画面，暗示人类可以在一定程度上改造自然，但是违背自然规律，盲目追求知识，妄图用科学征服自然的野心最终只能带来灾难性的后果。亚当和夏娃正是因为偷吃了智慧之果才失去了天真，被逐出了伊甸园。在一定程度上我们可以说，这正是自然对人类的贪欲的惩罚。17 世纪是崇尚科学和理性的时代，人类逐渐获得了前所未有的信心去了解自然、征服自然，也似乎不可避免地将人类凌驾于自然之上。生活在这个时代的弥尔顿所表现出的朴素的生态思想是难能可贵的，也对后世作家产生了不小的影响。

 思考题

1. Can you describe Adam's and Eve's life in the Garden of Eden?

2. What are the animals created by God in the excerpt? How do they live together in Eden?

3. What is the relationship between human beings and other creatures in the poem?

4. How does the excerpt show Milton's ecological thinking?

推荐阅读

Borlik, Todd A. *Ecocriticism and Early Modern English Literature: Green Pastures*. Routledge, 2011.

Buckham, Rebecca Lynn. *Reading Nature: The Georgic Spirit of "Paradise Lost", Early Modern England, and Twenty-first-century Ecocriticism*. Villanova University Press, 2009.

Pici, Nick. "Milton Times new Romans 'Eco-Eden: Place and Notions of the 'Green in *Paradise Lost*." In *College Literature*, vol. 28, issue 3 (2001).

Theis, Jeffery S. "The Environmental Ethics of *Paradise Lost*: Milton Times new Romans Exegesis of Genesis I-III." In *Milton Studies*, vol. 34 (1997).

—. *Writing the Forest in Early Modern England: A Sylvan Pastoral Nation*. Duquesne University Press, 2009.

王立、沈传河、岳庆云:《生态美学视野中的中外文学作品》,人民出版社,2007年。

玛丽·雪莱(Mary Shelley)

【作者简介】

玛丽·雪莱(1797—1851)出生在享有盛誉的知识分子家庭,父亲是哲学家、无神论者威廉·戈德温(William Godwin),母亲是女权运动最早的发起者、教育家和作家玛丽·沃斯通克拉夫特(Mary Wollstonecraft)。由于母亲早逝,玛丽一直由父亲抚养,虽然没有受过多少正规教育,但是她在父亲的影响下博览群书,自幼就喜爱创作,有很高的文学修养。

玛丽容貌出众,才智过人,她在1814年结识了当时已婚的浪漫派诗人珀西·雪莱,二人后来私奔,并且在雪莱的第一任妻子去世后正式结婚。婚后玛丽生育了四个孩子,不幸的是,三个先后夭折,雪莱也在一次沉船事故中早早去世。玛丽此后笔耕不辍,成为专业作家,在很艰难的情况下独自养大了她和雪莱唯一幸存的儿子。

玛丽在21岁时出版了她最著名的小说《弗兰肯斯坦》(*Frankenstein; or, The Modern Prometheus*)。她也撰写游记、自传,为杂志写稿,从事编辑工作等。除了《弗兰肯斯坦》,玛丽最重要的贡献是为亡夫编印遗作。1824年,她出版了《雪莱诗遗作》,1839年又发行了一套《雪莱诗集》。

受到家庭的熏陶,玛丽深受启蒙思想的影响,相信人类理性的力量,然而她并不如一般的启蒙主义者那样乐观地认为理性的发展必将使人性逐渐完善,必然带来光明的未来。玛丽对人类无节制地扩张自己的欲望,试图征服自然的做法是持否定态度的。以下选自《弗兰肯斯坦》的第二章、第四章和第六章。

Chapter 2

We[1] were brought up together; there was not quite a year difference in our ages. I need not say that we were strangers to any species of disunion or dispute[2]. Harmony was the soul of our companionship, and the diversity and contrast that subsisted in our characters drew us nearer together. Elizabeth was of a calmer and more concentrated disposition; but, with all my ardour, I was capable of a more intense application, and was more deeply smitten with the thirst for knowledge. She busied herself with following the aerial creations of the poets; and in the majestic and wondrous scenes which surrounded our Swiss home—the sublime shapes of the mountains; the changes of the seasons; tempest and calm; the silence of winter, and the life and turbulence of our Alpine summers—she found ample scope for admiration and delight. While my companion contemplated with a serious and satisfied spirit the magnificent appearances of things, I delighted in investigating their causes. The world was to me a secret which I desired to divine. Curiosity, earnest research to learn the hidden laws of nature, gladness akin to rapture, as they were unfolded to me, are among the earliest sensations I can remember.

On the birth of a second son, my junior by seven years, my parents gave up entirely their wandering life, and fixed themselves in their native country. We possessed a house in Geneva, and a campagne on Belrive, the eastern shore of the lake, at the distance of rather more than a league from the city. We resided principally in the latter, and the lives of my parents were passed in considerable seclusion. It was my temper to avoid a crowd, and to attach myself fervently to a few. I was indifferent, therefore, to my schoolfellows in general; but I united myself in the bonds of the closest friendship to one among them. Henry Clerval was the son of a merchant of Geneva. He was a boy of singular talent and fancy. He loved enterprise, hardship, and even danger, for its own sake. He was deeply read in books of chivalry and romance. He composed heroic songs, and began to write many a tale of enchantment and knightly adventure. He tried to make us act plays, and to enter into masquerades, in which the characters were drawn from the heroes of Roncesvalles, of the Round Table of King Arthur, and the chivalrous train who shed their blood to redeem the holy sepulchre[3] from the hands of the infidels.

No human being could have passed a happier childhood than myself. My parents were possessed by the very spirit of kindness and indulgence. We felt that they were not the tyrants to rule our lot according to their caprice, but the agents and creators of all the many delights which we enjoyed. When I mingled with other families, I distinctly discerned how peculiarly fortunate my lot was, and gratitude assisted the development of filial love.

My temper was sometimes violent, and my passions vehement; but by some law in my temperature they were turned, not towards childish pursuits, but to an eager desire to learn, and not to learn all things indiscriminately. I confess that neither the structure of languages, nor the code of governments, nor the politics of various states, possessed attractions for me. It was the secrets of heaven and earth that I desired to learn; and whether it was the outward substance of things, or the inner spirit of nature and the mysterious soul of man that occupied me, still my inquiries were directed to the metaphysical[4], or, in its highest sense, the physical secrets of the world.

Meanwhile Clerval occupied himself, so to speak, with the moral relations of things. The busy stage of life, the virtues of heroes, and the actions of men, were his theme; and his hope and his dream was to become one among those whose names are recorded in story, as the gallant and adventurous benefactors of our species. The saintly soul of Elizabeth shone like a shrine dedicated lamp in our peaceful home. Her sympathy was ours; her smile, her soft voice, the sweet glance of her celestial eyes[5], were ever there to bless and animate us. She was the living spirit of love to soften and attract: I might have become sullen in my study, rough through the ardour of my nature, but that she was there to subdue me to a semblance of her own gentleness. And Clerval—could aught ill entrench on the noble spirit of Clerval? —yet he might not have been so perfectly humane, so thoughtful in his generosity—so full of kindness and tenderness amidst his passion for adventurous exploit, had she not unfolded to him the real loveliness of beneficence, and made the doing good the end and aim of his soaring ambition[6].

I feel exquisite pleasure in dwelling on the recollections of childhood, before misfortune had tainted my mind, and changed its bright visions of extensive usefulness into gloomy and narrow reflections upon self. Besides, in drawing the picture of my early days, I also record those events which led, by insensible steps, to my after tale of misery: for when I would account to myself for the birth of that passion, which afterwards ruled my destiny, I find it arise, like a mountain river, from ignoble and almost forgotten sources; but, swelling as it proceeded, it became the torrent which, in its course, has swept away all my hopes and joys.

Chapter 4

One of the phenomena which had peculiarly attracted my attention was the structure of the human frame, and, indeed, any animal endued with life. Whence, I often asked myself, did the principle of life proceed? It was a bold question, and one which has ever been considered as a mystery; yet with how many things are we upon the brink of becoming acquainted[7], if cowardice or carelessness did not restrain our inquiries. I revolved these circumstances in my mind, and determined thenceforth to apply myself more particularly to those branches of natural philosophy which relate to physiology. Unless I had been animated by an almost supernatural enthusiasm, my application to this study would have been irksome, and almost intolerable. To examine the causes of life, we must first have recourse to death. I became acquainted with the science of anatomy: but this was not sufficient; I must also observe the natural decay and corruption of the human body. In my education my father had taken the greatest precautions that my mind should be impressed with no supernatural horrors. I do not ever remember to have trembled at a tale of superstition, or to have feared the apparition of a spirit. Darkness had no effect upon my fancy; and a churchyard was to me merely the receptacle of bodies deprived of life, which, from being the seat of beauty and strength, had become food for the worm. Now I was led to examine the cause and progress of this decay, and forced to spend days and nights in vaults[8] and charnel-houses[9]. My attention was fixed upon every object the most insupportable to the delicacy of the human feelings. I saw how the fine form of man was degraded and wasted; I beheld the corruption of death succeed to the blooming cheek of life; I saw how the worm inherited the wonders of the eye and brain. I paused, examining and analysing all the minutia of causation, as exemplified in the change from life to death, and death to life, until from the midst of this darkness a sudden light broke in upon me—a light so brilliant and wondrous, yet so simple, that while I became dizzy with the immensity of the prospect which it illustrated, I was surprised, that among so many men of genius who had directed their inquiries towards the same science, that I alone should be reserved to discover so astonishing a secret.

Remember, I am not recording the vision of a madman. The sun does not more certainly shine in the heavens, than that which I now affirm is true[10]. Some miracle might have produced it, yet the stages of the discovery were distinct and probable. After days and nights of incredible labour and fatigue, I succeeded in discovering the cause of generation and life; nay, more, I became myself capable of bestowing animation upon lifeless matter.

The astonishment which I had at first experienced on this discovery soon gave place to delight and rapture. After so much time spent in painful labour, to arrive at once at the summit of my desires was the most gratifying consummation of my toils. But this discovery was so great and overwhelming that all the steps by which I had been progressively led to it were obliterated, and I beheld only the result. What had been the study and desires of the wisest men since the creation of the world was now within my grasp. Not that, like a magic scene, it all opened upon me at once: the information I had obtained was of a nature rather to direct my endeavours so soon as I should point them towards the object of my search, than to exhibit that object already accomplished. I was like the Arabian who had been buried with the dead, and found a passage to life, aided only by one glimmering, and seemingly ineffectual, light.

I see by your eagerness, and the wonder and hope which your eyes express, my friend, that you expect to be informed of the secret with which I am acquainted; that cannot be: listen patiently until the end of my story, and you will easily perceive why I am reserved upon that subject. I will not lead you on, unguarded and ardent as I then was, to your destruction and infallible misery. Learn from me, if not by my precepts, at least by my example, how dangerous is the acquirement of knowledge, and how much happier that man is who believes his native town to be the world, than he who aspires to become greater than his nature will allow.

When I found so astonishing a power placed within my hands, I hesitated a long time concerning the manner in which I should employ it. Although I possessed the capacity of bestowing animation, yet to prepare a frame for the reception of it, with all its intricacies of fibres, muscles, and veins, still remained a work of inconceivable difficulty and labour. I doubted at first whether I should attempt the creation of a being like myself, or one of simpler organisation; but my imagination was too much exalted by my first success to permit me to doubt of my ability to give life to an animal as complex and wonderful as man. The materials at present within my command hardly appeared adequate to so arduous an undertaking; but I doubted not that I should ultimately succeed. I prepared myself for a multitude of reverses; my operations might be incessantly baffled, and at last my work be imperfect: yet, when I considered the improvement which every day takes place in science and mechanics, I was encouraged to hope my present attempts would at least lay the foundations of future success. Nor could I consider the magnitude and complexity of my plan as any argument of its impracticability[11]. It was with these feelings that I began the creation of a human being. As the minuteness of the parts formed a great hinderance to my speed, I resolved, contrary to my first intention, to make the being of a gigantic stature; that is to say, about eight feet in height, and proportionably large. After having formed this determination, and having spent some months in successfully collecting and arranging my materials, I began.

No one can conceive the variety of feelings which bore me onwards, like a hurricane, in the first enthusiasm of success. Life and death appeared to me ideal bounds, which I should first break through, and pour a torrent of light into our dark world. A new species would bless me as its creator and source; many happy and excellent natures would owe their being to me. No father could claim the gratitude of his child so completely as I should deserve theirs. Pursuing these reflections, I thought, that if I could bestow animation upon lifeless matter, I might in process of time (although I now found it impossible) renew life where death had apparently devoted the body to corruption.

These thoughts supported my spirits, while I pursued my undertaking with unremitting ardour. My cheek had grown pale with study, and my person had become emaciated with confinement. Sometimes, on the very brink of certainty, I failed; yet still I clung to the hope which the next day or the next hour might realise. One secret which I alone possessed was the hope to which I had dedicated myself; and the moon gazed on my midnight labours, while, with unrelaxed and breathless eagerness, I pursued nature to her hiding-places. Who shall conceive the horrors of my secret toil, as I dabbled among the unhallowed damps of the grave, or tortured the living animal to animate the lifeless clay? My limbs now tremble and my eyes swim[12] with the remembrance; but then a resistless, and almost frantic, impulse urged me forward; I seemed to have lost all soul or sensation but for this one pursuit. It was indeed but a passing trance that only made me feel with renewed acuteness so soon as, the unnatural stimulus ceasing to operate, I had returned to my old habits. I collected bones from charnel houses; and disturbed, with profane fingers, the tremendous secrets of the human frame. In a solitary chamber, or rather cell, at the top of the house, and separated from all the other apartments by a gallery and staircase, I kept my workshop of filthy creation: my eye-balls were starting from their sockets[13] in attending to the details of my employment. The dissecting room and the slaughterhouse furnished many of my materials; and often did my human nature turn with loathing from my occupation, whilst, still urged on by an eagerness which perpetually increased, I brought my work near to a conclusion.

The summer months passed while I was thus engaged, heart and soul, in one pursuit. It was a most beautiful season; never did the fields bestow a more plentiful harvest, or the vines yield a more luxuriant vintage: but my eyes were insensible to the charms of nature. And the same feelings which made me neglect the scenes around me caused me also to forget those friends who were so many miles absent, and whom I had not seen for so long a time. I knew my silence disquieted them; and I well remembered the words of my father:"I know that while you are pleased with yourself, you will think of us with affection, and we shall hear regularly from you. You must pardon me if I regard any interruption in your correspondence as a proof that your other duties are equally neglected."

I knew well, therefore, what would be my father's feelings; but I could not tear my thoughts from my employment, loathsome in itself, but which had taken an irresistible hold of my imagination. I wished, as it were, to procrastinate all that related to my feelings of affection until the great object, which swallowed up every habit of my nature, should be completed.

I then thought that my father would be unjust if he ascribed my neglect to vice, or faultiness on my part; but I am now convinced that he was justified in conceiving that I should not be altogether free from blame. A human being in perfection ought always to preserve a calm and peaceful mind, and never to allow passion or a transitory desire to disturb his tranquillity. I do not think that the pursuit of knowledge is an exception to this rule. If the study to which you apply yourself has a tendency to weaken your affections, and to destroy your taste for those simple pleasures in which no alloy can possibly mix, then that study is certainly unlawful, that is to say, not befitting the human mind. If this rule were always observed; if no man allowed any pursuit whatsoever to interfere with the tranquillity of his domestic affections, Greece had not been enslaved; Caesar would have spared his country; America would have been discovered more gradually; and the empires of Mexico and Peru had not been destroyed.

But I forget that I am moralising in the most interesting part of my tale; and your looks remind me to proceed.

My father made no reproach in his letters, and only took notice of my silence by inquiring into my occupations more particularly than before. Winter, spring, and summer passed away during my labours; but I did not watch the blossom or the expanding leaves—sights which before always yielded me supreme delight—so deeply was I engrossed in my occupation. The leaves of that year had withered before my work drew near to a close; and now every day showed me more plainly how well I had succeeded. But my enthusiasm was checked by my anxiety[14], and I appeared rather like one doomed by slavery to toil in the mines, or any other unwholesome trade, than an artist occupied by his favourite employment. Every night I was oppressed by a slow fever, and I became nervous to a most painful degree; the fall of a leaf startled me, and I shunned my fellow-creatures as if I had been guilty of a crime. Sometimes I grew alarmed at the wreck I perceived that I had become; the energy of my purpose alone sustained me: my labours would soon end, and I believed that exercise and amusement would then drive away incipient disease; and I promised myself both of these when my creation should be complete.

Chapter 6

Clerval had never sympathised in my tastes for natural science; and his literary pursuits differed wholly from those which had occupied me. He came to the university with the design of making himself complete master of the oriental languages, as thus he should open a field for the plan of life he had marked out for himself. Resolved to pursue no inglorious career, he turned his eyes toward the East, as affording scope for his spirit of enterprise. The Persian, Arabic, and Sanscrit languages engaged his attention, and I was easily induced to enter on the same studies. Idleness had ever been irksome to me, and now that I wished to fly from reflection, and hated my former studies, I felt great relief in being the fellow-pupil with my friend, and found not only instruction but consolation in the works of the orientalists. I did not, like him, attempt a critical knowledge of their dialects, for I did not contemplate making any other use of them than temporary amusement. I read merely to understand their meaning, and they well repaid my labours. Their melancholy is soothing, and their joy elevating, to a degree I never experienced in studying the authors of any other country. When you read their writings, life appears to consist in a warm sun and a garden of roses—in the smiles and frowns of a fair enemy, and the fire that consumes your own heart. How different from the manly and heroical poetry of Greece and Rome!

Summer passed away in these occupations, and my return to Geneva was fixed for the latter end of autumn; but being delayed by several accidents, winter and snow arrived, the roads were deemed impassable, and my journey was retarded until the ensuing spring. I felt this delay very bitterly; for I longed to see my native town and my beloved friends. My return had only been delayed so long from an unwillingness to leave Clerval in a strange place, before he had become acquainted with any of its inhabitants. The winter, however, was spent cheerfully; and although the spring was uncommonly late, when it came its beauty compensated for its dilatoriness.

The month of May had already commenced, and I expected the letter daily which was to fix the date of my departure, when Henry proposed a pedestrian tour in the environs of Ingolstadt, that I might bid a personal farewell to the country I had so long inhabited. I acceded with pleasure to this proposition: I was fond of exercise, and Clerval had always been my favourite companion in the rambles of this nature that I had taken among the scenes of my native country.

We passed a fortnight in these perambulations[15]; my health and spirits had long been restored, and they gained additional strength from the salubrious air I breathed, the natural incidents of our progress, and the conversation of my friend. Study had before secluded me from the intercourse of my fellow-creatures, and rendered me unsocial; but Clerval called forth the better feelings of my heart; he again taught me to love the aspect of nature, and the cheerful faces of children. Excellent friend! How sincerely did you love me, and endeavour to elevate my mind until it was on a level with your own! A selfish pursuit had cramped and narrowed me, until your gentleness and affection warmed and opened my senses; I became the same happy creature who, a few years ago, loved and beloved by all, had no sorrow or care. When happy, inanimate nature had the power of bestowing on me the most delightful sensations. A serene sky and verdant fields filled me with ecstasy. The present season was indeed divine; the flowers of spring bloomed in the hedges, while those of summer were already in bud. I was undisturbed by thoughts which during the preceding year had pressed upon me, notwithstanding my endeavours to throw them off, with an invincible burden.

Henry rejoiced in my gaiety, and sincerely sympathised in my feelings: he exerted himself to amuse me, while he expressed the sensations that filled his soul. The resources of his mind on this occasion were truly astonishing: his conversation was full of imagination; and very often, in imitation of the Persian and Arabic writers, he invented tales of wonderful fancy and passion. At other times he repeated my favourite poems, or drew me out into arguments, which he supported with great ingenuity.

We returned to our college on a Sunday afternoon: the peasants were dancing, and every one we met appeared gay and happy. My own spirits were high, and I bounded along with feelings of unbridled joy and hilarity.

注释

1. We：指弗兰肯斯坦和伊丽莎白。伊丽莎白是弗兰肯斯坦父母收养的孤儿，与弗兰肯斯坦以表兄妹相称，二人青梅竹马，情投意合。

2. I need not say that we were strangers to any species of disunion or dispute：自不必说，我们绝无纷争，从不争吵。

3. holy sepulchre：圣墓。

4. the metaphysical：超自然的。

5. celestial eyes：天使般的眼睛。

6. the doing good the end and aim of his soaring ambition：高涨的雄心壮志最终是为了行善。

7. upon the brink of becoming acquainted：几乎要了解。

8. vaults：墓穴。

9. charnel-houses：(旧时的)藏骸所。

10. The sun does not more certainly shine in the heavens, than that which I now affirm is true：这一切都有如日悬空中，千真万确。

11. Nor could I consider the magnitude and complexity of my plan as any argument of its impracticability：我的计划庞大复杂，但我不能因此认为这个计划无法实现。

12. my eyes swim：我感到头晕目眩。

13. my eye-balls were starting from their sockets：(因为全神贯注地做细致的工作)眼珠都瞪得好像快要掉出眼眶。

14. my enthusiasm was checked by my anxiety：我的激情被焦虑所抑制。

15. perambulations：漫步。

作品导读

《弗兰肯斯坦》的创作起源于拜伦、雪莱等人的一次夜谈。当时大家阅读了德国的神怪小说，并且谈论了不少哲学问题，最后拜伦提议在座的朋友们每人也写一篇神怪小说。虽然大家都动了笔，但最后只有玛丽完成了作品，并且在出版后轰动一时。这部小说被誉为英国文学史上第一篇科幻小说，带有浓厚的哥特风格，既有浪漫的气氛，也有令人毛骨悚然的情节，更重要的是，这部作品还带有深切的人文关怀，探索了人性中的黑暗，也深刻反思了理性时代以来崇尚科学与理性，割裂人与自然的思潮。

在《弗兰肯斯坦》中，科学家维克多·弗兰肯斯坦雄心勃勃地想要成为"现代普罗米修斯"，他希望通过创造生命来证明自己，并且最终用尸体拼凑出了一个有生命的怪物。这个面目可憎、奇丑无比的怪物起先对人类并无恶意，但在饱受歧视和冷遇后，他在失望中杀害了弗兰肯斯坦的朋友和亲人，最后与弗兰肯斯坦同归于尽。弗兰肯斯坦相信科学的力量，热心科学研究，这本身并没有错，但是他妄想征服自然，试图凌驾于自然之上，颠覆自然的生态伦理，这种人类中心主义的姿态却最终毁灭了家人、朋友和自己。弗兰肯斯坦曾目睹了大自然的巨大力量，例如在一次暴风雨中雷电彻底击毁了一棵老橡树，这其实是大自然对他的"暗示"，但是弗兰肯斯坦却一意孤行，离群索居，为了实现自己造物的雄心而不顾一切地投入到试验中。在这个过程中，他对活的或是死的生命都没有丝毫的敬畏，也疏远了亲人的感情，忽略了四季的变化，一心幻想有一天他所创造的"新的物种"将奉他为"造物之主"，对他"顶礼膜拜"，对他"感恩戴德"。事与愿违，弗兰肯斯坦手中诞生的"怪物"却并未对他产生这种情感。相反的，怪物威胁他说，自己虽为弗兰肯斯坦所创造，但却是弗兰肯斯坦的主人。这是对人类中心主义的一种反讽，暗示人与自然对抗的结果可能会是人和自然关系的失衡以及人类自身毁灭性灾难的到来。

与弗兰肯斯坦形成对比的是他的未婚妻伊丽莎白和挚友克莱瓦尔。伊丽莎白性格安静、专注，沉醉于瑞士优美的湖光山色中，自然的一切都让她感到钦佩和欣喜。伊丽莎白从未想过要征服自然，而是与自然建立了一种和谐的关系，在精神上同大自然交流融合。克莱瓦尔喜欢文学，热爱自然，在自然中他体会到了生命真正的意义。自然也赋予了他热情慷慨的性格，他对朋友永远都极富同情心。在弗兰肯斯坦受到疾病折磨的时候，是克莱瓦尔通过文学把弗兰肯斯坦重新带回充满"和煦的阳光"的生活，也是他提议进行了长达两周的远足，沿途的自然美景重新唤起了弗兰肯斯坦心中美好的情感，使他恢复了心灵的平静。

玛丽·雪莱通过《弗兰肯斯坦》这个生态伦理寓言表明，人本是自然的一部分，是自然的创造，自然是人类生存的条件，也对人类的心灵有着不可替代的净化作用。如果科学技术成了统治自然的工具，被人类过分贪婪地使用，其后果只能是自然规律遭到破坏，生态失衡，最终人类将为此付出沉重的代价。

思考题

1. Why does Frankenstein recall his childhood affectionately?
2. What is the implication of Frankenstein's father's blame on his son?
3. What is the lesson Frankenstein learns from his own experience?
4. What does the monster symbolize in the story?
5. Can you explain why today *Frankenstein* still has much significance from an

ecological perspective?

推荐阅读

Barclay, Bridgitte and Christy Tidwell (eds). *Gender and Environment in Science Fiction*. Lexington Books, 2019.

Carman, Colin. *The Radical Ecology of the Shelleys: Eros and Environment*. Routledge, 2019.

Feder, Helena. "'A Blot upon the Earth': Nature's 'Negative' and the Production of Monstrosity in *Frankenstein*." In *Journal of Ecocriticism*, vol. 2 (1), 2010.

Heymans, Peter. *Animality in British Romanticism: The Aesthetics of Species*. Routledge, 2012.

Smith, Andrew and William Hughes. *Ecogothic*. Manchester University Press, 2013.

Smith, Andrew. *The Cambridge Companion to Frankenstein*. Cambridge University Press, 2016.

Vakoch, Douglas A. ed. *Feminist Ecocriticism: Environment, Women, and Literature*. Lexington Books, 2012.

鲁枢元:《生态文艺学》,陕西人民出版社,2000年。

威廉·华兹华斯(William Wordsworth)

【作者简介】

威廉·华兹华斯(1770—1850)是著名的浪漫主义派诗人,曾在剑桥接受教育,后游历欧洲,深受法国大革命鼓舞。不过和当时很多英国知识分子一样,在耳闻目睹了革命的血腥和暴力之后,诗人的思想逐渐趋于保守。1798年,华兹华斯与好友柯尔律治合作出版了《抒情歌谣集》(*Lyrical Ballads*),正式宣告了英国文学浪漫主义时代的来临。这部诗集不仅收录了二人的诗歌,而且在第二版的序言中,华兹华斯还阐明了浪漫主义诗歌的基本原则,认为诗歌是"强烈情感的自然流露",主张诗人应该选用普通人的语言来写普通生活里的事件和情境,反对华丽的辞藻和过分的雕琢。他还认为诗人是"人性最坚强的保护者、支持者和维护者。他所到之处都播下人的情谊和爱"。

华兹华斯长期和柯尔律治、骚塞等人居住在风景优美、远离城市的湖区,寄情山水,在大自然里找慰藉。他的代表作品包括长诗《序曲》(*The Prelude*)、《丁登寺》("Lines Composed a Few Miles above Tintern Abbey")、《咏水仙》("I Wandered Lonely as a Cloud")、《孤独的割麦女》("The Solitary Reaper")等。他的诗歌清新优美,情景交融,寓意深刻,强调回归自然,人与自然和谐相处,具有强烈的生态意识。

Lines Written in Early Spring

I heard a thousand blended notes,
While in a grove I sate[1] reclined,
In that sweet mood when pleasant thoughts
Bring sad thoughts to the mind.

To her fair works[2] did Nature link
The human soul that through me ran;
And much it grieved my heart to think
What man has made of man.

Through primrose tufts[3], in that green bower,
The periwinkle[4] trailed its wreaths;
And 'tis my faith that every flower
Enjoys the air it breathes.

The birds around me hopped and played,
Their thoughts I cannot measure[3]:—
But the least motion which they made
It seemed a thrill of pleasure.

The budding twigs spread out their fan,
To catch the breezy air;
And I must think, do all I can,
That there was pleasure there.   20

If this belief from heaven be sent,
If such be Nature's holy plan,
Have I not reason to lament
What man has made of man?

 注释

1. sate: sit 的过去式和过去分词。
2. her fair works: 大自然的美妙杰作。
3. tuft: 小树丛。
4. periwinkle: 长春花。
5. measure: 揣测。

I Wandered Lonely as a Cloud

I wandered lonely as a cloud
That floats on high o'er vales and hills,
When all at once I saw a crowd,
A host[1], of golden daffodils;
Beside the lake, beneath the trees,   5
Fluttering and dancing in the breeze.

Continuous[2] as the stars that shine
And twinkle on the milky way,
They stretched in never-ending line
Along the margin of a bay[3]:   10
Ten thousand saw I at a glance,
Tossing their heads in sprightly dance.

The waves beside them danced; but they

Out-did the sparkling waves in glee:
A poet could not but be gay, 15
In such a jocund company:
I gazed—and gazed—but little thought
What wealth the show to me had brought:

For oft, when on my couch I lie
In vacant[4] or in pensive mood, 20
They flash upon that inward eye
Which is the bliss of solitude[5];
And then my heart with pleasure fills,
And dances with the daffodils.

 注释

1. host：一大群，许多。
2. continuous：延伸一片。
3. the margin of a bay：一湾湖水。
4. vacant：茫然，无聊。
5. that inward eye which is the bliss of solitude：诗人认为，在孤寂中回想自然美景是一种幸福。

 作品导读

《早春即景》是华兹华斯早期的作品，也是他的代表作之一，篇幅并不长，但在很大程度上定下了诗人整个诗歌创作的基调。诗歌开头就将读者引入到平静祥和的自然中陷入沉思。诗人认为人与自然本应有亲密的内在联系，但是人类文明却使人与自然、人与人产生了隔阂。在这首诗中，大自然被比作艺术家，她创造美的事物，也将诗人的灵魂与自然相连。华兹华斯崇拜自然，他认为自然有一些力量能"启发我们内在的心灵，为它灌输崇高的理想"。诗人也热爱大自然，在大自然中他能够感受到发自心底的欢乐。身处鸟语花香之中，华兹华斯仿佛置身于天堂，虽然无法确定跳跃的鸟儿和绽放的花蕾的感受，但是从花朵鲜艳的色彩和鸟儿欢快的叫声中，他可以推断世间万物都在享受大自然的清新和美丽，它们的每一个姿态和动作都显示了它们正在迸发的兴奋和快乐。

在这种美当中，诗人并没有尽情地享受自然的美丽，而是不禁有些感伤，想到"人怎样对待着人"。对于他来说，"大自然的神圣安排"就是让人与万物和谐共存，人本是大自然的一部分，自然给人们提供了一个有益身心健康的、自然的生活方式，但是文明的高度发展和对利益无休止的追求却使人们迷失了方向。

在《咏水仙》里，向往自由的诗人离开喧嚣的城市，独自在山谷中游荡，与自然融为一体。

在这种和谐中,他发现了律动的生命,一大片金色的水仙花在湖畔、树下随风起舞,像群星一样熠熠生辉地点缀在波光粼粼的河边,绵延不绝,与身处其中的诗人构成了一幅天人合一的画卷。诗歌用了一多半篇幅生动真实地描绘水仙花,引导读者感受自然的魅力,与诗人形成共鸣。

诗人早已敏锐地意识到了工业文明带来的弊端,因此厌倦了城市生活,孤独地在山谷中求索,寄情于山水之间。他将怒放的水仙花视为"同伴",在与它的交流中获得了极大的快乐。这种快乐不仅是感官上一时的快乐,而且带给了他宝贵的精神财富,值得他细细品味:在百无聊赖的时候,诗人在脑海中反复重温与水仙花的对话交流,诗情画意真正进入了他的生命,使他达到了诗意栖居的状态。在这种状态下,诗人悟出了自然对人类在道德上的教育意义,自然引导着人类,对自然的热爱也关联着对人类的热爱,纯净的自然让诗人体会到了生活的真谛。在诗歌的最后,诗人在脑海中与水仙共舞,人类与自然完美和谐地共同存在、共同发展,这正是诗人所追求的理想的栖居方式。

1. How does Wordsworth show the beauty of early spring?
2. In "Lines Written in Early Spring", how does Wordsworth make a comparison between the state of nature and the state of mankind?
3. What are the themes of "I Wandered Lonely as a Cloud"?
4. If Wordsworth had used *walked* instead of *wandered* in the first line, would he have ruined the poem?
5. Some critics argue that although he often describes nature and meditates on nature's significance, Wordsworth is still anthropocentric. What is your opinion?

推荐阅读

Bate, Jonathan. "Romantic Ecology Revisited." In *Wordsworth's Circle*. Vol. 24, issue 3 (1993).

Bennett, Andrew, ed. *William Wordsworth in Context*. Cambridge University Press, 2015.

Gill, Stephen, ed. *The Cambridge Companion to Wordsworth*. Cambridge University Press, 2003.

Hall, Dewey W., ed. *Victorian Ecocriticism: The Politics of Place and Early Environmental Justice*. Lexington Books, 2017.

Hess, Scott. *William Wordsworth and the Ecology of Authorship: the Roots of Environmentalism in Nineteenth-century Culture*. University of Virginia Press, 2012.

Heymans, Peter. *Animality in British Romanticism: The Aesthetics of Species*. Routledge, 2012.

Kroeber, Karl. *Ecological Literary Criticism: Romantic Imagining and the Biology *of the Mind*. Columbia University Press, 1994.

McGann, Jerome. *The Romantic Ideology: A Critical Investigation*. University of Chicago Press, 1983.

McKuick, James C. *Green Writing: Romanticism and Ecology*. St. Martin's, 2000.

格伦·A. 勒夫:《实用生态批评:文学、生物学及环境》,胡志红、王敬民、徐常勇译,北京大学出版社,2010年。

托马斯·哈代(Thomas Hardy)

【作者简介】

托马斯·哈代（1840—1928）是维多利亚时代晚期最具有代表性的小说家之一，也是20世纪初重要的现代派诗人。他横跨了两个世纪，早期创作以小说为主，当《无名的裘德》

受到了猛烈抨击后，他转而创作诗歌，创作了八部抒情诗集和气势恢宏的史诗《列王》(*Dynasts*)。哈代是一个承上启下的作家，他继承了维多利亚小说的现实主义传统，也为20世纪的英国文学开拓了道路。

哈代出生在英国南部多塞特郡的一个乡村里，在那里他度过了一生中的大多数时光，他的一系列"威塞克斯小说"就取材于家乡这片封闭、落后的土地。随着19世纪中后期工业的蓬勃发展，乡村自给自足的自然经济遭受了毁灭性的打击，乡村的生活方式、传统习俗等都发生了巨大的改变。深受进化论影响的哈代目睹了这些变化，他清楚地意识到社会的转变是不可避免的，工业社会代替农业社会是社会发展的必然，然而他同时又对逐渐逝去的田园牧歌生活感到深深的惋惜，同情面对变化无所适从的农民。他的作品用现实主义的笔法真实地反映了资本主义入侵英国乡村后引起的社会经济、政治、道德、风俗等方面的深刻变化以及人民的悲惨命运，也在很大程度上揭露了资产阶级道德、法律和宗教的虚伪性。

哈代一生创作了十五部长篇小说，他自己将其分为"性格与环境小说""幻想与浪漫小说"和"爱情阴谋故事"，其中最著名的当属"性格与环境小说"，包括《绿荫下》(*Under the Greenwood Tree*)、《远离尘嚣》(*Far from the Madding Crowd*)、《还乡》(*The Return of the Native*)、《卡斯特桥市长》(*The Mayor of Casterbridge*)、《林中人》(*The Woodlanders*)、《德伯家的苔丝》(*Tess of the D'Urbervilles*，简称《苔丝》)和《无名的裘德》(*Jude the Obscure*)等。

以下选自《苔丝》第十六章和第十七章，也是小说第三部分"旗鼓重整"的开头两章。

XVI[1]

On a thyme-scented, bird-hatching morning in May, between two and three years after the return from Trantridge—silent, reconstructive years for Tess Durbeyfield—she left her home for the second time.

Having packed up her luggage so that it could be sent to her later, she started in a hired trap for the little town of Stourcastle, through which it was necessary to pass on her journey, now in a direction almost opposite to that of her first adventuring. On the curve of the nearest hill she looked back regretfully at Marlott and her father's house, although she had been so anxious to get away.

Her kindred dwelling there would probably continue their daily lives as heretofore, with no great diminution of pleasure in their consciousness, although she would be far off, and they deprived of her smile. In a few days the children would engage in their games as merrily as ever, without the sense of any gap left by her departure. This leaving of the younger children she had decided to be for the best; were she to remain they would probably gain less good by her precepts than harm by her example.[2]

She went through Stourcastle without pausing and onward to a junction of highways, where she could await a carrier's van[3] that ran to the south-west; for the railways which engirdled this interior tract of country had never yet struck across it. While waiting, however, there came along a farmer in his spring cart, driving approximately in the direction that she wished to pursue. Though he was a stranger to her she accepted his offer of a seat beside him, ignoring that its motive was a mere tribute to her countenance. He was going to Weatherbury, and by accompanying him thither she could walk the remainder of the distance instead of travelling in the van by way of Casterbridge.

Tess did not stop at Weatherbury, after this long drive, further than to make a slight nondescript meal at noon at a cottage to which the farmer recommended her. Thence she started on foot, basket in hand, to reach the wide upland of heath dividing this district from the low-lying meads of a further valley in which the dairy stood that was the aim and end of her day's pilgrimage.

Tess had never before visited this part of the country, and yet she felt akin to the landscape. Not so very far to the left of her she could discern a dark patch in the scenery, which inquiry confirmed her in supposing to be trees marking the environs of Kingsbere—in the church of which parish the bones of her ancestors—her useless ancestors—lay entombed.

She had no admiration for them now; she almost hated them for the dance[4] they had led her; not a thing of all that had been theirs did she retain but the old seal and spoon. "Pooh—I have as much of mother as father in me!" she said. "All my prettiness comes from her, and she was only a dairymaid."

The journey over the intervening uplands and lowlands of Egdon, when she reached them, was a more troublesome walk than she had anticipated, the distance being actually but a few miles. It was two hours, owing to sundry wrong turnings, ere she found herself on a summit commanding the long-sought-for vale, the Valley of the Great Dairies, the valley in which milk and butter grew to rankness, and were produced more profusely, if less delicately, than at her home—the verdant plain so well watered by the river Var or Froom.

It was intrinsically different from the Vale of Little Dairies, Blackmoor Vale, which, save during her disastrous sojourn at Trantridge, she had exclusively known till now. The world was drawn to a larger pattern here. The enclosures numbered fifty acres instead of ten, the farmsteads were more extended, the groups of cattle formed tribes hereabout; there only families.[5] These myriads of cows stretching under her eyes from the far east to the far west outnumbered any she had ever seen at one glance before. The green lea was speckled as thickly with them as a canvas by van Alsloot[6] or Sallaert[7] with burghers. The ripe hue of the red and dun[8] kine[9] absorbed the evening sunlight, which the white-coated animals returned to the eye in rays almost dazzling, even at the distant elevation on which she stood.

The bird's-eye perspective before her was not so luxuriantly beautiful, perhaps, as that other one which she knew so well; yet it was more cheering. It lacked the intensely blue atmosphere of the rival vale, and its heavy soils and scents; the new air was clear, bracing, ethereal. The river itself, which nourished the grass and cows of these renowned dairies, flowed not like the streams in Blackmoor. Those were slow, silent, often turbid; flowing over beds of mud into which the incautious wader might sink and vanish unawares. The Froom waters were clear as the pure River of Life shown to the Evangelist[10], rapid as the shadow of a cloud, with pebbly shallows that prattled to the sky all day long. There the water-flower was the lily; the crow-foot[11] here.

Either the change in the quality of the air from heavy to light, or the sense of being amid new scenes where there were no invidious eyes upon her, sent up her spirits wonderfully. Her hopes mingled with the sunshine in an ideal photosphere which surrounded her as she bounded along against the soft south wind. She heard a pleasant voice in every breeze, and in every bird's note seemed to lurk a joy.

Her face had latterly changed with changing states of mind, continually fluctuating between beauty and ordinariness, according as the thoughts were gay or grave. One day she was pink and flawless; another pale and tragical. When she was pink she was feeling less than when pale; her more perfect beauty accorded with her less elevated mood; her more intense mood with her less perfect beauty. It was her best face physically that was now set against the south wind.

The irresistible, universal, automatic tendency to find sweet pleasure somewhere, which pervades all life, from the meanest to the highest, had at length mastered Tess. Being even now only a young woman of twenty, one who mentally and sentimentally had not finished growing, it was impossible that any event should have left upon her an impression that was not in time capable of transmutation.

And thus her spirits, and her thankfulness, and her hopes, rose higher and higher. She tried several ballads, but found them inadequate; till, recollecting the psalter that her eyes had so often wandered over of a Sunday morning before she had eaten of the tree of knowledge, she chanted:"O ye Sun and Moon...O ye Stars...ye Green Things upon the Earth...ye Fowls of the Air...Beasts and Cattle...Children of Men...bless ye the Lord, praise Him and magnify Him for ever!"[12]

She suddenly stopped and murmured:"But perhaps I don't quite know the Lord as yet."

And probably the half-unconscious rhapsody was a Fetishistic utterance in a Monotheistic setting; women whose chief companions are the forms and forces of outdoor

Nature retain in their souls far more of the Pagan fantasy of their remote forefathers than of the systematized religion taught their race at later date. However, Tess found at least approximate expression for her feelings in the old "Benedicite" that she had lisped from infancy; and it was enough. Such high contentment with such a slight initial performance as that of having started towards a means of independent living was a part of the Durbeyfield temperament. Tess really wished to walk uprightly[13], while her father did nothing of the kind; but she resembled him in being content with immediate and small achievements, and in having no mind for laborious effort towards such petty social advancement as could alone be effected by a family so heavily handicapped as the once powerful d'Urbervilles were now.

There was, it might be said, the energy of her mother's unexpended family, as well as the natural energy of Tess's years, rekindled after the experience which had so overwhelmed her for the time. Let the truth be told—women do as a rule live through such humiliations, and regain their spirits, and again look about them with an interested eye. While there's life there's hope is a conviction not so entirely unknown to the "betrayed" as some amiable theorists would have us believe.

Tess Durbeyfield, then, in good heart, and full of zest for life, descended the Egdon slopes lower and lower towards the dairy of her pilgrimage.

The marked difference, in the final particular, between the rival vales now showed itself. The secret of Blackmoor was best discovered from the heights around; to read aright the valley before her it was necessary to descend into its midst. When Tess had accomplished this feat she found herself to be standing on a carpeted level, which stretched to the east and west as far as the eye could reach.

The river had stolen from the higher tracts and brought in particles to the vale all this horizontal land; and now, exhausted, aged, and attenuated, lay serpentining along through the midst of its former spoils.

Not quite sure of her direction, Tess stood still upon the hemmed expanse of verdant flatness, like a fly on a billiard-table of indefinite length, and of no more consequence to the surroundings than that fly. The sole effect of her presence upon the placid valley so far had been to excite the mind of a solitary heron, which, after descending to the ground not far from her path, stood with neck erect, looking at her.

Suddenly there arose from all parts of the lowland a prolonged and repeated call—"Waow! waow! waow!"

From the furthest east to the furthest west the cries spread as if by contagion, accompanied in some cases by the barking of a dog. It was not the expression of the valley's consciousness that beautiful Tess had arrived, but the ordinary announcement of milking-time—half-past four o'clock, when the dairymen set about getting in the cows.

The red and white herd nearest at hand, which had been phlegmatically waiting for the call, now trooped towards the steading in the background, their great bags of milk swinging under them as they walked. Tess followed slowly in their rear, and entered the barton by the open gate through which they had entered before her. Long thatched sheds stretched round the enclosure, their slopes encrusted with vivid green moss, and their eaves supported by wooden posts rubbed to a glossy smoothness by the flanks of infinite cows and calves of bygone years, now passed to an oblivion almost inconceivable in its profundity. Between the post were ranged the milchers[14], each exhibiting herself at the present moment to a whimsical eye in the rear as a circle on two stalks, down the center of which a switch moved pendulum-wise; while the sun, lowering itself behind this patient row, threw their shadows accurately inwards upon the wall. Thus it threw shadows of these obscure and homely figures every evening with as much care over each contour as if it had been the profile of a court beauty on a palace wall; copied them as diligently as it had copied Olympian shapes on marble *façades* long ago, or the outline of Alexander, Caesar, and the Pharaohs.

They were the less restful cows that were stalled. Those that would stand still of their own will were milked in the middle of the yard, where many of such better behaved ones stood waiting now—all prime milchers, such as were seldom seen out of this valley, and not always within it; nourished by the succulent feed which the water-meads[15] supplied at this prime season of the year. Those of them that were spotted with white reflected the sunshine in dazzling brilliancy, and the polished brass knobs[16] of their horns glittered with something of military display. Their large-veined udders hung ponderous as sandbags, the teats sticking out like the legs of a gipsy's crock[17]; and as each animal lingered for her turn to arrive the milk oozed forth and fell in drops to the ground.

XVII

The dairymaids and men had flocked down from their cottages and out of the dairy-house with the arrival of the cows from the meads; the maids walking in pattens[18], not on account of the weather, but to keep their shoes above the mulch of the barton. Each girl sat down on her three-legged stool, her face sideways, her right cheek resting against the cow, and looked musingly along the animal's flank at Tess as she approached. The male milkers, with hat-brims turned down, resting flat on their foreheads and gazing on the ground, did not observe her.

One of these was a sturdy middle-aged man—whose long white "pinner"[19] was somewhat finer and cleaner than the wraps of the others, and whose jacket underneath had a presentable marketing aspect—the master-dairyman, of whom she was in quest, his double character as a working milker and butter maker here during six days, and on the seventh as a man in shining broad-cloth in his family pew at church, being so marked as to have inspired a rhyme:

Dairyman Dick[20]

All the week:—

On Sundays Mister Richard Crick.

Seeing Tess standing at gaze he went across to her.

The majority of dairymen have a cross manner at milking time, but it happened that Mr Crick was glad to get a new hand—for the days were busy ones now—and he received her warmly; inquiring for her mother and the rest of the family—(though this as a matter of form merely, for in reality he had not been aware of Mrs Durbeyfield's existence till apprised of the fact by a brief business-letter about Tess).

"Oh—ay, as a lad I knowed your part o' the country very well," he said terminatively. "Though I've never been there since. And an aged woman of ninety that use to live nigh here, but is dead and gone long ago, told me that a family of some such name as yours in Blackmoor Vale came originally from these parts, and that 'twere a old ancient race that had all but perished off the earth—though the new generations didn't know it. But, Lord, I took no notice of the old woman's ramblings, not I."

"Oh no—it is nothing," said Tess.

Then the talk was of business only.

"You can milk 'em clean, my maidy? I don't want my cows going azew[21] at this time o' year."

She reassured him on that point, and he surveyed her up and down. She had been staying indoors a good deal, and her complexion had grown delicate.

"Quite sure you can stand it? 'Tis comfortable enough here for rough folk; but we don't live in a cowcumber frame[22]."

She declared that she could stand it, and her zest and willingness seemed to win him over.

"Well, I suppose you'll want a dish o' tay, or victuals of some sort, hey? Not yet? Well, do as ye like about it. But faith, if 'twas I, I should be as dry as a kex[23] wi' travelling so far."

"I'll begin milking now, to get my hand in," said Tess.

She drank a little milk as temporary refreshment—to the surprise—indeed, slight contempt—of Dairyman Crick, to whose mind it had apparently never occurred that milk was good as a beverage.

"Oh, if ye can swaller that, be it so," he said indifferently, while holding up the pail that she sipped from. "'Tis what I hain't touched for years—not I. Rot the stuff; it would lie in my innerds like lead. You can try your hand upon she," he pursued, nodding to the nearest cow. "Not but what she do milk rather hard.[24] We've hard ones and we've easy ones, like other folks. However, you'll find out that soon enough."

When Tess had changed her bonnet for a hood, and was really on her stool under the cow, and the milk was squirting from her fists into the pail, she appeared to feel that she really had laid a new foundation for her future. The conviction bred serenity, her pulse slowed, and she was able to look about her.

The milkers formed quite a little battalion of men and maids, the men operating on the hardteated animals, the maids on the kindlier natures. It was a large dairy. There were nearly a hundred milchers under Crick's management, all told; and of the herd the master-dairyman milked six or eight with his own hands, unless away from home. These were the cows that milked hardest of all; for his journey-milkmen being more or less casually hired, he would not entrust this half-dozen to their treatment, lest, from indifference, they should not milk them fully; nor to the maids, lest they should fail in the same way for lack of finger-grip; with the result that in course of time the cows would "go azew"—that is, dry up. It was not the loss for the moment that made slack milking so serious, but that with the decline of demand there came decline, and ultimately cessation, of supply.

After Tess had settled down to her cow there was for a time no talk in the barton, and not a sound interfered with the purr of the milk-jets into the numerous pails, except a momentary exclamation to one or other of the beasts requesting her to turn round or stand still. The only movements were those of the milkers' hands up and down, and the swing of the cows' tails. Thus they all worked on, encompassed by the vast flat mead which extended to either slope of the valley—a level landscape compounded of old landscapes long forgotten, and, no doubt, differing in character very greatly from the landscape they composed now.

"To my thinking," said the dairyman, rising suddenly from a cow he had just finished off, snatching up his three-legged stool in one hand and the pail in the other, and moving on to the next hard-yielder in his vicinity, "to my thinking, the cows don't gie down their milk to-day as usual. Upon my life, if Winker[25] do begin keeping back like this, she'll not be worth going under by midsummer."

"'Tis because there's a new hand come among us," said Jonathan Kail. "I've noticed such things afore."

"To be sure. It may be so. I didn't think o't."

"I've been told that it goes up into their horns at such times," said a dairymaid.

"Well, as to going up into their horns," replied Dairyman Crick dubiously, as though even witchcraft might be limited by anatomical possibilities, "I couldn't say; I certainly could not. But as nott cows[26] will keep it back as well as the horned ones, I don't quite agree to it. Do ye know that riddle about the nott cows, Jonathan? Why do nott cows give less milk in a year than horned?"

"I don't!" interposed the milkmaid, "Why do they?"

"Because there bain't so many of 'em,"[27] said the dairyman. "Howsomever, these gam'sters[28] do certainly keep back their milk to-day. Folks, we must lift up a stave or two[29]—that's the only cure for't."

Songs were often resorted to in dairies hereabout as an enticement to the cows when they showed signs of withholding their usual yield; and the band of milkers at this request burst into melody—in purely business-like tones, it is true, and with no great spontaneity; the result, according to their own belief, being a decided improvement during the song's continuance. When they had gone through fourteen or fifteen verses of a cheerful ballad about a murderer who was afraid to go to bed in the dark because he saw certain brimstone flames around him, one of the male milkers said—

"I wish singing on the stoop didn't use up so much of a man's wind! You should get your harp, sir; not but what a fiddle is best."

Tess, who had given ear to this, thought the words were addressed to the dairyman, but she was wrong. A reply, in the shape of "Why?" came as it were out of the belly of a dun cow in the stalls; it had been spoken by a milker behind the animal, whom she had not hitherto perceived.

"Oh yes; there's nothing like a fiddle," said the dairyman. "Though I do think that bulls are more moved by a tune than cows—at least that's my experience. Once there was an old aged man over at Mellstock—William Dewy by name—one of the family that used to do a good deal of business as tranters over there—Jonathan, do ye mind?—I knowed the man by sight as well as I know my own brother, in a manner of speaking. Well, this man was a coming home along from a wedding, where he had been playing his fiddle, one fine moonlight night, and for shortness' sake he took a cut across Forty-acres, a field lying that way, where a bull was out to grass. The bull seed William, and took after him, horns aground, begad; and though William runned his best, and hadn't MUCH drink in him (considering 'twas a wedding, and the folks well off), he found he'd never reach the fence and get over in time to save himself. Well, as a last thought, he pulled out his fiddle as he runned, and struck up a jig[30], turning to the bull, and backing towards the corner. The bull softened down, and stood still, looking hard at William Dewy, who fiddled on and on; till a sort of a smile stole over the bull's face. But no sooner did William stop his playing and turn to get over hedge than the bull would stop his smiling and lower his horns towards the seat of William's breeches. Well, William had to turn about and play on, willy-nilly; and 'twas only three o'clock in the world, and 'a knowed that nobody would come that way for hours, and he so leery and tired that 'a didn't know what to do. When he had scraped till about four o'clock he felt that he verily would have to give over soon, and he said to himself, 'There's only this last tune between me and eternal welfare! Heaven save me, or I'm a done man.' Well, then he called to mind how he'd seen the cattle kneel o' Christmas Eves in the dead o'night.[31] It was not Christmas Eve then, but it came into his head to play a trick upon the bull. So he broke into the 'Tivity Hymm[32], just as at Christmas carol-singing; when, lo and behold, down went the bull on his bended knees, in his ignorance, just as if 'twere the true 'Tivity night and hour. As soon as his horned friend were down, William turned, clinked off like a long-dog, and jumped safe over hedge, before the praying bull had got on his feet again to take after him. William used to say that he'd seen a man look a fool a good many times, but never such a fool as that bull looked when he found his pious feelings had been played upon, and 'twas not Christmas Eve. ... Yes, William Dewy, that was the man's name; and I can tell you to a foot where's he a-lying in Mellstock Churchyard at this very moment—just between the second yew-tree and the north aisle."

"It's a curious story; it carries us back to medieval times, when faith was a living thing!"

The remark, singular for a dairy-yard, was murmured by the voice behind the dun cow; but as nobody understood the reference, no notice was taken, except that the narrator seemed to think it might imply scepticism as to his tale.

"Well, 'tis quite true, sir, whether or no. I knowed the man well."

"Oh yes; I have no doubt of it," said the person behind the dun cow.

Tess's attention was thus attracted to the dairyman's interlocutor, of whom she could see but the merest patch, owing to his burying his head so persistently in the flank of the milcher. She could not understand why he should be addressed as "sir" even by the dairyman himself. But no explanation was discernible; he remained under the cow long enough to have milked three, uttering a private ejaculation now and then, as if he could not get on.

"Take it gentle, sir; take it gentle," said the dairyman. "'Tis knack, not strength, that does it."

"So I find," said the other, standing up at last and stretching his arms. "I think I have finished her, however, though she made my fingers ache."

Tess could then see him at full length. He wore the ordinary white pinner and leather leggings of a dairy-farmer when milking, and his boots were clogged with the mulch of the yard; but this was all his local livery. Beneath it was something educated, reserved, subtle, sad, differing.

But the details of his aspect were temporarily thrust aside by the discovery that he was one whom she had seen before. Such vicissitudes had Tess passed through since that time that for a moment she could not remember where she had met him; and then it flashed upon her that he was the pedestrian who had joined in the club-dance at Marlott—the passing stranger who had come she knew not whence, had danced with others but not with her, and slightingly left her, and gone on his way with his friends.

The flood of memories brought back by this revival of an incident anterior to her troubles produced a momentary dismay lest, recognizing her also, he should by some means discover her story. But it passed away when she found no sign of remembrance in him. She saw by degrees that since their first and only encounter his mobile face had grown more thoughtful, and had acquired a young man's shapely moustache and beard—the latter of the palest straw colour where it began upon his cheeks, and deepening to a warm brown farther from its root. Under his linen milking-pinner he wore a dark velveteen jacket, cord breeches[33] and gaiters[34], and a starched white shirt. Without the milking-gear nobody could have guessed what he was. He might with equal probability have been an eccentric landowner or a gentlemanly ploughman. That he was but a novice at dairy work she had realized in a moment, from the time he had spent upon the milking of one cow.

Meanwhile many of the milkmaids had said to one another of the newcomer, "How pretty she is!" with something of real generosity and admiration, though with a half hope that the auditors would qualify the assertion—which, strictly speaking, they might have done, prettiness being an inexact definition of what struck the eye in Tess. When the milking was finished for the evening they straggled indoors, where Mrs Crick, the dairyman's wife—who was too respectable to go out milking herself, and wore a hot stuff gown in warm weather because the dairymaids wore prints[35]—was giving an eye to the leads[36] and things.

Only two or three of the maids, Tess learnt, slept in the dairy-house besides herself, most of the helpers going to their homes. She saw nothing at supper-time of the superior milker who had commented on the story, and asked no questions about him, the remainder of the evening being occupied in arranging her place in the bed-chamber. It was a large room over the milk-house, some thirty feet long; the sleeping-cots of the other three indoor milkmaids being in the same apartment. They were blooming young women, and, except one, rather older than herself. By bedtime Tess was thoroughly tired, and fell asleep immediately.

But one of the girls, who occupied an adjoining bed, was more wakeful than Tess, and would insist upon relating to the latter various particulars of the homestead into which she had just entered. The girl's whispered words mingled with the shades, and, to Tess's drowsy mind, they seemed to be generated by the darkness in which they floated.

"Mr Angel Clare—he that is learning milking, and that plays the harp—never says much to us. He is a pa'son's son, and is too much taken up wi' his own thoughts to notice girls. He is the dairyman's pupil—learning farming in all its branches. He has learnt sheep-farming at another place, and he's now mastering dairy-work.... Yes, he is quite the gentleman-born. His father is the Reverent Mr Clare at Emminster—a good many miles from here."

"Oh—I have heard of him," said her companion, now awake. "A very earnest clergyman, is he not?"

"Yes—that he is—the earnestest man in all Wessex, they say—the last of the old Low Church[37] sort, they tell me—for all about here be what they call High. All his sons, except our Mr Clare, be made pa'sons too."

Tess had not at this hour the curiosity to ask why the present Mr Clare was not made a parson like his brethren, and gradually fell asleep again, the words of her informant coming to her along with the smell of the cheeses in the adjoining cheeseloft, and the measured dripping of the whey from the wrings[38] downstairs.

注释

1. 第16章和第17章是小说第三部分"旗鼓重整"的开始两章。在这两章里,苔丝来到牛奶厂,在那里愉快地工作和生活。

2. gain less good by her precepts than harm by her example:身教优于言教。

3. van:运货车,客车。

4. dance：指的是祖先们让苔丝担了贵族后裔之名，引发了后来的不幸。

5. there only families：指苔丝熟悉的小牛奶厂的牛只是一家一家地养着。

6. van Alsloot：16 世纪末、17 世纪初画家，现存作品有《布鲁塞尔行会游行》等。

7. Sallaert：16 世纪末、17 世纪初画家，现存作品有《比箭》《布鲁塞尔行会游行》等。哈代此处指的是行会游行图。

8. dun：暗褐色的。

9. kine：母牛。

10. the Evangelist：福音教徒，指圣约翰。

11. the crow-foot：水毛茛。

12. 一首赞扬上帝的颂歌，名为《赞扬颂》（或译作《万物颂》），晨祷时与赞美上帝的《天主颂》交替而唱，内容是呼叫天地万物，令他们永远赞扬上帝。

13. to walk uprightly：大意是挺起腰杆做人。

14. the milchers：乳牛。

15. water-meads：水草场，按时放水灌溉的草场，多在河滨。

16. brass knobs：牛犄角上戴的铜箍，防止牛角触伤别的牛。

17. crock：一种用来烹饪的三足锅。

18. pattens：木头套鞋。

19. pinner：围裙。

20. Dick：Richard 的昵称。

21. going azew：停止分泌乳汁。

22. a cowcumber frame：黄瓜暖架，木头框架上盖有玻璃，是一种防风保暖的措施。

23. as dry as a kex：干得像柴一样。

24. Not but what she do milk rather hard：挤起来有点费劲。

25. Winker：一头牛的名字。

26. nott cows：没有犄角的牛。

27. there bain't so many of 'em：没犄角的牛压根就很少。

28. gam'sters：倔强胆大的畜生。

29. lift up a stave or two：唱几首歌。

30. a jig：吉格舞曲，一种三拍子的快步舞曲。

31. 据说圣诞前夜，牛在牛棚里跪着欢迎耶稣的诞生。这是一种迷信的说法。

32. Tivity Hymm：《圣诞颂》，颂扬耶稣诞生的颂诗，圣诞节演唱。

33. cord breeches：灯芯绒马裤。

34. gaiters：绑腿，裹腿。

35. print：印花布，印花布做的服装。

36. leads：盛牛奶的铅桶。

37. Low Church：低教派。与后面提到的高教派 High (Church) 相对，是英国国教的两个派别。

38. wrings：压干酪的机器。

**作品导读**

在哈代的小说中,"性格与环境小说"最突出地表现了哈代对自然、对生态的看法。尽管哈代对现代生态思想是陌生的,但他长期生活在乡间的经历,他对渐渐被破坏殆尽的乡村环境和乡村生活方式的怀念都决定了他独特的生态视角。很多哈代的研究者都发现,作家笔下的多塞特郡地貌多样,既神奇又充满生命力,苔丝生活的小山村纯净美丽,而《还乡》的女主人公游苔莎生活的爱敦荒原则广袤苍凉。大自然不仅起到提供故事背景、烘托主题的作用,也具有自己独立的内在精神,与人物的思想和命运息息相通。苔丝出生在风光旖旎、有着优美传说的布蕾谷,在那里她汲取大自然的精华,成长为勤劳质朴的少女,天然地具有美丽的容貌和与之相称的纯朴的道德感。苔丝还是干农活的行家里手,并且热爱乡间的劳动,能够很好地与自然融为一体。更重要的是,苔丝的命运变化也遵循自然季节交替变化的规律,她去城里认亲和去大奶牛场工作都是在气候宜人的春季,而她的命运转折都发生在深秋或者隆冬。

在经历了失去孩子的悲伤后,苔丝重新鼓起勇气去寻找新的生活。作家花了不少笔墨描述大奶牛场周围的自然风光:这里给人"畅快爽朗之感","空气清新、爽利、缥缈、空灵"。在新的环境中,苔丝也摆脱了过去的烦恼,兴致"高到令人惊异的程度"。"她在每一阵的微风里,都听到悦耳的声音,在每一只鸟儿的歌唱中,都觉到隐而未发的快乐。"在这样愉快的心境下,苔丝开始高声地唱起《万物颂》,她歌唱太阳、月亮与星辰,还有飞鸟、野兽和家畜。这本是一首赞扬上帝的颂歌,但是哈代特别指出,对于苔丝这种"以户外大自然的形体和力量作为主要伙伴的女人",与其说她是在赞颂基督教的上帝(正是基督教的二元论使人与自然不再平等和谐),不如说她主要还是受到异教的影响,也就是说,苔丝歌颂的就是神秘美丽的大自然本身。

在这片郁郁葱葱的土地上,人类并不是主宰者,而只是自然的一部分,甚至是非常渺小的一部分。站在四面环山的田野里,苔丝"好像一个苍蝇,落到一个大的没有限度的台球台子上似的","对于四围的景物,丝毫无足轻重",不过是引起了一只苍鹭的注意。万物同祖同源是达尔文进化论的重要思想,它使哈代充分意识到,人和大自然中的其他生物是平等的,并无优越之处。这一点在对奶牛场的描述中也得到了印证。奶牛场不仅水草充足肥美,而且所有人对待奶牛就像对待自己的同类一样。每头奶牛都有显示它们性格或者外貌的名字,而当奶出得不好的时候,大家还会用合唱来催奶,并且真心相信这种方法行之有效。为了证实动物确实能听懂音乐,奶牛场老板还讲了小提琴手和公牛的故事。提琴手对着咆哮而来的公牛拉起欢快的舞曲,而这头牛不仅喜欢听音乐,甚至听到《圣诞颂》还会下跪祈祷。也许歌唱使奶牛增产不过是迷信,公牛的故事也只是传说,但这些细节表明,在奶牛场人们尊重奶牛,像朋友一样对待它们,人与其他生物和谐地生活在一起,一切都让人身心愉悦。这说明,哈代很早就对工业革命以来愈演愈烈的人类中心论进行了反思,并且在自己的小说中对其进行了批判。

1. How do you understand that Tess is "a daughter of nature"?

2. Why is Tess so happy to work on the dairy farm?

3. On the diary farm people believe that singing songs can improve milk production. Comment on this plot.

4. Analyze Thomas Hardy's ecological thinking.

5. Can you use eco-critical theories you have learned to interpret Tess's doomed tragic destiny?

推荐阅读

Armbruster, Karla and Kathleen. R. Wallace, ed. *Beyond Nature Writing: Expanding the Boundaries of Ecocriticism*. University Press of Virginia, 2001.

Hall, Dewey W. (ed). *Victorian Ecocriticism: The Politics of Place and Early Environmental Justice*. Lexington Books, 2017.

Mazzeno, Laurence W. and Ronald D. Morrison (eds). *Victorian Writers and the Environment: Ecocritical Perspectives*. Routledge, 2017.

Taylor, P. W. *Respect for Nature: A Theory of Environmental Ethics*. Princeton University Press, 1986.

Worster, D. *The Wealth of Nature: Environmental History and the Ecological Imagination*. Oxford University Press, 1993.

李美华:《英国生态文学》,学林出版社,2008年。

威廉·巴特勒·叶芝(William Butler Yeats)

【作者简介】

叶芝(1865—1939)是爱尔兰著名诗人、剧作家和散文家,也是爱尔兰文艺复兴运动的领袖,1923年获诺贝尔文学奖,获奖的理由是他"用鼓舞人心的诗篇,以高度的艺术形式表达了整个民族的精神风貌"。

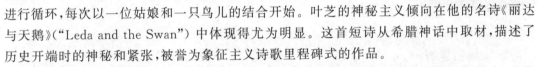

叶芝早年的创作浪漫主义色彩浓厚,诗歌多取材于爱尔兰本土的传奇与民谣,崇尚自然,风格华丽,善于营造梦幻般的氛围,带有朴素的生态思想。《茵尼斯弗利岛》("The Lake Isle of Innisfree")就属于这一时期的杰作。诗人受到美国文学家大卫·梭罗的影响,向往过一种与大自然亲密接触的农耕生活,因此整首诗有追寻世外桃源,逃避现实的倾向。

叶芝一生都对神秘主义和唯灵论有浓厚的兴趣,他在诗歌创作中形成了自己复杂的神秘主义体系。他认为历史以2000年为周期进行循环,每次以一位姑娘和一只鸟儿的结合开始。叶芝的神秘主义倾向在他的名诗《丽达与天鹅》("Leda and the Swan")中体现得尤为明显。这首短诗从希腊神话中取材,描述了历史开端时的神秘和紧张,被誉为象征主义诗歌里程碑式的作品。

在意象派诗人庞德等人的影响下,在积极参加爱尔兰民族主义政治运动的实践中,叶芝的诗歌风格在他创作的中后期逐渐发生了比较大的变化,更加质朴无华,关注精神的意象和细节。艾略特认为,叶芝的诗歌不单能带来"经验和喜悦",还具有"更重要的历史意义","他的历史就是他们时代的历史,没有他便不能理解那些历史"。

The Sad Shepherd

There was a man whom Sorrow named his Friend,
And he, of his high comrade Sorrow dreaming,
Went walking with slow steps along the gleaming
And humming Sands, where windy surges wend[1]:
And he called loudly to the stars to bend
From their pale thrones and comfort him, but they
Among themselves laugh on and sing alway[2]:
And then the man whom Sorrow named his friend
Cried out, Dim sea, hear my most piteous story!
The sea Swept on and cried her old cry still,
Rolling along in dreams from hill to hill.
He fled the persecution of her glory

And, in a far-off, gentle valley stopping,
Cried all his story to the dewdrops glistening.
But naught they heard, for they are always listening, 15
The dewdrops, for the sound of their own dropping.
And then the man whom Sorrow named his friend
Sought once again the shore, and found a shell,
And thought, I will my heavy story tell
Till my own words, re-echoing, shall send 20
Their sadness through a hollow, pearly heart;
And my own tale again for me shall sing,
And my own whispering words be comforting,
And lo! my ancient burden may depart.
Then he sang softly nigh[3] the pearly rim; 25
But the sad dweller by the sea-ways lone
Changed all he sang to inarticulate moan
Among her wildering whirls, forgetting him.

注释

1. wend:行,走,往,去。
2. alway:即 always。
3. nigh:(在时间、地点、关系等方面)接近地,靠近地。

The Stolen Child

WHERE dips the rocky highland
Of Sleuth Wood[1] in the lake,
There lies a leafy island
Where flapping herons[2] wake
The drowsy water rats; 5
There we've hid our faery vats,
Full of berrys
And of reddest stolen cherries.
Come away, O human child!
To the waters and the wild 10
With a faery, hand in hand,
For the world's more full of weeping than you can understand.

Where the wave of moonlight glosses
The dim gray sands with light,

Far off by furthest Rosses³   15
We foot it all the night,
Weaving olden dances
Mingling hands and mingling glances
Till the moon has taken flight;
To and fro we leap   20
And chase the frothy bubbles,
While the world is full of troubles
And anxious in its sleep.
Come away, O human child!
To the waters and the wild   25
With a faery, hand in hand,
For the world's more full of weeping than you can understand.

Where the wandering water gushes
From the hills above Glen-Car⁴,
In pools among the rushes   30
That scarce could bathe a star,
We seek for slumbering trout
And whispering in their ears
Give them unquiet dreams;
Leaning softly out   35
From ferns that drop their tears
Over the young streams.
Come away, O human child!
To the waters and the wild
With a faery, hand in hand,   40
For the world's more full of weeping than you can understand.

Away with us he's going,
The solemn-eyed:
He'll hear no more the lowing⁵
Of the calves on the warm hillside   45
Or the kettle on the hob
Sing peace into his breast,
Or see the brown mice bob
Round and round the oatmeal chest.
For he comes, the human child,   50
To the waters and the wild
With a faery, hand in hand,

For the world's more full of weeping than he can understand.

注释

1. Sleuth Wood：斯硫斯丛林，位于斯拉哥郡。
2. herons：苍鹭。
3. Rosses：罗赛斯，斯拉哥附近的一个海滨渔村。
4. Glen-Car：格伦卡，斯拉哥境内的一个湖名。
5. lowing：牛的哞哞叫声。

作品导读

《悲伤的牧羊人》描述了一个与"悲哀"做伴，想要向自然倾诉自己的伤心事的牧羊人。尽管在生活中是失意的，悲伤的牧羊人在面对自然时依然趾高气扬，颐指气使，妄想让天上的星星俯身听他的故事，给他安慰。然而星星只是窃笑，牧羊人只得放低身段，去向海洋和露珠诉说，依然没有得到任何回应，最后只能自我安慰地向贝壳倾诉，希望回声能够帮助自己忘却烦恼。令他感到失望的是，就连贝壳也没有如他所愿清晰地回响他的歌声，他只落得被自然遗忘的下场。

这首诗中的牧羊人在很大程度上代表着空虚、无聊的现代人，因为无法与人进行真正的沟通，所以转而向自然求助。与传统的牧羊人不同，叶芝笔下悲伤的牧羊人不是将自己融入自然，与自然和谐相处，而是把自己，或者说人类，当做宇宙的中心，理所当然地希望自然倾听自己的烦恼。然而星星、海洋、露珠和贝壳都被叶芝赋予了生命，他们或"窃笑"，或"追袭"，或"压根儿没管"，或"遗忘"牧羊人的倾诉。他们在自己的"歌吟""喊声""滴滴答答"声"呻吟"中体现出，自然万物不是被动的、沉默的客体，而是有着独立于人的存在与价值。自然有着自己的喜怒哀乐，人不过是宇宙中一个渺小的存在，一个微不足道的环节。如果人类总是凌驾于自然之上，对自然失去敬畏，不能平等地对待自然，其结果只能是像悲哀的牧羊人一样，被自然抛弃。

《被盗的孩子》是叶芝早期的代表作之一，取材于古老的爱尔兰民间传说，描写仙子引诱孩子离家出走的故事："来，人之子呀，/到湖滨旷野来吧，/手拉手，与仙人一道。"诗中描绘了一个伊甸园般神奇美妙的自然世界，在那里人可以摆脱尘世的无尽烦恼，与精灵共舞。

在诗歌的第一节，叶芝描绘了生机勃勃的小岛，岛上森林郁郁葱葱，生长着味道鲜美的草莓和樱桃。在第二节中，诗人描写了美丽的沙滩和海浪，在月光下人与精灵快乐地共舞，自由自在地享受美妙的时光。在诗歌的第三节中，"我们"在睡梦中的鳟鱼耳边轻轻诉说，看到"年轻的溪水"上"蕨类在垂泪"，"我们"悄然离去。这一切都构成一幅优美灵动的画面，人与自然融为一体，成为自然的一部分。徜徉其中，读者也禁不住希望自己就是那个被盗的孩子，可以和精灵在林中共舞，在泉边散步，品尝大自然慷慨的馈赠。

在夜幕的笼罩中，大自然的一切都显得那么和谐优美，充满神秘的感觉，使人忘却忧伤和烦恼。与之形成鲜明对比的是人类世界。"世界充满苦恼/连觉也睡不好"，有太多的悲伤和泪水,让"人之子"无法理解。叶芝生活在动荡的世纪之交,深切地体会到现代工业社会的悲哀,厌恶都市生活,因此产生了脱离现实,逃向仙境的倾向。大自然纯洁美丽,魅惑着都市人远离尘嚣,返璞归真。叶芝的思想虽然略显消极,希望从逃避遁世中获得安宁,但这种热爱自然,渴望回归自然,寻求与自然和谐相处,达到精神生态的平衡的生态思想在叶芝的时代是难能可贵的。

思考题

1. Explain Yeats's eco-critical thinking by analyzing the image of the Shepherd in "The Sad Shepherd".
2. What is nature's attitude to the sad shepherd?
3. Why does the faery steal the child?
4. How does Yeats create a stunning fairyland to his readers?
5. What is (are) the theme(s) of "The Stolen Child"?

推荐阅读

Clark, Timothy. *The Cambridge Introduction to Literature and the Environment*. Cambridge University Press, 2011.

Garrard, Greg. *Ecocriticism*. Routledge, 2004.

Genet, Jacqueline (ed). *Rural Ireland, Real Ireland*? Colin Smythe, 1996.

Muller, Sabine Lenore and Tina-Karen Pusse (eds). *From Ego to Eco: Mapping Shifts from Anthropocentrism to Ecocentrism*. Brill, 2018.

Parham, John ed. *The Environmental Tradition in English Literature*. Ashgate, 2002.

Wenzell, Tim. *Emerald Green: An Ecocritical Study of Irish Literature*. Cambridge Scholars Pub., 2009.

胡志红:《西方生态批评研究》,中国社会科学出版社,2006年。

雷毅:《深层生态学思想研究》,清华大学出版社,2001年。

第三编　探索自然
——生态视域中的美国经典文学

背景介绍

美国是当代生态文学和生态批评的发起地。1962年美国作家蕾切尔·卡森（Rachel Carson）的散文集《寂静的春天》（*Silent Spring*）的问世，标志着世界生态文学时代的来临。1978年，美国学者威廉·鲁克尔特（William Rueckert）在《衣阿华评论》上发表文章《文学与生态学：一次生态批评实验》（"Literature and Ecology: An Experiment in Ecocriticism"），首次提出"生态批评"概念，以此为起点，文学与自然环境、社会现状与精神生态的联系成为文学研究的一个新视域。生态批评在美国的兴起并非偶然，其中不仅是因为美国文学批评界有着善于推陈出新的理论探索传统，还因为美国文学与自然有着不可分割的天然联系。在北美这片远离欧亚文明的新大陆上，自然与人、环境状况与科技发展、生态思想与工具理性的争斗一直在美国文化与文学发展中交织演变，也造就了生态批评对美国文学无所不在的解读。

从历史上溯源，早在哥伦布发现新大陆之前的许多世纪，生态意识已存在于北美印第安的文化中。从这个意义上说，美国的生态文学最早可追溯到美国印第安传统文学。在16世纪西班牙殖民者踏上美洲大陆之前，印第安人已创作了多种形式的文学作品，如反映本民族历史的神话传说、颂扬英雄事迹的戏剧、敬神的诗歌和抒情诗等。虽然这些大多已经失传，但是，与其他大陆的早期部落文化传统一样，现代人在印第安人的祭神典仪与曲词文学中、在有关印第安起源神话与其他传说中，依然可以发现自然与神明的合二为一。例如，在阿兹特克人（Aztec）的纳瓦特尔（Nāhuatl）诗歌和印加人（Inca）的克丘亚（Qhichwa）诗歌中，有大量描写花卉禽兽和自然之美的抒情诗。这种本土的生态文学传统在当代作家中依然保存。在美国生态批评家唐奈·德莱斯（Donelle N. Dreese）所著《生态批评：环境文学与美国印第安文学中的自我与地域》（*Ecocriticism: Creating Self and Place in Environmental and American Indian Literatures*）一书表明，美国文学的生态传统在印第安本土文学中有着充分表现，文学的"地域"特征与自我、社区以及人类意识的形成息息相关。作者还通过对美国印第安文学中所表现出的非殖民化倾向的讨论，其间存在的"领土"问题，把批判矛头指向了美国当今的环境种族主义者，把地域环境问题与政治意识形态关联起来。[1]

自从17世纪欧洲殖民者走上美洲大陆，美国进入殖民时期文学（1650—1750），这个时期的文学以叙史、散文、诗歌为主。在最早的移民开拓新大陆的时期，以清教徒为主的欧洲移民奋力求生，垦荒种植，人与自然的抗衡与协作是文学

---

[1] 乔国强：“读唐奈·德莱斯《生态批评：环境文学与美国印第安文学中的自我与地域》”，《外国文学评论》，2005（01）：169—170。

创作的主题。在随后独立革命时期的文学中(1750—1810),北美作家们对新大陆欣欣向荣的景象的赞美与民族独立意识相融合,形成了具有美国特色的民族文学,迎来了美国文学的成熟时期。从19世纪初开始,美国浪漫主义文学盛极一时,华盛顿·欧文(Washington Irving)的短篇小说和札记,埃德加·爱伦·坡(Edgar Allen Poe)的小说及诗歌,尤其是詹姆斯·费尼莫尔·库柏(James Fenimore Cooper)的系列小说《皮袜子故事集》(*The Leatherstocking Tales*),以殖民前后的美洲印第安人、林中人以及英法殖民者之间的斗争为主线,凸显了自然生态与文明发展之间的复杂矛盾。紧接着美国文学进入其黄金期——被称为美国"文艺复兴"的创作高峰期(1830—1860),最重要的是"超验主义"文学流派的兴起,其中爱默生(Ralph Waldo Emerson)和梭罗(Henry David Thoreau)这两位代表人物都对自然、人性和文明发展做了经典阐释,其作品成为当代生态批评与生态文学研究必读的文本。

从19世纪中期到19世纪中叶,美国文学迅猛发展,涌现了大批的经典作家。有惠特曼(Walt Whitman)、狄金森(Emily Dickinson)、弗罗斯特(Robert Frost)、朗费罗(Henry Longfellow)这样把浪漫主义与现代主义相结合的诗人,有梅尔维尔(Herman Melville)、海明威(Ernest Hemingway)、尤金·奥尼尔(Eugene O'Neill)、福克纳(William Faulkner)、菲兹杰拉德(F. Scott Fitzgerald)、薇拉·凯瑟(Willa Cather)这样反映社会现实和历史的小说家,他们的作品或宏大或细腻,从不同角度描绘了美国现代社会的全景。自然不可避免地成为了这些作品的核心议题之一。在两位美国学者编写的《早期美国自然作家:传纪百科》[①]一书中,列举了52位早期美国自然作家,包括约翰·詹姆斯·奥杜尔本(John James Audubon)、科克兰德(Caroline Stansbury Kirkland)、杰斐逊(Thomas Jefferson)、梭罗、爱默生、莱特(Mabel Osgood Wright)等用文笔书写自然的著名和非著名作家、自然学者和环境主义者。早期美国自然作家在他们的作品中呈现自然之美,他们不仅是细心而热情的自然观察者,而且是自然界各个部分应该协调一致的生态学思想表述者。他们开启了美国现代自然写作(Nature Writing)的先河。

从生态视角研读美国经典作家的经典作品,不难发现人与自然的关系始终是美国文学主要的叙述线索,也是众多作家苦心孤诣追寻的思想脉络。因此,本编从生态批评的角度出发,分别就散文、诗歌、小说这几种主要文体,精选了美国经典文学中具有代表性的六位作家,从他们作品中节选了具有生态意义的作品,从生态批评的角度予以解读,管窥生态思想在美国经典文学中的体现。

[①] Patterson, Daniel and Roger Thompson. *Early American Nature Writers: A Biographical Encyclopedia*. Greenwood Publishing Group, 2008.

亨利·大卫·梭罗(Henry David Thoreau)

【作者简介】

亨利·大卫·梭罗(1817—1862),19 世纪美国作家、思想家、诗人,美国超验主义运动代表人物之一。在他 45 年的人生历程中,他只自费出版了两本书和为数不多的文章和诗歌,生前籍籍无名,却在身后留下大量的日记和未发表的著作。20 世纪后半叶之后,梭罗作为思想家与作家的声誉日隆。尤其是他的文学创作和生态思想,开辟了现代生态文学和生态批评的滥觞。

1817 年 7 月 12 日,梭罗生于美国马萨诸塞州康科德城,父亲是个铅笔制造商。1837 年从哈佛大学毕业后,梭罗回乡执教两年。1839 年,他与兄长约翰在康科德和梅里麦克的河流上作过一次难忘的旅行。十年后,梭罗出版了第一本书《康科德河和梅里麦克河上的一星期》(*A Week on the Concord and Merrimack Rivers*, 1849),分七章记载了这七天的旅行。1840 年后,梭罗不断改变自己的生活方式,在父亲的铅笔厂帮过工,做过家庭教师,讲过学。1841 年,他住在思想家爱默生家里,做助手兼门徒,并开始尝试写作,为《日晷》(*The Dial*)季刊撰写散文和诗歌。

1845 年 7 月 4 日,梭罗借了一柄斧头,孤身来到无人居住的瓦尔登湖边的山林中,自建一所小木屋居住,耕作豆田,打猎捕鱼,尝试过一种简单从容的生活。他在这里住了两年零两个月又两天的时间,1847 年 9 月 6 日,他完成尝试回到康科德。他把这期间的所作所为、所思所想写成了散文集,这就是 1854 年出版的《瓦尔登湖,又名林中生活》(*Walden, or Life in the Woods*, 1854)。离开瓦尔登湖之后,他还曾漫游过缅因森林和科德角,发表演讲,研究物种,书写日记和游记。1862 年,他因肺病逝于康科德,终年 45 岁。他留下的 39 卷《日记》在他去世后得到整理,陆续出版。

梭罗不是隐居避世者,相反,他一生都积极参与社会政治生活,努力寻求最佳的人生方式。他信仰独立、自由、人与自然和谐共处的人生境界,反对任何形式的专制压迫和物质羁绊。他为抗议美国南部的蓄奴制,曾拒付人头税,为此被捕入狱,一天后被友人救出。1859 年,他支持反对美国蓄奴制度的运动领导人约翰·布朗。在布朗被逮捕、被处绞刑后,他发表了为布朗辩护和呼吁的演讲,并为他鸣钟悼念。他写的《论公民的不服从》("Civil Disobedience")一文,阐述公民对政府有不服从的权利,对英国工党和费边主义者、印度圣雄甘地的"非暴力不合作运动",以及马丁·路德·金、托尔斯泰、罗曼·罗兰都产生了一定影响。以下选文来自他的《瓦尔登湖》。

Where I Lived, and What I Lived For

I went to the woods because I wished to live deliberately, to front only the essential facts of life, and see if I could not learn what it had to teach, and not, when I came to die, discover that I had not lived. I did not wish to live what was not life, living is so dear; nor did I wish to practise resignation, unless it was quite necessary. I wanted to live deep and suck out all the marrow of life[1], to live so sturdily and Spartan-like[2] as to put to rout[3] all that was not life, to cut a broad swath[4] and shave close, to drive life into a corner, and reduce it to its lowest terms, and, if it proved to be mean, why then to get the whole and genuine meanness of it, and publish its meanness to the world; or if it were sublime, to know it by experience, and be able to give a true account of it in my next excursion. For most men, it appears to me, are in a strange uncertainty about it, whether it is of the devil or of God, and have somewhat hastily concluded that it is the chief end of man here to "glorify God and enjoy him forever."[5]

Still we live meanly, like ants; though the fable tells us that we were long ago changed into men; like pygmies[6] we fight with cranes; it is error upon error, and clout upon clout, and our best virtue has for its occasion a superfluous and evitable wretchedness. Our life is frittered away by detail. An honest man has hardly need to count more than his ten fingers, or in extreme cases he may add his ten toes, and lump the rest. Simplicity, simplicity, simplicity! I say, let your affairs be as two or three, and not a hundred or a thousand; instead of a million count half a dozen, and keep your accounts on your thumb-nail. In the midst of this chopping sea of civilized life, such are the clouds and storms and quicksands[7] and thousand-and-one items to be allowed for, that a man has to live, if he would not founder and go to the bottom and not make his port at all, by dead reckoning[8], and he must be a great calculator indeed who succeeds. Simplify, simplify. Instead of three meals a day, if it be necessary eat but one; instead of a hundred dishes, five; and reduce other things in proportion. Our life is like a German Confederacy[9], made up of petty states, with its boundary forever fluctuating, so that even a German cannot tell you how it is bounded at any moment. The nation itself, with all its so-called internal improvements, which, by the way are all external and superficial, is just such an unwieldy and overgrown establishment, cluttered with furniture and tripped up by its own traps, ruined by luxury and heedless expense, by want of calculation and a worthy aim, as the million households in the land; and the only cure for it, as for them, is in a rigid economy, a stern and more than Spartan simplicity of life and elevation of purpose. It lives too fast. Men think that it is essential that the Nation have commerce, and export ice, and talk through a telegraph, and ride thirty miles an hour, without a doubt, whether they do or not; but whether we should live like baboons[10] or like men, is a little uncertain. If we do not get out sleepers[11], and forge rails, and devote days and nights to the work, but go to tinkering upon our lives to improve them, who will build railroads? And if railroads are not built, how shall we get to heaven in season? But if we stay at home and mind our business, who will want railroads? We do not ride on the railroad; it rides upon us. Did you ever think what those sleepers are that underlie the railroad? Each one is a man, an Irishman, or a Yankee man[12]. The rails are laid on them, and they are covered with sand, and the cars run smoothly over them. They are sound sleepers, I assure you. And every few years a new lot is laid down and run over; so that, if some have the pleasure of riding on a rail, others have the misfortune to be ridden upon. And when they run over a man that is walking in his sleep, a supernumerary sleeper in the wrong position, and wake him up, they suddenly stop the cars, and make a hue and cry about it, as if this were an exception. I am glad to know that it takes a gang of men for every five miles to keep the sleepers down and level in their beds as it is, for this is a sign that they may sometime get up again.

Why should we live with such hurry and waste of life? We are determined to be starved before we are hungry. Men say that a stitch in time saves nine[14], and so they take a thousand stitches today to save nine tomorrow. As for work, we haven't any of any consequence. We have the Saint Vitus' dance[15], and cannot possibly keep our heads still. If I should only give a few pulls at the parish bell-rope, as for a fire, that is, without setting the bell, there is hardly a man on his farm in the outskirts of Concord, notwithstanding that press of engagements which was his excuse so many times this morning, nor a boy, nor a woman, I might almost say, but would forsake all and follow that sound, not mainly to save property from the flames, but, if we will confess the truth, much more to see it burn, since burn it must, and we, be it known, did not set it on fire—or to see it put out, and have a hand in it, if that is done as handsomely; yes, even if it were the parish church itself. Hardly a man takes a half-hour's nap after dinner, but when he wakes he holds up his head and asks, "What's the news?" as if the rest of mankind had stood his sentinels[16]. Some give directions to be waked every half-hour, doubtless for no other purpose; and then, to pay for it, they tell what they have dreamed. After a night's sleep the news is as indispensable as the breakfast. "Pray tell me anything new that has happened to a man anywhere on this globe"—and he reads it over his coffee and rolls, that a man has had his eyes gouged out this morning on the Wachito River[17]; never dreaming the while that he lives in the dark unfathomed mammoth cave of this world, and has but the rudiment[18] of an eye himself.

Solitude

This is a delicious evening, when the whole body is one sense, and imbibes delight through every pore. I go and come with a strange liberty in Nature, a part of herself. As I walk along the stony shore of the pond in my shirt-sleeves, though it is cool as well as cloudy and windy, and I see nothing special to attract me, all the elements are unusually congenial to me. The bullfrogs[19] trump to usher in the night, and the note of the whip-poor-will[20] is borne on the rippling wind from over the water. Sympathy with the fluttering alder and poplar[21] leaves almost takes away my breath; yet, like the lake, my serenity is rippled but not ruffled. These small waves raised by the evening wind are as remote from storm as the smooth reflecting surface. Though it is now dark, the wind still blows and roars in the wood, the waves still dash, and some creatures lull the rest with their notes. The repose is never complete. The wildest animals do not repose, but seek their prey now; the fox, and skunk, and rabbit, now roam the fields and woods without fear. They are Nature's watchmen—links which connect the days of animated life.

When I return to my house I find that visitors have been there and left their cards, either a bunch of flowers, or a wreath of evergreen, or a name in pencil on a yellow walnut leaf or a chip. They who come rarely to the woods take some little piece of the forest into their hands to play with by the way, which they leave, either intentionally or accidentally. One has peeled a willow wand, woven it into a ring, and dropped it on my table. I could always tell if visitors had called in my absence, either by the bended twigs or grass, or the print of their shoes, and generally of what sex or age or quality they were by some slight trace left, as a flower dropped, or a bunch of grass plucked and thrown away, even as far off as the railroad, half a mile distant, or by the lingering odor of a cigar or pipe. Nay, I was frequently notified of the passage of a traveler along the highway sixty rods[22] off by the scent of his pipe.

There is commonly sufficient space about us. Our horizon is never quite at our elbows. The thick wood is not just at our door, nor the pond, but somewhat is always clearing, familiar and worn by us, appropriated and fenced in some way, and reclaimed from Nature. For what reason have I this vast range and circuit, some square miles of unfrequented forest, for my privacy, abandoned to me by men? My nearest neighbor is a mile distant, and no house is visible from any place but the hill-tops within half a mile of my own. I have my horizon bounded by woods all to myself; a distant view of the railroad where it touches the pond on the one hand, and of the fence which skirts the woodland road on the other. But for the most part it is as solitary where I live as on the prairies. It is as much Asia or Africa as New England. I have, as it were, my own sun and moon and stars, and a little world all to myself. At night there was never a traveller passed my house, or knocked at my door, more than if I were the first or last man; unless it were in the spring, when at long intervals some came from the village to fish for pouts[23]—they plainly fished much more in the Walden Pond of their own natures, and baited their hooks with darkness—but they soon retreated, usually with light baskets, and left "the world to darkness and to me," and the black kernel of the night was never profaned by any human neighborhood. I believe that men are generally still a little afraid of the dark, though the witches are all hung, and Christianity and candles have been introduced.

Conclusion

Rather than love, than money, than fame, give me truth. I sat at a table where were rich food and wine in abundance, and obsequious[24] attendance, but sincerity and truth were not; and I went away hungry from the inhospitable board. The hospitality was as cold as the ices. I thought that there was no need of ice to freeze them. They talked to me of the age of the wine and the fame of the vintage[25]; but I thought of an older, a newer, and purer wine, of a more glorious vintage, which they had not got, and could not buy. The style, the house and grounds and "entertainment" pass for nothing with me. I called on the king, but he made me wait in his hall, and conducted like a man incapacitated for hospitality. There was a man in my neighborhood who lived in a hollow tree. His manners were truly regal. I should have done better had I called on him.

How long shall we sit in our porticoes[26] practising idle and musty[27] virtues, which any work would make impertinent? As if one were to begin the day with long-suffering, and hire a man to hoe his potatoes; and in the afternoon go forth to practise Christian meekness and charity with goodness aforethought[28]! Consider the China pride and stagnant self-complacency of mankind. This generation inclines a little to congratulate itself on being the last of an illustrious line; and in Boston and London and Paris and Rome, thinking of its long descent, it speaks of its progress in art and science and literature with satisfaction. There are the Records of the Philosophical Societies, and the public Eulogies of Great Men! It is the good Adam contemplating his own virtue. "Yes, we have done great deeds, and sung divine songs, which shall never die"—that is, as long as we can remember them. The learned societies and great men of Assyria[29]—where are they? What youthful philosophers and experimentalists we are! There is not one of my readers who has yet lived a whole human life. These may be but the spring months in the life of the race. If we have had the seven-years' itch[30], we have not seen the seventeen-year locust[31] yet in Concord. We are acquainted with a mere pellicle of the globe on which we live. Most have not delved six feet beneath the surface, nor leaped as many above it. We know not where we are. Beside, we are sound asleep nearly half our time. Yet we esteem ourselves wise, and have an established order on the surface. Truly, we are deep thinkers, we are ambitious spirits! As I stand over the insect crawling amid the pine needles on the forest floor, and endeavoring to conceal itself from my sight, and ask myself why it will cherish those humble thoughts, and bide its head from me who might, perhaps, be its benefactor, and impart to its race some cheering information, I am reminded of the greater Benefactor and Intelligence that stands over me the human insect.

There is an incessant influx of novelty into the world, and yet we tolerate incredible dullness. I need only suggest what kind of sermons are still listened to in the most enlightened countries. There are such words as joy and sorrow, but they are only the burden of a psalm, sung with a nasal twang, while we believe in the ordinary and mean. We think that we can change our clothes only. It is said that the British Empire is very large and respectable, and that the United States are a first-rate power. We do not believe that a tide rises and falls behind every man which can float the British Empire like a chip, if he should ever harbor it in his mind. Who knows what sort of seventeen-year locust will next come out of the ground? The government of the world I live in was not framed, like that of Britain, in after-dinner conversations over the wine.

The life in us is like the water in the river. It may rise this year higher than man has ever known it, and flood the parched uplands; even this may be the eventful year, which will drown out all our muskrats[33]. It was not always dry land where we dwell. I see far inland the banks which the stream anciently washed, before science began to record its freshets[34]. Every one has heard the story which has gone the rounds of New England, of a strong and beautiful bug which came out of the dry leaf of an old table of apple-tree wood, which had stood in a farmer's kitchen for sixty years, first in Connecticut, and afterward in Massachusetts—from an egg deposited in the living tree many years earlier still, as appeared by counting the annual layers beyond it; which was heard gnawing out for several weeks, hatched perchance by the heat of an urn. Who does not feel his faith in a resurrection and immortality strengthened by hearing of this? Who knows what beautiful and winged life, whose egg has been buried for ages under many concentric layers of woodenness in the dead dry life of society, deposited at first in the alburnum[35] of the green and living tree, which has been gradually converted into the semblance of its well-seasoned tomb—heard perchance gnawing out now for years by the astonished family of man, as they sat round the festive board—may unexpectedly come forth from amidst society's most trivial and handselled furniture, to enjoy its perfect summer life at last!

I do not say that John or Jonathan[36] will realize all this; but such is the character of that morrow which mere lapse of time can never make to dawn. The light which puts out our eyes[37] is darkness to us. Only that day dawns to which we are awake. There is more day to dawn. The sun is but a morning star.

 注释

1. the marrow of life:生命的精华。
2. Spartan-like:像斯巴达人一样。斯巴达,古希腊最强大的城邦之一(存在时间大约在公元前 10 世纪到前 2 世纪左右),其居民以崇尚武力、坚韧强悍著称。
3. put to rout:打垮,打败。
4. swath:(割草机、飓风等经过时留下的)刈痕。
5. to "glorify God and enjoy him forever":出自《威斯敏斯特小教理问答》(*Westminster Shorter Catechism*)。威斯敏斯特议会为了让孩童和初信主的信徒有效地学习真道,于 1647 年按《威斯敏斯特信仰宣言》编写了《威斯敏斯特小教理问答》,包含 107 条的问与答,简短易读,字句浅显,每个问题多以一个句子来回答,是神学入门的必备。次年(1648)又出版了《威斯敏斯特大教理问答》。这部《问答》的第一个问题就是:What is the chief end of man?(人类的主旨是什么?)回答是:Man's chief end is to glorify God, and to enjoy him forever.(人类的主旨是荣耀上帝,并永远以他为乐。)
6. pygmies:pygmy,特别矮小的人或动物,侏儒。
7. quicksands:流沙,危险而捉摸不定的事物。
8. dead reckoning:(航海中不看自然状况而进行的)推算航行法,在信息匮乏情况下进行的推算。
9. German Confederacy:德意志邦联,指的是 19 世纪前期德国各个地方政权割据的状况,直至 1871 年才在俾斯麦的领导下成立了以普鲁士为主体的统一的德意志帝国。

10. baboon:狒狒,生活在非洲的一种猴科动物,雄性凶猛,杂食。

11. sleeper:(铁路上的)轨枕,枕木。

12. Yankee man:(俗语)美国佬,(尤其是)来自美国北部的美国佬。

13. hue and cry:喧叫声;责难声;抗议声。

14. a stitch in time saves nine:(英语谚语)一针及时省九针;小洞不补大洞吃苦。

15. the Saint Vitus' dance:圣维斯特舞蹈病,一种常由风湿病毒引起的疾病,因为链球菌侵入大脑的运动中心而影响神经冲动向肌肉的传递,由此导致肌肉无意义的非主动活动,症状为手脚笨拙和做怪脸。名称源自于欧洲的中世纪,当时得了这种狂舞怪病的人会向圣维斯特(演员和舞者的保护神)祈祷以求早日康复。

16. stood his sentinels:给他站岗放哨。

17. the Wachito River:流经路易斯安那州北部和阿肯色州南部的一条河流,19世纪的时候被认为是逃犯经常光顾的地方,现名 the Ouachita River。

18. rudiment:退化的器官。

19. bullfrog:牛蛙,独居的水栖蛙,因其叫声大且洪亮酷似牛叫而得名,为北美最大的蛙类。

20. the whip-poor-will:三声夜鹰,夜鹰科北美洲夜出鸟,由其强有力且不慌不忙的鸣声(whip-poor-will,第一及第三音节重)而得名,可不停地反复连叫400次,生活在靠近开阔地的林中。

21. alder and poplar:赤杨和白杨,两种桦木科落叶乔木。

22. rod:杆,一种长度单位,大约5.03米。

23. pout:大头鱼类(如鲶鱼、鳕鱼等)。

24. obsequious:奉承的,谄媚的。

25. vintage:(葡萄酒的)制造年代,佳酿。

26. portico:柱廊;门廊。

27. musty:发霉的,落伍的。

28. aforethought:事先考虑的;预谋的;故意的。

29. Assyria:亚述,古代西亚奴隶制国家。属于闪米特族的亚述人建立亚述尔城后逐渐形成贵族专制的奴隶制城邦;公元前612年,亚述帝国为新巴比伦和米底联军灭亡。亚述帝国曾以英勇善战著称。

30. the seven-years' itch:七年之痒。这里不是指婚姻的厌倦期(这个含义到1955年玛丽莲·梦露主演的同名电影上映之后才得以风行)。在19世纪早期的美国,"七年之痒"指的是一种顽固的皮肤病,后逐渐演变成比喻一切令人不快而时间久长的事物。

31. seventeen-year locust:十七年蝉,一种北美昆虫,并不常见,因为其蛹需要13—17年方能孵化成蝉。

32. pellicle:薄皮;薄膜。

33. muskrat:麝鼠,北美洲本土较大的水栖啮齿目动物。

34. freshet:洪水,汛期。

35. alburnum:木质,白材。

36. John or Jonathan:指的是英国人和美国人,英国的外号是 John Bull(约翰牛),在喜剧舞台上经常用 John 和 Jonathan 来指代英美两国。

37. The light which puts out our eyes:使得我们双目失明的光芒。梭罗曾听人说,印度有苦行僧故意直视太阳,以使自己目盲来表现虔诚。

 作品导读

梭罗的散文集《瓦尔登湖》在 1854 年发表时并没有引起关注,然而随着时光推移,这部作品逐渐成为美国文学的经典,继而被视为世界文学中不可或缺的一颗明珠,被认为是现代生态文学的开山之作。

在瓦尔登湖畔那个自建的小木屋里,梭罗独自生活了两年零两个月又两天的时间,做一个自种自收的农夫。在农耕之余,他读书、思考,写下了散文集《瓦尔登湖》来记录自己的所思所想,为这次生活实验镌刻下哲学的印记。在这部文字优美的作品中,梭罗没有把思路局限在自我之中,而是把自我这个个体投入到大自然的怀抱里,使得"我"所代表的"人"成为自然的一部分,与鸟兽同出没,和草木共呼吸,用最为简单质朴的生活方式来对抗欲望给人类带来的无穷烦恼和灾难,用亲身实践来证明人的幸福不是源自物质获取,而是来自纯净天然的人与自然之关系。

节选的第一节取自《瓦尔登湖》第二章"我生活的地方,我为何生活",在这一节中梭罗解释了自己深入到丛林中的湖畔生活的原因:"我到林中去,因为我希望谨慎地生活,只面对生活的基本事实,看看我是否学得到生活要教育我的东西,免得到了临死的时候,才发现我根本就没有生活过"(徐迟译)。梭罗的离群独居,不是要逃离生活,而是因为他如此热爱生活,不想把有限的生命消耗在为利益而奔波的碌碌之中。在这种思想下,他产生了反对物质文明无限发展的想法,呼吁人类尽量简化自己的物质需求,不要为走得更远、知道得更多、为了未雨绸缪而牺牲了当前的安宁喜乐。

第二节选自第五章"独处",作者首先对周边的自然环境做了细致优美的描写,然后引发出他的"超验"之思。梭罗喜欢独处,并不因此而感觉寂寞。相反,他在独处中思考、劳作,与自然为伴,心情愉悦,因为"任何大自然的事物中,都能找出最甜蜜温柔,最天真和鼓舞人的伴侣"(徐迟译)。在梭罗看来,只要跟自然在一起,可以"不以物喜,不以己悲",成败得失都是相对而言,不足忧虑。人在自然中从不孤独,他可以从同类中获得关爱,更能从自然中思索出生命之精髓。

第三节选自本书最后一章"结束语",是梭罗离开瓦尔登湖之后、即将结束这部散文集之际写下的感言。梭罗坦承了他对真理和天然的热爱,又一次抨击了人类为追求"成功"而浪费生命的愚行,讴歌了生命本身的伟大,呼唤人们认清生命的本质,用乐观的态度珍爱有限之生,投入无垠之思。

以上三节只截取了《瓦尔登湖》中的些许鳞爪,唯有细读全文才能领略梭罗的诗人品味、哲人情怀。梭罗在世时并未看见,他的《瓦尔登湖》在后世成为美国生态文学最经典的作品,促成了 20 世纪美国自然文学流派的诞生,影响了诸多生态作家与生态批评家(如奥尔多·利奥波德、爱德华·艾比等人);不仅如此,这部书成为世界经典,在各个国家引起强烈反响和共鸣,这是因为梭罗的"瓦尔登湖"情结反映了整个人类的共同感受,为人与自然如何相处提供了最为优美纯净的范例。

思考题

1. According to Thoreau, why did he go to the woods and what did he live for?
2. What did a simple life mean to Thoreau?
3. Why did Thoreau call certain wild animals "Nature's watchmen"?
4. What do you think of what Thoreau said about "the China pride and stagnant self-complacency of mankind"?
5. In your opinion, why did Thoreau not stay at Walden for good?

推荐阅读

Bickman, Martin. *Walden: Volatile Truths*. Macmillan Publishing Company, 1992.

Gould, RebeccaKneale. "Thoreau, Race and Environmental Justice: Deepening the Conversation." *The Concord Saunterer*, vol. 25, 2017.

Harding, Walter. *The Days of Henry Thoreau: A Biography*. Dover Publications (2nd edition), 2011.

Hess, Scott. "Thoreau's Legacy for Climate Change." *The Concord Saunterer*, New Series, vol. 28 (2020).

Lyon, Thomas J. *The Incomparable Land: A Guide of American Nature Writing*. Milkweed Editions; Revised edition, 2001.

McIntosh, James. *Thoreau as Romantic Naturalist: His Shifting Stance toward Nature*. Cornell University Press, 1974.

Richardson, Robert. D., Jr. *Henry Thoreau: A Life of the Mind*. University of California Press, 1986.

Ross, Austin Bernard. "Confucianism, Transcendentalism, and the 'Dao' of Henry David Thoreau." *The Concord Saunterer*, vol. 26, 2018.

Saunders, Judith P. "Biophilia in Thoreau's *Walden*." *South Atlantic Review*, vol. 79, no. 1—2, 2014.

Sherman, Paul. *The Shores of America: Thoreau's Inward Exploration*. Russell & Russell Pub. 1971.

Thoreau, Henry David. *Walden and Other Writings*. Empire Books, 2012.

陈茂林:《诗意栖居:亨利·大卫·梭罗的生态批评》,浙江大学出版社,2009年。

程虹:《寻归荒野》,生活·读书·新知三联书店,2001年。

梭罗:《瓦尔登湖》,徐迟译,上海译文出版社,2004年。

孙霄:"宗教典故与生态书写——以梭罗《瓦尔登湖》为讨论中心",《山东社会科学》,2019(12)。

邹建军,白阳明:"梭罗的地理漫游与生态自我的实现及其当代启示",《文艺评论》,2018(05)。

拉尔夫·沃尔多·爱默生
（Ralph Waldo Emerson）

【作者简介】

拉尔夫·沃尔多·爱默生(1803—1882)出生于美国马萨诸塞州波士顿附近的康科德的一个牧师家庭，是随笔作家、诗人和演讲家，19世纪中期哲学思潮超验主义运动的领军人物。在就读哈佛期间，爱默生曾阅读大量英国浪漫主义作家的作品。毕业后曾执教两年，之后进入哈佛神学院，担任基督教唯一神教派牧师，并开始布道。1832年以后，爱默生到欧洲各国游历，结识了浪漫主义先驱华兹华斯和柯尔律治，接受了他们的先验论思想，对他思想体系的形成具有很大影响。

回到波士顿后，爱默生经常布道、演讲，并与梭罗、霍桑、阿尔柯、玛格丽特·福勒等人举行小型聚会，探讨神学、哲学和社会学问题。这种聚会当时被称为"超验主义俱乐部"(the Transcendental Club)，爱默生也自然而然地成为超验主义的领袖。1837年爱默生发表著名演讲《美国学者》("The American Scholar")，宣告美国文学已脱离英国文学而独立，被誉为美国思想文化领域的"独立宣言"。1840年爱默生任超验主义刊物《日晷》(*The Dial*)的主编，进一步宣扬超验主义思想。他的演讲词汇编成书，这就是他的名作《论文集》(*Essays*)，经典篇章有《论自然》《论超灵》《论补偿》《论爱》《论友谊》等，其中的思想被称为超验主义的核心、美国最重要的世俗宗教；他本人则被冠以"美国的文艺复兴领袖"之美誉。1882年4月27日，爱默生在波士顿逝世，享年79岁。

爱默生的散文《论自然》(*Nature*)最早创作于1836年9月，被称作超验主义理论的《圣经》。与梭罗关注人类与自然环境之关系的生态意识有所不同，爱默生偏重于现代意义上的自然生态意识、自然与西方传统文化建构的关系，以及生态问题背后的文化机制因素。他更注意资本主义文明自身机制的生态缺陷与补救。其文学创作与思想观念对美国文化从近代向现代转型有着重要实践意义，但同样不免具有理想主义色彩和时代局限性。

以下片段选自《论自然》的"导言"和第一章"自然"部分。

Introduction

Our age is retrospective. It builds the sepulchers[1] of the fathers. It writes biographies, histories, and criticism. The foregoing generations beheld God and nature face to face; we, through their eyes. Why should not we also enjoy an original relation to the universe? Why should not we have a poetry and philosophy of insight and not of tradition, and a religion by revelation to us, and not the history of theirs? Embosomed for a season in nature, whose floods of life stream around and through us, and invite us by the powers they supply, to action proportioned to nature, why should we grope among the dry bones of the past, or put the living generation into masquerade[2] out of its faded wardrobe? The sun shines to-day also. There is more wool and flax[3] in the fields. There are new lands, new men, new thoughts. Let us demand our own works and laws and worship.

Undoubtedly we have no questions to ask which are unanswerable. We must trust the perfection of the creation so far, as to believe that whatever curiosity the order of things has awakened in our minds, the order of things can satisfy. Every man's condition is a solution in hieroglyphic[4] to those inquiries he would put. He acts it as life, before he apprehends it as truth. In like manner, nature is already, in its forms and tendencies, describing its own design. Let us interrogate the great apparition that shines so peacefully around us. Let us inquire, to what end is nature?

All science has one aim, namely, to find a theory of nature. We have theories of races and of functions, but scarcely yet a remote approach to an idea of creation. We are now so far from the road to truth, that religious teachers dispute and hate each other, and speculative men are esteemed unsound and frivolous[5]. But to a sound judgment, the most abstract truth is the most practical. Whenever a true theory appears, it will be its own evidence. Its test is, that it will explain all phenomena. Now many are thought not only unexplained but inexplicable; as language, sleep, madness, dreams, beasts, sex.

Philosophically considered, the universe is composed of Nature and the Soul. Strictly speaking, therefore, all that is separate from us, all which Philosophy distinguishes as the NOT ME, that is, both nature and art, all other men and my own body, must be ranked under this name, NATURE. In enumerating the values of nature and casting up their sum, I shall use the word in both senses;—in its common and in its philosophical import. In inquiries so general as our present one, the inaccuracy is not material; no confusion of thought will occur. Nature, in the common sense, refers to essences unchanged by man; space, the air, the river, the leaf. Art is applied to the mixture of his will with the same things, as in a house, a canal, a statue, a picture. But his operations taken together are so insignificant, a little chipping, baking, patching, and washing, that in an impression so grand as that of the world on the human mind, they do not vary the result.

Chapter I

To go into solitude, a man needs to retire as much from his chamber as from society. I am not solitary whilst I read and write, though nobody is with me. But if a man would be alone, let him look at the stars. The rays that come from those heavenly worlds, will separate between him and what he touches. One might think the atmosphere was made transparent with this design, to give man, in the heavenly bodies, the perpetual presence of the sublime[6]. Seen in the streets of cities, how great they are! If the stars should appear one night in a thousand years, how would men believe and adore; and preserve for many generations the remembrance of the city of God which had been shown! But every night come out these envoys of beauty, and light the universe with their admonishing smile.

The stars awaken a certain reverence, because though always present, they are inaccessible; but all natural objects make a kindred[8] impression, when the mind is open to their influence. Nature never wears a mean appearance. Neither does the wisest man extort her secret, and lose his curiosity by finding out all her perfection. Nature never became a toy to a wise spirit. The flowers, the animals, the mountains, reflected the wisdom of his best hour, as much as they had delighted the simplicity of his childhood.

When we speak of nature in this manner, we have a distinct but most poetical sense in the mind. We mean the integrity of impression made by manifold natural objects. It is this which distinguishes the stick of timber of the wood-cutter, from the tree of the poet. The charming landscape which I saw this morning, is indubitably made up of some twenty or thirty farms. Miller owns this field, Locke that, and Manning the woodland beyond. But none of them owns the landscape. There is a property in the horizon which no man has but he whose eye can integrate all the parts, that is, the poet. This is the best part of these men's farms, yet to this their warranty-deeds[9] give no title.

To speak truly, few adult persons can see nature. Most persons do not see the sun. At least they have a very superficial seeing. The sun illuminates only the eye of the man, but shines into the eye and the heart of the child. The lover of nature is he whose inward and outward senses are still truly adjusted to each other; who has retained the spirit of infancy even into the era of manhood. His intercourse with heaven and earth, becomes part of his daily food. In the presence of nature, a wild delight runs through the man, in spite of real sorrows. Nature says,—he is my creature, and maugre[10] all his impertinent griefs, he shall be glad with me. Not the sun or the summer alone, but every hour and season yields its tribute of delight; for every hour and change corresponds to and authorizes a different state of the mind, from breathless noon to grimmest midnight. Nature is a setting that fits equally well a comic or a mourning piece. In good health, the air is a cordial of incredible virtue. Crossing a bare common, in snow puddles, at twilight, under a clouded sky, without having in my thoughts any occurrence of special good fortune, I have enjoyed a perfect exhilaration. I am glad to the brink of fear.[11] In the woods too, a man casts off his years, as the snake his slough[12], and at what period soever[12] of life, is always a child. In the woods, is perpetual youth. Within these plantations of God, a decorum and sanctity reign, a perennial festival is dressed, and the guest sees not how he should tire of them in a thousand years. In the woods, we return to reason and faith. There I feel that nothing can befall me in life,—no disgrace, no calamity, (leaving me my eyes,) which nature cannot repair. Standing on the bare ground,—my head bathed by the blithe air, and uplifted into infinite space,—all mean egotism vanishes. I become a transparent eye-ball; I am nothing; I see all; the currents of the Universal Being circulate through me; I am part or particle of God. The name of the nearest friend sounds then foreign and accidental: to be brothers, to be acquaintances,—master or servant, is then a trifle and a disturbance. I am the lover of uncontained and immortal beauty. In the wilderness, I find something more dear and connate than in streets or villages. In the tranquil landscape, and especially in the distant line of the horizon, man beholds somewhat as beautiful as his own nature.

The greatest delight which the fields and woods minister, is the suggestion of an occult[14] relation between man and the vegetable. I am not alone and unacknowledged. They nod to me, and I to them. The waving of the boughs in the storm, is new to me and old. It takes me by surprise, and yet is not unknown. Its effect is like that of a higher thought or a better emotion coming over me, when I deemed I was thinking justly or doing right.

Yet it is certain that the power to produce this delight, does not reside in nature, but in man, or in a harmony of both. It is necessary to use these pleasures with great temperance. For, nature is not always tricked in holiday attire, but the same scene which yesterday breathed perfume and glittered as for the frolic[15] of the nymphs, is overspread with melancholy today. Nature always wears the colors of the spirit. To a man laboring under calamity, the heat of his own fire hath sadness in it. Then, there is a kind of contempt of the landscape felt by him who has just lost by death a dear friend. The sky is less grand as it shuts down over less worth in the population.

注释

1. sepulcher：坟墓，埋葬地。
2. masquerade：伪装，化装舞会。
3. wool and flax：羊毛和亚麻（当时两种常见的农产品）。
4. hieroglyphic：象形文字，难以辨别的文字。
5. unsound and frivolous：不明智而轻佻琐碎的。
6. the sublime：超凡高尚（的事物或精神）。
7. envoys of beauty：美的使者。
8. kindred：同类的，相似的，有亲缘关系的。
9. warranty-deed：地契保证书，确认买卖关系和财产所有权的法律文书。
10. maugre：不管 (in spite of)。
11. I am glad to the brink of fear：我欢喜到近乎恐惧的地步。brink：边缘。
12. slough：(蛇等动物的)蜕皮。
13. soever：无论(任何)。
14. occult：超乎自然的，神秘的。
15. frolic：嬉戏，游玩。

作品导读

《论自然》是爱默生早期的经典之作，其开篇即洋溢着积极乐观的探索精神，提出不因循守旧、要亲自追寻意义的科学态度。他用科学和哲学来探究"自然"的本源：从哲学意义上

说,整个宇宙是由自然和精神构成;从基本意义上说,自然是指不能人为改变的本质。真正热爱自然者是那些能真正做到内外如一的人;是那些能将一颗童心带到成年时代的人。

在爱默生的笔下,人与自然不是二元对立,而是紧密相连、和谐统一的整体。人的灵魂在最纯净的时候与自然融为一体,不分彼此。他在《论自然》的第一章里提出了著名的论述"透明的眼球"(transparent eyeball):"我变成了一个透明的眼球,我是一个'无',我看见了一切,普遍的存在进入到我的血脉,在我周身流动。我成为上帝的一部分或一分子。"在他看来,自然与人紧密相连,自然规律与人的思想规律具有一致性。在宇宙这一大体系中,人的"天性"(nature)与大自然(Nature)是不可分割的,都是宇宙的一部分。爱默生把人与自然等同起来,找出了两者的共同点:都源于宇宙,都有相似的运动和规律。从这个意义上,人与自然不存在对立关系,而是同根同源。

与梭罗以自然环境为主体描述对象的生态思想相比,爱默生对自然的态度要更加"超验"——即他提出了"自然是精神之象征"这一命题。自然被赋予了具备上帝一般的神性,爱默生更倾向于从哲学、社会的层面来解读自然,而不是像梭罗那样沉浸在自然荒野中,成为一个生态保护主义者。所以有生态学者认为,与梭罗相比,爱默生不算是真正的生态主义者,而是一个泛神论者。他更看重人在自然中所处的地位和所发生的作用,是人与自然之和谐,而不是以自然为主导。而梭罗则更倾向于认为顺其自然是人与自然和谐关系的要诀。这两位美国作家从不同角度探究了人与自然之关系,也给生态批评提供了两种蓝本。当研究者认为梭罗所提出的亲近自然、远离尘嚣的简单生活模式是典型的生态主义样板之时,爱默生则提供了把自然与人的灵魂合二为一的哲学观,让人在自然的熏陶下更好地接近神性和灵性,达到"超灵"(Oversoul)境界。

思考题

1. What does Emerson think of the retrospective age?
2. According to Emerson, what is the aim of all science?
3. How does Emerson think of the relationship between Nature and the Soul?
4. Why does Emerson say that "few adult persons can see nature"?
5. What are the similarities and differences between Thoreau and Emerson in their ecological views?

推荐阅读

Davis, Clark. "Emerson's Telescope: Jones Very and Romantic Individualism." *The New England Quarterly*, vol. 91, no. 3, 2018.

Emerson, Ralph Waldo. *Nature and Other Essays*. Dover Publications, 2012.

——. *The Laws of Nature: Excerpts from the Writings of Ralph Waldo Emerson*. North Atlantic Books, 2010.

Guardiano, Nicholas. "Ecstatic Naturalism and Aesthetic Transcendentalism on the Creativity of Nature." *American Journal of Theology & Philosophy*, vol. 37, no. 1, 2016.

McMurry, Andrew. *Environmental Renaissance：Emerson, Thoreau, and the Systems of Nature*. University of Georgia Press，2003.

Thoreau & Emerson. *Thoreau and Emerson：Nature and Spirit*. Audio Partners，1997.

—. *Nature Walking*. Beacon Press；Reissue edition，1994.

胡志红:"崇高、自然、种族:崇高美学范畴的生态困局、重构及其意义——少数族裔生态批评视野",《外语与外语教学》,2020(02)。

孙霄:"美国文艺复兴时期的生态转向与中国视野",《中国比较文学》,2022(03)。

朱新福:《美国经典作家的生态视域和自然思想》,上海外语教育出版社,2015年。

艾米莉·狄金森(Emily Dickinson)

【作者简介】

艾米莉·狄金森(1830—1886)是美国最富传奇性的抒情女诗人。她出生在马萨诸塞州阿默斯特镇的一个正统家庭,父亲是该镇的首席律师。狄金森没有受过高深的教育,只在阿默斯特附近的一所女子学校读过一年书便回家隐居,自我幽闭。她常身穿白衣,避不见客,在孤独中埋头写诗30年,直至56岁时患肾病去世。她生前籍籍无名,只发表了七首诗,却留下一千七百多首诗歌和大量书信,逐渐被后世文坛认可,被视为20世纪现代主义诗歌的先驱之一,与美国文学之父欧文、诗人惠特曼比肩。

狄金森的诗富于睿智,用词变化多端,新奇的比喻随手抛掷,旧字新用,自铸伟词。在形式上富于独创性,大多使用17世纪英国宗教圣歌作者艾萨克·沃茨(Isaac Watts, 1674—1748)的传统格律形式,多押半韵,但又做了许多变化,例如在诗句中使用许多短破折号,既可代替标点,又使正常的抑扬格音步节奏产生突兀的起伏跳动。她擅长用平凡亲切的语言描写爱情、死亡和自然;痛苦与狂喜,死亡与永生,都是狄金森诗歌的重要主题。这位传奇女诗人远离尘世,更愿意与自然亲近,所以自然在她近一千八百首诗作中占了将近三分之一的篇幅。她在独居和想象中尽情表达自然界蕴含的美,用简洁灵动的诗句描绘了自然万物的和谐统一。

以下是狄金森的五首自然诗。

"Nature" is what we see

"Nature" is what we see—
The Hill—the Afternoon—
Squirrel—Eclipse—the Bumble bee[1]—
Nay[2]—Nature is Heaven—
Nature is what we hear—
The Bobolink[3]—the Sea—
Thunder—the Cricket—
Nay—Nature is Harmony—
Nature is what we know—
Yet have no art to say—
So impotent Our Wisdom is
To her Simplicity.

A Bird Came Down

A bird came down the walk:
He did not know I saw;
He bit an angle-worm[4] in halves
And ate the fellow, raw.

And then he drank a dew
From a convenient grass,
And then hopped sidewise to the wall
To let a beetle pass.

He glanced with rapid eyes
That hurried all abroad,—
They looked like frightened beads, I thought;
He stirred his velvet head

Like one in danger; cautious,
I offered him a crumb,
And he unrolled his feathers
And rowed him softer home

Than oars divide the ocean,
Too silver for a seam,
Or butterflies, off banks of noon,
Leap, splashless, as they swim.

A Dying Tiger—moaned for Drink

A Dying Tiger—moaned for Drink—
I hunted all the Sand—
I caught the Dripping of a Rock
And bore it in my Hand—

His Mighty Balls[5]—in death were thick—
But searching—I could see
A Vision on the Retina[6]
Of Water—and of me—

'Twas[7] not my blame—who sped too slow—
'Twas not his blame—who died

While I was reaching him—
But 'twas—the fact that He was dead—

The Black Berry[8]—wears a Thorn in his side

The Black Berry—wears a Thorn in his side—
But no Man heard Him cry—
He offers His Berry, just the same
To Partridge[9]—and to Boy—

He sometimes holds upon the Fence—
Or struggles to a Tree—
Or clasps a Rock, with both His Hands—
But not for Sympathy—

We—tell a Hurt—to cool it—
This Mourner—to the Sky
A little further reaches—instead—
Brave Black Berry—

Sunset at Night—is natural

Sunset at Night—is natural—
But Sunset on the Dawn
Reverses Nature—Master—
So Midnight's—due—at Noon.

Eclipses be—predicted—
And Science bows them in—
But do one face us suddenly—
Jehovah's Watch[10]—is Wrong.

注释

1. bumble bee:熊蜂,一种体型较大的蜂科动物。
2. nay:不但如此;而且。
3. Bobolink:一种美洲候鸟,与画眉鸟同属,擅鸣唱。
4. angle-worm:钓饵虫,蚯蚓。
5. balls:眼球(eyeballs)。
6. retina:视网膜。
7. 'Twas:(略写)It was。

8. black berry:黑莓,一种浆果类植物,果实旁长有尖刺。
9. partridge:鹧鸪,雉鸡的一种。
10. Jehovah's Watch:耶和华的钟表。耶和华(Jehovah),《圣经·旧约》中所记载的上帝的名字,被认为是造物主。"耶和华的表"指的是自然运行的规律。

作品解读

以上节选的五首诗,如果从生态批评的视角加以解读,不难发现狄金森对自然万物由衷的热爱,以及她在诗作中融入自然之乐,既能感受自然的无私和慷慨,又对自然充满了深切的生态关怀。

细读起来,第一首《自然即所见》,作者把自然定为人的一切所见、所闻、所知,山川树木,晨曦昏晓,花鸟虫鱼,风雨雷电,无不是自然之一部分。而相对于如此简单朴素之自然,人类的智慧又显得如此无力。作者在诗行中尽情推崇自然,以自然之天然来对照人类理性的无力,彰显出作者对自然生态的尊崇和热爱,完全打破了人类中心理念,把淳朴的自然万物奉为一切的根本。第二首则用生动的笔调描述"我"偷窥一只鸟如何捕虫、饮露、给甲壳虫让路。"我"仔细观察这只鸟灵动的眼珠、它的灵敏警惕,在"我"想给它喂食时,它却展翅飞走了。这个自然的精灵有着它自己的生存之道,非人类可以干涉。第三首是写一只垂死的老虎,呻吟着要水喝。当诗中的"我"终于在岩石间找到水捧回给它,那只老虎已经瞳孔放大,带着对水的渴望死去了。"我"并没有自责或者怪罪老虎的死亡,只是无奈地呈现这个事实——老虎已经死了。不管这首白描诗有何寓意,"我"对老虎的关爱和对它死亡的痛心跃然纸上。第四首《带刺的黑莓》则赞美了黑莓虽然带刺,却无私地把自己浆果奉献给鸟儿和孩子,在岩石篱笆间顽强求生,从不寻求同情。人类会以诉说的方式来减轻伤痛,而黑莓却把它的悲怆举向天空。作者在黑莓这一普通植物身上发现了奉献、坚强和坚韧;与之相比,爱抱怨的人类显得黯然失色。第五首《夜晚的日落是自然》,写的是自然界的一个奇特现象——日食。虽然人类科技已经可以做到预测日食,可是一旦人们忽然遇到一次日食,依然会觉得上帝定好的天时运转出了错。作者通过这一奇异的天象来表现自然的变化多端,非人力和宗教可以概括。

狄金森的自然诗歌风格清新,感情纯朴,既有人类对自然的观察仰慕,也有人与其他物种之间的互动交流,更有人作为万物的一种对纯粹的大自然所持有的感恩与冥想,无不显示出诗人热爱自然、希冀人与自然和谐共生的生态视野。

思考题

1. According to Dickinson, what is Nature in essence?
2. How did "I" think of the bird that refused "my" offer of crumb?
3. What did the author intend to convey in the death of the tiger?
4. Why does the black berry wear a thorn since it is so generous?

5. How do eclipses observe Jehovah's Watch?

推荐阅读

Davies, Terence, and Maria Garcia. "The Quiet Passion of Emily Dickinson: An Interview with Terence Davies." *Cinéaste*, vol. 42, no. 3, 2017.

Dickinson, Emily. *Dickinson: Selected Poems and Commentaries*. Belknap Press: Reprint edition, 2012.

——. *The Complete Poems of Emily Dickinson*. Back Bay Books, 1976.

Legault, Paul. *The Emily Dickinson Reader: An English-to-English Translation of Emily Dickinson's Complete Poems*. McSweeney's, 2012.

Lundin, Roger. *Emily Dickinson and the Art of Belief*. Wm. B. Eerdmans Publishing Co., 2004.

Socarides, Alexandra. *Dickinson Unbound: Paper, Process, Poetics*. Oxford University Press, 2012.

Stearns, Catherine. "Emily Dickinson's War Poetry." *The North American Review*, vol. 301, no. 3, 2016.

艾米莉·狄金森:《狄金森诗选》,蒲隆译,上海译文出版社,2010年。

黄国文:"自然诗歌中的元功能和语法隐喻分析——以狄金森的一首自然诗歌为例",《外语教学》,2018,39(03)。

李玲,张跃军:"艾米莉·狄金森的家园书写与文化身份",《中南大学学报》(社会科学版),2020,26(06)。

尚玲玲:《艾米莉·狄金森的永恒观及其诗歌创作研究》,浙江工商大学出版社,2021年。

宋秀葵、周青:"艾米莉·狄金森的自然诗作:生态文学的典范",《山东社会科学》,2007(09)。

王玮:《艾米莉·狄金森的"空间诗学"研究》,上海三联书店,2019年。

罗伯特·弗罗斯特(Robert Frost)

【作者简介】

罗伯特·弗罗斯特(1874—1963)是20世纪最著名的美国诗人之一,与艾略特并称为美国现代诗歌的两大巨匠。他生于旧金山,长于马赛诸塞州,就读于哈佛大学,因肺病辍学,经营过农场,做过教师,徒步漫游过许多地方,写过很多诗歌,被称为"新英格兰的农民诗人"。最初他的诗作并未引起出版界兴趣。直至1912年他举家迁居英国,在伦敦结识了埃兹拉·庞德、托马斯·休姆等著名诗人,才在朋友们帮助下出版了第一部抒情诗集《少年的意志》(*A Boy's Will*, 1913),次年又出版了叙事诗集《波士顿以北》(*North of Boston*, 1914),踏上成为知名诗人的大道。

第一次世界大战开始后,他于1915年返回美国,成为享誉大西洋两岸的名诗人,先后在阿默斯特学院、密歇根大学和哈佛大学等院校执教或从事研究工作。他曾四次获得美国文坛最高奖——普利策文学奖,晚年是美国非官方的"桂冠诗人",曾以86岁的高龄在1961年肯尼迪总统的就职典礼上朗诵他的诗篇《全才》("The Gift Outright")。

在美国,弗罗斯特是家喻户晓的诗人,其诗歌以其独特风格和深刻思想而深受喜爱、备受关注。无论是他的抒情短诗,还是情节感人的叙事诗,都成为脍炙人口的经典之作。他对自然的热爱和沉思主要体现在其抒情诗的创作中,他的田园山水诗描述了新英格兰乡村的秀丽景色和那里淳朴的农居生活,并把自己对生活的感悟融合其中,发人深省。他创作了许多流传久远的自然诗篇,如《雪夜林边驻马》("Stopping by Woods on a Snowy Evening")、《美景易逝》("Nothing Gold Can Stay")、《荒野》("Desert Places")、《既不远,也不深》("Neither out Far nor in Deep")及《未选之路》("The Road Not Taken")等。弗罗斯特善于使用质朴清新的语言来描述真切的感受。他的世界观并不单一,他把世界看成是一个交织着善与恶的混合体,时而慈悲慷慨,时而暴戾残酷。总体上来说,弗罗斯特热爱自然胜于热爱文明,他对工业发展对自然的损伤感受尤其痛切。他的理想是人与自然的和谐共存,这在他的许多诗作中都能窥到端倪。

以下是弗罗斯特的三首自然诗歌。

God's Garden

God made a beatous[1] garden
With lovely flowers strown,
But one straight, narrow pathway

That was not overgrown.
And to this beauteous garden
He brought mankind to live,
And said:"To you, my children,
These lovely flowers I give.
Prune ye my vines and fig trees,[2]
With care my flowerets[3] tend,
But keep the pathway open
Your home is at the end."

Then came another master,
Who did not love mankind,
And planted on the pathway
Gold flowers for them to find.
And mankind saw the bright flowers,
That, glitt'ring[4] in the sun,
Quite hid the thorns of av'rice[5]
That poison blood and bone;
And far off many wandered,
And when life's night came on,
They still were seeking gold flowers,
Lost, helpless and alone.

O, cease to heed the glamour
That blinds your foolish eyes,
Look upward to the glitter
Of stars in God's clear skies.
Their ways are pure and harmless
And will not lead astray,
Bid aid your erring footsteps
To keep the narrow way.[6]
And when the sun shines brightly
Tend flowers that God has given
And keep the pathway open
That leads you on to heaven.

A Brook in the City

The firm house[7] lingers, though averse to square
With the new city street it has to wear

A number in.⁸ But what about the brook
That held the house as in an elbow-crook⁹?
I ask as one who knew the brook, its strength
And impulse, having dipped a finger length
And made it leap my knuckle¹⁰, having tossed
A flower to try its currents where they crossed.
The meadow grass could be cemented down¹¹
From growing under pavements of a town;
The apple trees be sent to hearth-stone flame.
Is water wood to serve a brook the same?
How else dispose of an immortal force
No longer needed? Staunch it at its source
With cinder loads dumped down? The brook was
thrown Deep in a sewer dungeon¹² under stone
In fetid darkness still to live and run—
And all for nothing it had ever done
Except forget to go in fear perhaps.
No one would know except for ancient maps
That such a brook ran water. But I wonder
If from its being kept forever under
The thoughts may not have risen that so keep
This new-built city from both work and sleep.

The Last Mowing

There's a place called Far-away Meadow
We never shall mow in again,
Or such is the talk at the farmhouse:
The meadow is finished with men.
Then now is the chance for the flowers
That can't stand mowers and plowers.
It must be now, through, in season
Before the not mowing brings trees on,
Before trees, seeing the opening,
March into a shadowy claim.
The trees are all I'm afraid of,
That flowers can't bloom in the shade of;
It's no more men I'm afraid of;
The meadow is done with the tame.
The place for the moment is ours
For you, oh tumultuous flowers,

To go to waste and go wild in,
All shapes and colors of flowers,
I needn't call you by name.

注释

1. beatous:(=beauteous) 美丽的。
2. Prune ye my vines and fig trees:你们要修剪我的葡萄藤和无花果树。ye 即为 you, 这句用作祈使句。
3. floweret:小花。
4. glitt'ring:(=glittering) 闪亮发光的。
5. av'rice:(=avarice) 贪婪。
6. Bid aid your erring footsteps to keep the narrow way:请让你们迷失的脚步再踏上那窄道。bid 这里表示祈使,相当于 let。
7. The firm house:那所坚固的屋子,house 指的是 farmhouse。
8. though averse to square with the new city street it has to wear a number in:虽不愿和城市街道相同,却不得不挂上一个门牌号码。square with 与……相符。number 门牌号码。
9. elbow-crook:臂弯,肘的内侧。
10. leap my knuckle:在我的指间跳跃。
11. be cemented down:被封在水泥下面。
12. sewer dungeon:下水道,阴沟。

作品导读

罗伯特·弗罗斯特是美国当代最受欢迎的诗人之一。不同于艾略特那类阳春白雪般的学者型诗人,弗罗斯特是一位质朴无华的"草根诗人"。正因如此,他才能用他仰慕的眼睛和诗人的文笔去发现和描绘这样一个质朴清新的大自然,才能为人类文明的无限发展对自然的危害做出沉痛的叹息。

本文所选的第一首诗《上帝的花园》中,作者用优美的语言、对照的手法,描绘了两种人生选择:一是在上帝的花园中,一条直直的甬道通向满是鲜花、藤蔓、无花果树的园林,人类可以在这个朴素的花园中劳作,与自然为伴。另一个园地有一个邪恶的主人,在园中的甬道旁种了金子做的花,引诱人类追寻这闪耀的虚荣,偏离了上帝指引的自然之路,把人生陷入不知餍足的贪婪之中,终于走向孤独和无望。诗人敦促人们看穿金花所代表的欲望,遵循上帝的意旨,回到自然的怀抱,如此才能到达天堂。

第二首诗《城中的小溪》用隐喻的手法,反映了工业文明对自然环境的粗暴摧残,使得原本朴素天然的生存环境荡然无存,让位于以金钱和消费为主导的工业社会。"那幢农舍依然存在,虽说它厌恶/与新城街道整齐划一,但不得不/挂上了门牌号。可是那条小溪呢?/那条像手臂环抱着农舍的小溪呢?/我问,作为一个熟悉那小溪的人/我知道它的力量和冲动,我曾经/把手伸进溪水让浪花在指尖跳舞/我曾经把花抛进水中测它的流速/……"(曹明伦译)在作者笔下,没有声色俱厉的批判,只有黯然怀旧的叹息。现代人必须眼睁睁地看着工业文明入侵自然:"除了远古地图没谁会知道/一条如此流动的小溪。但我怀疑/它是否想永远呆在下面,而不显现/曾经奔流的身影,使这新建的/城市,既不能工作也无法入眠。"

第三首《最后一片牧草地》也流露出同样的惆怅和忧思:"有一片被叫作偏远牧场的草地/我们再也不会去那儿收割牧草/或者说这是农舍里的一次谈话/说那片草场与割草人缘分已尽。这下该是野花们难得的机会/它们可以不再害怕割草机和耕犁/不过必须趁现在,得抓紧时机,因为不再种草树木就会逼近……"在诗人笔下,这最后一片牧草地象征着最后一个未经人类破坏的纯净的自然。这里有青青的牧草和恣意开放的野花,然而开阔的美景背后却是诗人对人类文明的迷茫和深深担忧。

弗罗斯特是一位从乡野走进城市的诗人,他的创作灵感更多地来自自然而不是城市,因此,他对文明对自然的侵袭感觉尤其痛切。他知道人类发展对自然的侵蚀不可避免,他也无力去改变这个趋向,所以他自己作为一个哀悼者,以一个热爱自然者的心去感受无可挽回的过去,无论是被城市掩埋了的小溪,还是那片最后的牧草地,都在他的诗歌里找到了永恒。这种永恒即为弗罗斯特所代表的生态忧思,也是人类思考自己与环境、与未来之关系的一种诗意呈现,在许多自然保护者那里得到了共鸣。

思考题

1. What does the God's garden symbolize?
2. What do the gold flowers reflect?
3. What happened to the brook in the city?
4. What does the last mowing stand for?
5. Compare Frost's nature poetry with Dickinson's from an ecocritical perspective.

推荐阅读

Frost, Robert. *The Poetry of Robert Frost: The Collected Poems*. Ed. Edward Connery Lathem. Holt Paperbacks, 2002.

Kendall, Tim. *The Art of Robert Frost*. Yale University Press, 2012.

Newman, Lea. *Robert Frost: The People, Places, and Stories Behind His New England Poetry*. New England Pr Inc, 2000.

Parini, Jay. *Robert Frost: A Life*. Picador; Reprint edition, 2000.

Penny, Jonathon. "Out of the Garden: The Nature of Revelation in Romanticism, Naturalism, and Modernism." *Dialogue: A Journal of Mormon Thought*, vol. 52, no. 4, 2019.

Smith, Virginia. "The Varieties of Natural Experience: The Importance of Place Names in the Poetry of Robert Frost." *The Robert Frost Review*, no. 25, 2015.

Stanlis, Peter. *Robert Frost: The Poet as Philosopher*. Intercollegiate Studies

Institute, 2008.

蔡培琳,刘立辉:"存在之链和生命树:弗罗斯特诗歌的动态自然观",《河北学刊》,2020,40(04)。

刘金侠:"中西诗歌中物我关系的对比研究——以柳宗元和弗罗斯特为例",《山东社会科学》,2010(12)。

刘瑞英:"罗伯特·弗罗斯特的生态智慧",《中国农业大学学报》(社会科学版),2010(03)。

罗伯特·弗罗斯特:《弗罗斯特集——诗全集、散文和戏剧作品》,曹明伦译,辽宁教育出版社,2002年。

肖锦凤:《生态批评与道家哲学视阈下的弗罗斯特诗歌研究》,西南财经大学出版社,2016年。

杰克·伦敦(Jack London)

【作者简介】

杰克·伦敦,原名为约翰·格利菲斯·伦敦(John Griffith London,1876—1916),美国现代现实主义作家。他生于破产农民家庭,一生充满传奇色彩,生活经验之丰富在世界作家中独树一帜。他从小以出卖劳力为生,曾卖报、卸货、当童工。成年后当过水手、工人,曾去阿拉斯加淘金,得了坏血症,后专门从事文学创作。艰辛的求生历程赋予了他作品中现实主义风格和多样化的题材,并从中展示出其独特个性,使他成为美国文学史上具有世界声望的"阳刚型作家"。他成名之后获得了名誉和财富,却饱受病痛折磨和情感挫折。1916年11月21日晚,他因服用过量吗啡去世,是误服药量还是自杀,至今成谜。

伦敦一生共写了19部长篇小说、150多篇短篇小说和故事,3部剧本,以及论文、特写等。他不仅多产,而且作品极具特色,文笔刚劲质朴,情节生动,他笔下的人物常置身于极端严酷的境地中以求生,在生死攸关的危机中表现勇猛、坚忍和真情这些优良品质。这种"严酷的真实"会使读者受到强烈的心灵震撼。他的作品中有描写北方淘金者生活的短篇小说集,包括1900年至1902年发表的《狼的儿子》(Son of the Wolf)等3部集子,通称"北方故事";有描写兽性般残忍和利己主义的长篇小说《海狼》(The Sea-Wolf,1904);有号召工人阶级抛开幻想、准备坚持长期武装斗争的政治幻想小说《铁蹄》(The Iron Heel,1908);有描写劳动者出身的现实主义作家因理想破灭而投海自杀的自传体长篇小说《马丁·伊登》(Martin Eden,1909)。而最著名的,莫过于他以狗为主角写成的名作《野性的呼唤》(The Call of the Wild,1903)和《白獠牙》(White Fang,1906),前者是一条狗变成了狼的故事,而后者是狼被驯化成狗的故事。动物的天性是野性还是驯服？伦敦没有给出明确的答案,他只用细致入微的描写来客观地呈现人与动物、动物与自然之间微妙的依存与矛盾关系。

以下节选自《野性的呼唤》第七章。

Chapter VII The Sounding of the Wild

Spring came on once more, and at the end of all their wandering they found, not the Lost Cabin[1], but a shallow place in a broad valley where the gold showed like yellow butter across the bottom of the washing-pan. They sought no farther. Each day they worked earned them thousands of dollars in clean dust and nuggets, and they worked every day. The gold was sacked in moose-hide bags, fifty pounds to the bag, and piled like so much firewood outside the spruce-bough lodge. Like giants they toiled, days flashing on the heels of days like dreams as they heaped the treasure up.

There was nothing for the dogs to do, save the hauling in of meat now and again that Thornton[3] killed, and Buck spent long hours musing by the fire. The vision of the short-legged hairy man[4] came to him more frequently, now that there was little work to be done; and often, blinking by the fire, Buck wandered with him in that other world which he remembered.

The salient thing of this other world seemed fear. When he watched the hairy man sleeping by the fire, head between his knees and hands clasped above, Buck saw that he slept restlessly, with many starts and awakenings, at which times he would peer fearfully into the darkness and fling more wood upon the fire. Did they walk by the beach of a sea, where the hairy man gathered shell-fish and ate them as he gathered, it was with eyes that roved everywhere for hidden danger and with legs prepared to run like the wind at its first appearance. Through the forest they crept noiselessly, Buck at the hairy man's heels; and they were alert and vigilant, the pair of them, ears twitching and moving and nostrils quivering, for the man heard and smelled as keenly as Buck. The hairy man could spring up into the trees and travel ahead as fast as on the ground, swinging by the arms from limb to limb, sometimes a dozen feet apart, letting go and catching, never falling, never missing his grip. In fact, he seemed as much at home among the trees as on the ground; and Buck had memories of nights of vigil spent beneath trees wherein the hairy man roosted, holding on tightly as he slept.

And closely akin to the visions of the hairy man was the call still sounding in the depths of the forest. It filled him with a great unrest and strange desires. It caused him to feel a vague, sweet gladness, and he was aware of wild yearnings and stirrings for he knew not what. Sometimes he pursued the call into the forest, looking for it as though it were a tangible thing, barking softly or defiantly, as the mood might dictate. He would thrust his nose into the cool wood moss, or into the black soil where long grasses grew, and snort with joy at the fat earth smells; or he would crouch for hours, as if in concealment, behind fungus-covered trunks of fallen trees, wide-eyed and wide-eared to all that moved and sounded about him. It might be, lying thus, that he hoped to surprise this call he could not understand. But he did not know why he did these various things. He was impelled to do them, and did not reason about them at all.

Irresistible impulses seized him. He would be lying in camp, dozing lazily in the heat of the day, when suddenly his head would lift and his ears cock up, intent and listening, and he would spring to his feet and dash away, and on and on, for hours, through the forest aisles and across the open spaces where the niggerheads[5] bunched. He loved to run down dry watercourses, and to creep and spy upon the bird life in the woods. For a day at a time he would lie in the underbrush where he could watch the partridges[6] drumming and strutting up and down. But especially he loved to run in the dim twilight of the summer midnights, listening to the subdued and sleepy murmurs of the forest, reading signs and sounds as man may read a book, and seeking for the mysterious something that called—

called, waking or sleeping, at all times, for him to come.

One night he sprang from sleep with a start, eager-eyed, nostrils quivering and scenting, his mane bristling in recurrent waves. From the forest came the call (or one note of it, for the call was many noted), distinct and definite as never before,—a long-drawn howl, like, yet unlike, any noise made by husky dog. And he knew it, in the old familiar way, as a sound heard before. He sprang through the sleeping camp and in swift silence dashed through the woods. As he drew closer to the cry he went more slowly, with caution in every movement, till he came to an open place among the trees, and looking out saw, erect on haunches, with nose pointed to the sky, a long, lean, timber wolf[7].

He had made no noise, yet it ceased from its howling and tried to sense his presence. Buck stalked into the open, half crouching, body gathered compactly together, tail straight and stiff, feet falling with unwonted care. Every movement advertised commingled threatening and overture of friendliness. It was the menacing truce[8] that marks the meeting of wild beasts that prey. But the wolf fled at sight of him. He followed, with wild leapings, in a frenzy to overtake. He ran him into a blind channel, in the bed of the creek where a timber jam barred the way. The wolf whirled about, pivoting on his hind legs after the fashion of Joe[9] and of all cornered husky dogs, snarling and bristling, clipping his teeth together in a continuous and rapid succession of snaps.

Buck did not attack, but circled him about and hedged him in with friendly advances. The wolf was suspicious and afraid; for Buck made three of him in weight, while his head barely reached Buck's shoulder. Watching his chance, he darted away, and the chase was resumed. Time and again he was cornered, and the thing repeated, though he was in poor condition, or Buck could not so easily have overtaken him. He would run till Buck's head was even with his flank, when he would whirl around at bay[10], only to dash away again at the first opportunity.

But in the end Buck's pertinacity was rewarded; for the wolf, finding that no harm was intended, finally sniffed noses with him. Then they became friendly, and played about in the nervous, half-coy way with which fierce beasts belie their fierceness. After some time of this the wolf started off at an easy lope in a manner that plainly showed he was going somewhere. He made it clear to Buck that he was to come, and they ran side by side through the sombre twilight, straight up the creek bed, into the gorge from which it issued, and across the bleak divide where it took its rise.

On the opposite slope of the watershed they came down into a level country where were great stretches of forest and many streams, and through these great stretches they ran steadily, hour after hour, the sun rising higher and the day growing warmer. Buck was wildly glad. He knew he was at last answering the call, running by the side of his wood brother toward the place from where the call surely came. Old memories were coming upon him fast, and he was stirring to them as of old he stirred to the realities of which they were the shadows. He had done this thing before, somewhere in that other and dimly remembered world, and he was doing it again, now, running free in the open, the unpacked earth underfoot, the wide sky overhead.

They stopped by a running stream to drink, and, stopping, Buck remembered John Thornton. He sat down. The wolf started on toward the place from where the call surely came, then returned to him, sniffing noses and making actions as though to encourage him. But Buck turned about and started slowly on the back track. For the better part of an hour the wild brother ran by his side, whining softly. Then he sat down, pointed his nose upward, and howled. It was a mournful howl, and as Buck held steadily on his way he heard it grow faint and fainter until it was lost in the distance.

John Thornton was eating dinner when Buck dashed into camp and sprang upon him in a frenzy of affection, overturning him, scrambling upon him, licking his face, biting his hand—"playing the general tom-fool[11]," as John Thornton characterized it, the while he shook Buck back and forth and cursed him lovingly.

For two days and nights Buck never left camp, never let Thornton out of his sight. He followed him about at his work, watched him while he ate, saw him into his blankets at night and out of them in the morning. But after two days the call in the forest began to sound more imperiously than ever. Buck's restlessness came back on him, and he was haunted by recollections of the wild brother, and of the smiling land beyond the divide and the run side by side through the wide forest stretches. Once again he took to wandering in the woods, but the wild brother came no more; and though he listened through long vigils, the mournful howl was never raised.

He began to sleep out at night, staying away from camp for days at a time; and once he crossed the divide at the head of the creek and went down into the land of timber and streams. There he wandered for a week, seeking vainly for fresh sign of the wild brother, killing his meat as he travelled and travelling with the long, easy lope that seems never to tire. He fished for salmon in a broad stream that emptied somewhere into the sea, and by this stream he killed a large black bear, blinded by the mosquitoes while likewise fishing, and raging through the forest helpless and terrible. Even so, it was a hard fight, and it aroused the last latent remnants of Buck's ferocity. And two days later, when he returned to his kill and found a dozen wolverines[12] quarrelling over the spoil, he scattered them like chaff; and those that fled left two behind who would quarrel no more.

The blood-longing became stronger than ever before. He was a killer, a thing that preyed, living on the things that lived, unaided, alone, by virtue of his own strength and prowess, surviving triumphantly in a hostile environment where only the strong survived. Because of all this he became possessed of a great pride in himself, which communicated itself like a contagion to his physical being. It advertised itself in all his movements, was apparent in the play of every muscle, spoke plainly as speech in the way he carried himself, and made his glorious furry coat if anything more glorious. But for the stray brown on his muzzle and above his eyes, and for the splash of white hair that ran midmost down his chest, he might well have been mistaken for a gigantic wolf, larger than the largest of the breed. From his St. Bernard father[13] he had inherited size and weight, but it was his shepherd mother[14] who had given shape to that size and weight. His muzzle was the long wolf muzzle, save that was larger than the muzzle of any wolf; and his head, somewhat broader, was the wolf head on a massive scale.

His cunning was wolf cunning, and wild cunning; his intelligence, shepherd intelligence and St. Bernard intelligence; and all this, plus an experience gained in the fiercest of schools, made him as formidable a creature as any that intelligence roamed the wild. A carnivorous animal living on a straight meat diet, he was in full flower, at the high tide of his life, overspilling with vigor and virility. When Thornton passed a caressing hand along his back, a snapping and crackling followed the hand, each hair discharing its pent magnetism at the contact. Every part, brain and body, nerve tissue and fibre, was keyed to the most exquisite pitch; and between all the parts there was a perfect equilibrium or adjustment. To sights and sounds and events which required action, he responded with lightning-like rapidity. Quickly as a husky dog could leap to defend from attack or to attack, he could leap twice as quickly. He saw the movement, or heard sound, and responded in less time than another dog required to compass the mere seeing or hearing. He perceived and determined and responded in the same instant. In point of fact the three actions of perceiving, determining, and responding were sequential; but so infinitesimal were the intervals of time between them that they appeared simultaneous. His muscles were surcharged with vitality, and snapped into play sharply, like steel springs. Life streamed through him in splendid flood, glad and rampant, until it seemed that it would burst him asunder in sheer ecstasy and pour forth generously over the world.

"Never was there such a dog," said John Thornton one day, as the partners watched Buck marching out of camp.

注释

1.《野性的呼唤》讲述的是美国19世纪大淘金时代,一只名叫巴克(Buck)的狗在阿拉斯加的荒野中历尽磨难,最后回归狼群的故事。本章"荒原的鸣响"是该书的最后一章。

2. the Lost Cabin:失踪的木屋,小说中淘金者们传言可以淘到很多金子的一个神秘的金矿所在地。

3. Thornton:John Thornton:约翰·桑顿,小说中救了巴克的淘金者,是巴克最后一位主人。

4. the short-legged hairy man:短腿、长毛的人,是巴克臆想出的一个野人形象,代表着野性。

5. niggerheads:磊磊的岩石,因为形状、颜色与黑人的头颅相似而得名。

6. partridge:松鸡。

7. timber wolf:(一种产于北美的)大灰狼;林狼。

8. truce:休战,停战。

9. Joe:曾经和巴克一起拉过雪橇的一条狗的名字。

10. at bay：陷入困境，陷入绝境。
11. the general tom-fool：大傻瓜。
12. wolverine：狼獾，又名貂熊，是生活在寒温带的一种鼬科动物，凶猛而灵活。
13. St. Bernard father：巴克的父亲是一只圣伯纳德犬（St. Bernard dog），这个犬种来自意大利和瑞士阿尔卑斯山，体型庞大，过去曾用于雪山救援。
14. shepherd mother：巴克的母亲是一只苏格兰牧羊犬（Scotch shepherd dog），这是一种负责牧羊、畜牧的犬种，灵活机智，敏感活跃。

 作品导读

杰克·伦敦曾经说过："我的故事有双重性质，表面上是一个简单的故事，任何一个孩子都能读懂——尽是情节、变化和色彩。那下面的才是真正的故事，有哲理，很复杂，充满含义。"这一点在《野性的呼唤》里得到印证。在这个又名"荒野的呼唤"故事里，杰克·伦敦讲述了一只本来居住在加利福尼亚养尊处优的良犬巴克的故事。它如何被家里的厨师偷卖掉，几经辗转，成为阿拉斯加严寒地区淘金者的雪橇狗。在多次艰苦卓绝的求生过程中，巴克逐渐回归野性，狗性逐渐让位于狼性。这一过程充满了自然天性与驯良人性之间的交织与角斗，而作者将巴克这只天性中带有狼的凶横与机敏的混血犬投放在淘金时代蛮荒的北极地区，使得巴克逐渐适应了"弱肉强食"的丛林法则，最终天性中的野性占据了主导。在它挚爱的主人被印第安人杀害之后，它为主人报了仇，也断绝了它跟人类温情的最后一点牵挂，从此回归荒野，成为领导群狼的头狼。

节选的这一段是该小说的最后一章：巴克跟随主人桑顿来到了一处溪流边，这里金砂遍布，只需搬运即可。巴克在闲暇中越来越感到荒野对它的诱惑，它的狼性渐渐复苏。一个夜晚，它与一条林狼在林中相遇，在追逐中结成伴侣，并肩飞奔。巴克不舍桑顿，没有追随林狼而去，但它却越来越逡巡在丛林里，倾听荒野的呼唤。这是巴克由狗变狼的重要环节，为下文桑顿遇害后巴克终于加入狼群做好了铺垫。

从生态角度来看，《野性的呼唤》与作者的另一部小说《白獠牙》形成了狗与狼的反向流变，展现了人与自然之间截然相反的两种互动。在《白獠牙》中，一只充满野性的小灰狼历尽艰辛最终在主人的呵护下变成了狗，而《野性的呼唤》则是作为狗的巴克在苦难中变成了狼。很多评论都把巴克回归荒野视为回归自然的必由之路，值得欢呼，却忽略了杰克·伦敦在小说中所埋藏的人文情怀——巴克是因为人世间再无可恋才投身狼群。如果它亲爱的主人桑顿还活着，它不会离开主人投向荒野。阿拉斯加恶劣的生存环境使巴克由一只由人喂养的宠物狗变成自行猎食的荒原狼，为了生存，它必须去除身上狗的特性，唤醒心中埋藏的原始野性，如此才能存活下去。而"白獠牙"却是在"善良的呼唤"（The Call of Kind）下心甘情愿地成为人类的朋友。因此，我们可以说，只有人与其他物种之间平等相待、友好相处，才是人与自然和谐共生之道。

思考题

1. How did Buck respond to the sounding in the depths of the forest?
2. What did Buck do when he saw the timber wolf in the night?
3. Why did not Buck follow the timber wolf forward to where the call came?
4. What characteristics did Buck inherit from his parents?
5. Why did John Thornton say there was never such a dog as Buck?

推荐阅读

Berkove, Lawrence I. *Jack London（Critical Insights）*. Salem Press Inc，2011.
Brandt, Kenneth K. *Jack London*. Liverpool University Press，2018.
Haley, James L. *Wolf：The Lives of Jack London*. Basic Books，2001.
London, Jack. *The Call of the Wild，White Fang ＆ To Build a Fire*. Modern Library，2002.
Nagler, Michelle. *Jack London：A Biography*. Scholastic Paperbacks，2002.
崔小清："回归生命的本源——从《野性的呼唤》看杰克·伦敦的人生哲学"，《西安外国语大学学报》，2014，22(02)。
杰克·伦敦：《野性的呼唤》，刘荣跃译，上海译文出版社，2011年。
——：《野性的呼唤·白牙》，吕艺红等译，长江文艺出版社，2011年。
马新："杰克·伦敦的边疆情结——从北疆到亚太作品解析"，《国外文学》，2021(03)。
杨才英，钟婷："从及物性看《野性的呼唤》中的生态关怀"，《北京科技大学学报》(社会科学版)，2020，36(03)。
虞建华：《杰克·伦敦研究》，上海外语教育出版社，2009年。

薇拉·凯瑟(Willa Cather)

【作者简介】

薇拉·凯瑟(1873—1947),美国著名女作家。出生在弗吉尼亚州,9 岁时随父母迁居到中西部的内布拉斯加州,积累了丰富的西部边疆生活体验,成为她日后创作的主要源泉。她从内布拉斯加大学毕业后先后做过中学教员、记者和杂志编辑,1912 年开始专事写作。陆续发表了《亚历山大的桥》(*Alexander's Bridge*,1912)、《啊,拓荒者!》(*O Pioneers!*,1913)、《我的安东尼娅》(*My Ántonia*,1918)、《云雀之歌》(*The Song of the Lark*,1915)、《我们自己人》(*One of Ours*,1922)、《迷途的女人》(*A Lost Lady*,1923)、《教授的住宅》(*The Professor's House*,1925)及《大主教之死》(*Death Comes for the Archbishop*,1927)等作品,还有 4 部短篇小说集和几部中长篇小说。她从自己的亲身经历和所闻所见着手,充分利用自己少年时期在中西部大草原的生活经验,以简洁朴素的文笔,塑造了众多"拓荒时代"的典型人物,尤其是勤劳坚强的女性角色,与辽阔高原的自然环境相应和,有着高爽纯洁的思想境界和舒缓清新的艺术风格,使得她被誉为美国文学史上反映中西部生活最杰出的现代作家之一。

薇拉·凯瑟公认的代表作是小说《我的安东尼娅》,讲述了一位从东欧移民到美国的波希米亚姑娘历尽艰辛、顽强成长的历程,生动地刻画了一位像西部高原一样坚韧的女拓荒者形象。她的身上所体现的美国早期开拓者的力量,与她所处身的淳朴的自然环境融为一体,使得这部小说成为生态女性主义文学经典文本之一。

以下选自《我的安东尼娅》第 17 章。

XVII

When spring came, after that hard winter, one could not get enough of the nimble air. Every morning I wakened with a fresh consciousness that winter was over. There were none of the signs of spring for which I used to watch in Virginia, no budding woods or blooming gardens. There was only—spring itself; the throb of it, the light restlessness, the vital essence of it everywhere: in the sky, in the swift clouds, in the pale sunshine, and in the warm, high wind—rising suddenly, sinking suddenly, impulsive and playful like a big puppy that pawed you and then lay down to be petted. If I had been tossed down blindfold[1] on that red prairie[2], I should have known that it was spring.

Everywhere now there was the smell of burning grass. Our neighbours burned off their pasture before the new grass made a start, so that the fresh growth would not be mixed with the dead stand of last year. Those light, swift fires, running about the country, seemed a part of the same kindling[3] that was in the air.

The Shimerdas[4] were in their new log house by then. The neighbours had helped them to build it in March. It stood directly in front of their old cave, which they used as a cellar. The family were now fairly equipped to begin their struggle with the soil. They had four comfortable rooms to live in, a new windmill—bought on credit—a chicken-house and poultry. Mrs. Shimerda had paid grandfather ten dollars for a milk cow, and was to give him fifteen more as soon as they harvested their first crop.

When I rode up to the Shimerdas' one bright windy afternoon in April, Yulka[5] ran out to meet me. It was to her, now, that I gave reading lessons; Antonia was busy with other things. I tied my pony and went into the kitchen where Mrs. Shimerda was baking bread, chewing poppy seeds[6] as she worked. By this time she could speak enough English to ask me a great many questions about what our men were doing in the fields. She seemed to think that my elders withheld helpful information, and that from me she might get valuable secrets. On this occasion she asked me very craftily when grandfather expected to begin planting corn. I told her, adding that he thought we should have a dry spring and that the corn would not be held back by too much rain, as it had been last year.

She gave me a shrewd glance. "He not Jesus[7]," she blustered[8]; "he not know about the wet and the dry."

I did not answer her; what was the use? As I sat waiting for the hour when Ambrosch[9] and Antonia would return from the fields, I watched Mrs. Shimerda at her work. She took from the oven a coffee-cake[10] which she wanted to keep warm for supper, and wrapped it in a quilt stuffed with feathers. I have seen her put even a roast goose in this quilt to keep it hot. When the neighbours were there building the new house, they saw her do this, and the story got abroad that the Shimerdas kept their food in their featherbeds.

When the sun was dropping low, Antonia came up the big south draw with her team. How much older she had grown in eight months! She had come to us a child, and now she was a tall, strong young girl, although her fifteenth birthday had just slipped by. I ran out and met her as she brought her horses up to the windmill to water them. She wore the boots her father had so thoughtfully taken off before he shot himself, and his old fur cap. Her outgrown cotton dress switched about her calves, over the boot-tops. She kept her sleeves rolled up all day, and her arms and throat were burned as brown as a sailor's. Her neck came up strongly out of her shoulders, like the bole of a tree out of the turf. One sees that draught-horse neck[11] among the peasant women in all old countries.

She greeted me gaily, and began at once to tell me how much ploughing she had done that day. Ambrosch, she said, was on the north quarter, breaking sod with the oxen.

"Jim, you ask Jake how much he ploughed to-day. I don't want that Jake get more done in one day than me. I want we have very much corn this fall."

While the horses drew in the water, and nosed each other, and then drank again, Antonia sat down on the windmill step and rested her head on her hand.

"You see the big prairie fire from your place last night? I hope your grandpa ain't lose no stacks[12]?"

"No, we didn't. I came to ask you something, Tony. Grandmother wants to know if you can't go to the term of school that begins next week over at the sod schoolhouse. She says there's a good teacher, and you'd learn a lot."

Antonia stood up, lifting and dropping her shoulders as if they were stiff. "I ain't got time to learn. I can work like mans now. My mother can't say no more how Ambrosch do all and nobody to help him. I can work as much as him. School is all right for little boys. I help make this land one good farm."

She clucked[13] to her team and started for the barn. I walked beside her, feeling vexed. Was she going to grow up boastful like her mother, I wondered? Before we reached the stable, I felt something tense in her silence, and glancing up I saw that she was crying. She turned her face from me and looked off at the red streak of dying light, over the dark prairie.

I climbed up into the loft and threw down the hay for her, while she unharnessed her team. We walked slowly back toward the house. Ambrosch had come in from the north quarter, and was watering his oxen at the tank.

Antonia took my hand. "Sometime you will tell me all those nice things you learn at the school, won't you, Jimmy?" she asked with a sudden rush of feeling in her voice. "My father, he went much to school. He know a great deal; how to make the fine cloth like what you not got here. He play horn and violin, and he read so many books that the priests in Bohemie come to talk to him. You won't forget my father, Jim?" "No," I said, "I will never forget him."

Mrs. Shimerda asked me to stay for supper. After Ambrosch and Antonia had washed the field dust from their hands and faces at the wash-basin by the kitchen door, we sat down at the oilcloth-covered table. Mrs. Shimerda ladled meal mush[15] out of an iron pot and poured milk on it. After the mush we had fresh bread and sorghum molasses[16], and coffee with the cake that had been kept warm in the feathers. Antonia and Ambrosch were talking in Bohemian; disputing about which of them had done more ploughing that day. Mrs. Shimerda egged[17] them on, chuckling while she gobbled her food.

Presently Ambrosch said sullenly in English: "You take them ox tomorrow and try the sod plough. Then you not be so smart."

His sister laughed. "Don't be mad. I know it's awful hard work for break sod. I milk the cow for you tomorrow, if you want."

Mrs. Shimerda turned quickly to me. "That cow not give so much milk like what your grandpa say. If he make talk about fifteen dollars, I send him back the cow."

"He doesn't talk about the fifteen dollars," I exclaimed indignantly. "He doesn't find fault with people."

"He say I break his saw when we build, and I never," grumbled Ambrosch.

I knew he had broken the saw, and then hid it and lied about it. I began to wish I had not stayed for supper. Everything was disagreeable to me. Antonia ate so noisily now, like a man, and she yawned often at the table and kept stretching her arms over her head, as if they ached. Grandmother had said, "Heavy field work'll spoil that girl. She'll lose all her nice ways and get rough ones." She had lost them already.

After supper I rode home through the sad, soft spring twilight. Since winter I had seen very little of Antonia. She was out in the fields from sunup until sundown. If I rode over to see her where she was ploughing, she stopped at the end of a row to chat for a moment, then gripped her plough-handles, clucked to her team, and waded on down the furrow, making me feel that she was now grown up and had no time for me. On Sundays she helped her mother make garden or sewed all day. Grandfather was pleased with Antonia. When we complained of her, he only smiled and said, "She will help some fellow get ahead in the world."

Nowadays Tony could talk of nothing but the prices of things, or how much she could lift and endure. She was too proud of her strength. I knew, too, that Ambrosch put upon her some chores a girl ought not to do, and that the farm-hands around the country joked in a nasty way about it. Whenever I saw her come up the furrow, shouting to her beasts, sunburned, sweaty, her dress open at the neck, and her throat and chest dust-plastered, I used to think of the tone in which poor Mr. Shimerda, who could say so little, yet managed to say so much when he exclaimed, "My Antonia!"

注释

1. blindfold:蒙住眼睛。
2. red prairie:指的位于美国中西部内布拉斯加州的大草原,因多红色砂砾和红草而看似红色草原。文中的"我"是从弗吉尼亚州迁居至此的。
3. kindling:点火,可燃物。
4. The Shimerdas:西姆达一家,即女主人公安东尼娅一家。他们是波西米亚人,从中欧移民到美国。安东尼娅是这家的长女,她的父亲西姆达先生因不适应新环境持枪自杀而死。
5. Yulka:尤尔佳,安东尼娅的妹妹。
6. poppy seed:罂粟种子。
7. He not Jesus:他又不是耶稣。安东尼娅的母亲西姆达太太初学英语,语法不正确。他们一家人讲英语都会出现语法错误。
8. bluster:吆喝着,大声说。
9. Ambrosch:埃姆布罗什,安东尼娅的兄弟。
10. coffee cake:早餐点心。
11. draught-horse neck:像拉重物的马的脖子。
12. ain't lose no stacks:(=didn't lose any stacks)没有损失草垛。
13. cluck:嘴里发出啧啧声。这里是呼唤牲口。
14. Bohemie:即 Bohemia,波希米亚,以前为中欧一古国,现为捷克一部分。
15. mush:浓粥,糊糊。

16. sorghum molasses：高粱糖浆，高粱饴。
17. egg：怂恿，煽动。

作品解读

　　《我的安东尼娅》是薇拉·凯瑟的代表作，虽然故事的叙述者是一个移民到内布拉斯加草原的男孩，但自然和女性是凯瑟的草原小说中两个永恒的平行结构。内布拉斯加州的大草原有母性的大地，女性则是大自然最亲密的伙伴。根据生态女性主义者的观点，人类与自然相互联系，相互影响，共同发展，而女性在其生理特性和社会性上都比男性更接近自然。在《我的安东尼娅》中，凯瑟向读者展示了她对自然和女性之间关系的关怀，并创造出安东尼娅这样一个热爱大自然，并能像自然一样顽强生长、与各种生物和谐共生的主人公。

　　所选这一部分是安东尼娅的父亲自杀后，"我"来到她家所见到的情景。安东尼娅的父亲是家里的顶梁柱，在东欧的故乡他是一位技艺精湛的裁缝、多才多艺的波西米亚人。移民到美国大草原之后，由于不适应这里的农耕劳作和生活方式，他开枪自杀了。安东尼娅是父亲的掌上明珠，父亲死后，她只能与一个喜欢夸夸其谈的母亲相依为命，还有两个弟妹需要照顾。15岁的安东尼娅没有沉溺于悲伤，而是坚强地担负起与家人共建家园的责任，"我"所见到的安东尼娅，如同严冬过后的草原之春，历经沧桑之后更加顽强生长，不屈不挠。她放弃了学业，驾着牲口犁田耙地。在"我"的眼里，在风吹日晒下满身尘土、不停劳作的安东尼娅，是这片大草原上的移民者们坚忍不拔的象征。

　　在这部作品中，"我"是一个暗中爱慕安东尼娅的美国少年，从他的眼中看到的她，充满野性的美与活力。安东尼娅的生活从未富足或者顺利过，但她从未被艰辛所驯服，也从未丧失过内心的热情、对生活的热爱。在小说的结尾，安东尼娅已是一位红颜不再的中年妇女，与她那同是波西米亚人的丈夫一起，生活在这片满是红草的大草原上，生养了一大群活泼健壮的儿女，自由、快乐、坚强，像这片草原一样生机勃勃，永不妥协。

思考题

1. What did "I" think of the spring in the prairie?
2. What was Mrs. Shimerda's attitude toward her neighbors?
3. Why did Antonia cry when she refused to return school?
4. How did "I" think of Antonia in her field work?
5. What would happen to Antonia in her life?

推荐阅读

Calder, Alex. "Beyond Possession: Animals and Gifts in Willa Cather's Settler Colonial Fictions." *Western American Literature*, vol. 52, no. 1, 2017.

Cather, Willa. *Cather: Stories, Poems, and Other Writings*. Library of America, 1992.

—. *My Antonia*. Simon & Brown, 2012.

Lewis, Edith. *Willa Cather Living: A Personal Record*. University of Nebraska Press, 2000.

Schilling, Richard. *Portraits of the Prairie: The Land that Inspired Willa Cather*. University of Nebraska Press, 2011.

Squire, Kesley. *Willa Cather: The Critical Conversation*. NED-New edition. Boydell & Brewer, 2020.

谭晶华:《薇拉·凯瑟的生态视野》,北京师范大学出版社,2011年。

薇拉·凯瑟:《我的安东妮亚》,周微林译,湖南师范大学出版社,1998年。

许燕:《包容与排斥:薇拉·凯瑟小说的美国化主题研究》,湖南人民出版社,2012年。

熊盈盈:"生态美学视域下薇拉·凯瑟主要小说研究",《芒种》,2022(07)。

杨海燕:《重访红云镇:薇拉·凯瑟生态女性主义研究》,四川大学出版社,2006年。

第四编　融入自然——当代英美生态文学

背景介绍

20世纪以来，生态思潮在世界范围内呈现出井喷式发展势态。生态文学作为这一股生态思潮的重要组成部分，在以利奥波德和卡森为代表的众多杰出生态思想家和生态文学家的推动下，从20世纪60年代以来得到了快速的发展。生态文学在20世纪后半叶开始迅猛发展有其深刻的外部原因和内部因素。

20世纪见证了人类科学技术的飞速发展，人类自此进入了一个全新的历史时期。然而与此同时，人类也面临了有史以来最严重的生存危机。人类对现代化交通工具以及其他现代化产品的大量使用使得石油、天然气等不可再生能源日益减少，甚至濒临枯竭；人类活动所带来的二氧化碳的过度排放导致全球性气温升高、冰川融化、海平面上升；人为造成的生态环境的破坏所造成的后果是越来越频繁的极端灾难性气候事件。上述这些生态灾难直接威胁着人类作为一个整体的生存和发展。面对这一空前严重的生存危机，许多有识之士开始对人类过去的行为进行积极的反省和批判，同时思考应对这一危机的方法和措施。于是在20世纪，特别是60年代以来，生态思潮在全球范围内形成了波澜壮阔的繁荣之势。生态文学作为生态思潮的一个必不可少的分支，也承担起了重要的责任。生态文学的使命在于思索并挖掘导致生态灾难的深层次的思想根源，反思、批判反生态的人类思想传统，同时通过富含生态思想的文学作品，推动生态思想的传播和发展。这可以说是生态文学在20世纪迅速发展的重要外部原因。

而从文学的内部角度来看，生态文学在20世纪后半叶的发展也和文学发展趋势的变化密不可分。20世纪初期的现代主义文学在非理性哲学和现代心理学的影响下，把重心集中在人的精神世界或是说内部世界，而几乎不再关注外部客观世界。因此，以乔伊斯、伍尔芙为代表的意识流作家不再刻意追求文学对客观世界的模仿，而是聚焦于人的主观精神世界的刻画、挖掘和分析。然而到了60年代，这种文学"向内转"的趋势却几乎停滞，文学又开始"向外转"，或是说"向社会转""向意义和使命转"。在这样的趋势下，文学作品又开始重新关注外部世界，关注人类社会，关注人和自然的关系。从这个意义上来讲，生态文学的蓬勃发展自然合乎情理。

20世纪生态文学所体现出的思想大致可以划分为以下三个主要方面：生态整体观思想；欲望动力论批判和唯发展论批判；征服、统治自然思想批判。

生态整体观的思想并不是20世纪出现的新事物，把世界视为一个有机的整体的思想在西方早已有之。但利奥波德提出的生态整体主义的基本价值评判标准奠定了生态伦理的基础，同时大大推进了生态整体观的发展。利奥波德在其代表作《沙乡年鉴》(*A Sand County Almanac*)中提出，"有助于维持生命共同体的和谐、稳定和美丽的事就是正确的，反之则是错误的"。他的"ISB原则"

(integrity, stability and beauty)得到了西方学界的普遍认同。利奥波德的学说对长期以来的人类中心主义的哲学观点是致命的打击。在人类以往对大自然开发和利用的历史中，在自身利益与其他物种或是大自然利益发生冲突时，往往是以维系自身发展为借口，对大自然进行肆意破坏和掠夺。但根据利奥波德的原则，人类在大自然世界中的活动也必须遵循生态整体利益的原则，在维护生态整体和谐的前提条件下对大自然进行合理的开发和利用。因此生态整体主义思想是生态思潮中最重要最基本的思想。生态思潮中另一位重要人物便是美国女作家卡森。她在生态文学史上是一位里程碑式的人物。她的作品，特别是代表作《寂静的春天》(Silent Spring)推动了全球生态环境保护事业的进程，引发了全球范围内的生态思潮。该书对当时在全球范围内普遍使用的人工杀虫剂DDT所带来的生态影响进行了深刻的反思。DDT虽然能杀死害虫，但其毒性却保留在害虫体内，并转移到以害虫为食的鸟类以及其他生物体内。最终的结果便是整个生态系统遭到破坏，原本应该是鸟语花香的春天却如此寂静。生物学家卡森在书中用大量的科学事实向人们证明，人类并不是万物的"中心"，不能完全按照自己的意志去彻底消灭某一种生物或者不顾一切地去扶持另一种生物。只有把大自然看做是一个整体，尊重大自然的规律以及自然界中的每一个物种，人类才能够得到长久的生存和发展。

欲望动力论指的是人类为了不断满足自己的各种欲望而不停地工作、创造、探索、占有。必须承认，这些行为在整个人类的历史上推动了社会的进步。但另一方面，人类所生存的地球的资源总量却是有限的，如果人类放纵自己欲望的增长，通过不断地向自然索取资源来发展自身，甚至纯粹为了发展而发展，那么地球资源耗尽的那天便是人类的末日。许多生态思想家和文学家对唯发展论的观点进行了批判。美国作家艾比在代表作《沙漠独居者》(Desert Solitaire)中尖锐地指出，"为发展而发展是癌细胞的疯狂裂变和扩散"。他进一步一针见血地指出，不惜一切代价、哪怕是牺牲生态平衡和人的健康的发展，其实质上并不是满足所有人类的需要，而是满足工业化的需要，满足那些"寡头和政客"的需要。艾比认为人类应该在满足基本生存条件，在自然能够承载的范围内逐步提高生活水平的前提下，与自然和谐相处，同时注重自身精神层面的发展。艾比是一个激进的生态主义者，他提出了著名的生态防卫观，即为了保护生态而对破坏生态的行为进行有意破坏。在其另一部作品《有意破坏帮》(The Monkey Wrench Gang)里，小说主人公为了保护生态环境的原貌，向修建巨型水坝等破坏生态环境、扭曲自然规律的行为进行了有意的"生态性的破坏"(eco-sabotage)。

征服、统治自然是人类社会古已有之且根深蒂固的思想。在西方，对人类征服、统治自然的肯定和赞颂可以一直追溯到《圣经》。英国小说家笛福的《鲁滨孙漂流记》也是人类征服自然、统治自然思想的象征。20世纪的生态文学家们对这一历史悠久的错误思想也进行了猛烈地批判。卡森尖锐地指出，人类之所以"征服"自然，是因为还没有意识到人类其实就是自然这个整体的其中一部分。人类的科技能力在当今急剧膨胀，然而人类的意识却尚未成熟到正确地认识到自己在自然界中的地位。这样的结果便是，人类征服了自然，同时也是毁灭了自己。美国著名诗人、"垮掉的一代"的旗帜性人物斯耐德对人类征服、改造自然的行为进行了质疑和反思。他在论文集《荒野的实践》(*The Practice of the Wild*)中，通过自己的经历，对什么是"荒蛮的、贫瘠的"土地，什么又是"文明的、肥沃的"土地的标准进行了质疑，并呼吁人们尊重大自然。英国当代著名小说家麦克尤恩也在自己2010年的最新作品《日光》(*Solar*，又译为《太阳能》)中，以全球变暖这一热门话题为切入点，对人类究竟该如何以科学技术为武器，改造大自然、解决气候变化难题进行了探讨。

蕾切尔·卡森(Rachel Carson)

【作者简介】

蕾切尔·卡森(1907—1964)是20世纪美国最著名的生态文学家,在生态文学史上是一位里程碑式的人物。她的作品,特别是代表作《寂静的春天》(Silent Spring)推动了全球生态环境保护事业的进程,引发了全球范围内的生态思潮。卡森去世以后,美国总统吉米·卡特为她追发了总统自由勋章。

卡森在职业生涯之初供职于美国联邦渔业管理局,在20世纪50年代开始了职业文学创作。1951年她出版了第一部作品《我们周围的海洋》(The Sea Around Us),并凭借此书获得国家图书奖。她的接下来的两部作品——《海的边缘》(The Edge of the Sea)和《海风下》(Under the Sea Wind)均获得了广泛好评。从50年代末期开始,卡森逐渐将注意力转向环境问题,特别是由在当时广泛使用的人工合成的杀虫剂所引起的环境污染问题。1962年,她出版了《寂静的春天》一书,引发了全国关于环境问题的热烈讨论,激发了全民对人工杀虫剂的滥用的深刻反思,最终导致DDT以及其他杀虫剂在全美范围内的禁用。但此书的意义远不止如此。《寂静的春天》此后逐渐在全球范围内引起了热议,并直接掀起了轰轰烈烈的环境保护运动,改变了人们关于大自然和环境的看法,激发并推动了全球性生态思潮。《寂静的春天》被普遍认为是生态文学史上划时代的作品。

下面是该书第八章的节选。

8. And No Birds Sing (excerpt)

OVER INCREASINGLY large areas of the United States, spring now comes unheralded by the return of the birds, and the early mornings are strangely silent where once they were filled with the beauty of bird song. This sudden silencing of the song of birds, this obliteration of the color and beauty and interest they lend to our world have come about swiftly, insidiously, and unnoticed by those whose communities are as yet unaffected.

From the town of Hinsdale, Illinois, a housewife wrote in despair to one of the world's leading ornithologists[1], Robert Cushman Murphy, Curator Emeritus of Birds at the American Museum of Natural History.

Here in our village the elm trees have been sprayed for several years [she wrote in

1958]. When we moved here six years ago, there was a wealth of bird life; I put up a feeder and had a steady stream of cardinals, chickadees, downies and nuthatches[2] all winter, and the cardinals and chickadees brought their young ones in the summer.

After several years of DDT[3] spray, the town is almost devoid of robins and starlings[4]; chickadees have not been on my shelf for two years, and this year the cardinals are gone too; the nesting population in the neighborhood seems to consist of one dove pair and perhaps one catbird family.

It is hard to explain to the children that the birds have been killed off, when they have learned in school that a Federal law protects the birds from killing or capture. "Will they ever come back?" they ask, and I do not have the answer. The elms are still dying, and so are the birds. Is anything being done? Can anything be done? Can I do anything?

A year after the federal government had launched a massive spraying program against the fire ant, an Alabama woman wrote: "Our place has been a veritable bird sanctuary for over half a century. Last July we all remarked, "There are more birds than ever." Then, suddenly, in the second week of August, they all disappeared. I was accustomed to rising early to care for my favorite mare that had a young filly. There was not a sound of the song of a bird. It was eerie, terrifying. What was man doing to our perfect and beautiful world? Finally, five months later a blue jay appeared and a wren[5]."

The autumn months to which she referred brought other somber reports from the deep South, where in Mississippi, Louisiana, and Alabama the Field Notes published quarterly by the National Audubon Society and the United States Fish and Wildlife Service noted the striking phenomenon of "blank spots weirdly empty of virtually all bird life". The Field Notes are a compilation of the reports of seasoned observers who have spent many years afield in their particular areas and have unparalleled knowledge of the normal bird life of the region. One such observer reported that in driving about southern Mississippi that fall she saw "no land birds at all for long distances". Another in Baton Rouge reported that the contents of her feeders had lain untouched "for weeks on end", while fruiting shrubs in her yard, that ordinarily would be stripped clean by that time, still were laden with berries. Still another reported that his picture window, "which often used to frame a scene splashed with the red of 40 or 50 cardinals and crowded with other species, seldom permitted a view of as many as a bird or two at a time." Professor Maurice Brooks of the University of West Virginia, an authority on the birds of the Appalachian region, reported that the West Virginia bird population had undergone "an incredible reduction".

One story might serve as the tragic symbol of the fate of the birds—a fate that has already overtaken some species, and that threatens all. It is the story of the robin, the bird known to everyone. To millions of Americans, the season's first robin means that the grip of winter is broken. Its coming is an event reported in newspapers and told eagerly at the breakfast table. And as the number of migrants grows and the first mists of green appear in the woodlands, thousands of people listen for the first dawn chorus of the robins throbbing in the early morning light. But now all is changed, and not even the return of the birds may be taken for granted.

The survival of the robin, and indeed of many other species as well, seems fatefully linked with the American elm[6], a tree that is part of the history of thousands of towns from the Atlantic to the Rockies, gracing their streets and their village squares and college campuses with majestic archways of green. Now the elms are stricken with a disease that afflicts them throughout their range, a disease so serious that many experts believe all efforts to save the elms will in the end be futile. It would be tragic to lose the elms, but it would be doubly tragic if, in vain efforts to save them, we plunge vast segments of our bird populations into the night of extinction. Yet this is precisely what is threatened.

The so-called Dutch elm disease entered the United States from Europe about 1930 in elm burl logs imported for the veneer industry. It is a fungus[7] disease; the organism invades the water-conducting vessels of the tree, spreads by spores carried by the flow of sap, and by its poisonous secretions as well as by mechanical clogging causes the branches to wilt and the tree to die. The disease is spread from diseased to healthy trees by elm bark beetles. The galleries which the insects have tunneled out under the bark of dead trees become contaminated with spores of the invading fungus, and the spores adhere to the insect body and are carried wherever the beetle flies. Efforts to control the fungus disease of the elms have been directed largely toward control of the carrier insect. In community after community, especially throughout the strongholds of the American elm, the Midwest and New England, intensive spraying has become a routine procedure.

What this spraying could mean to bird life, and especially to the robin, was first made clear by the work of two ornithologists at Michigan State University, Professor George Wallace and one of his graduate students, John Mehner. When Mr. Mehner began work for the doctorate in 1954, he chose a research project that had to do with robin populations. This was quite by chance, for at that time no one suspected that the robins were in danger. But even as he undertook the work, events occurred that were to change its character and indeed to deprive him of his material.

Spraying for Dutch elm disease began in a small way on the university campus in 1954. The following year the city of East Lansing (where the university is located) joined in, spraying on the campus was expanded, and, with local programs for gypsy moth and mosquito control also under way, the rain of chemicals increased to a downpour.

During 1954, the year of the first light spraying, all seemed well. The following spring the migrating robins began to return to the campus as usual. Like the bluebells in Tomlinson's haunting essay "The Lost Wood", they were "expecting no evil" as they reoccupied their familiar territories. But soon it became evident that something was wrong. Dead and dying robins began to appear in the campus. Few birds were seen in their normal foraging activities or assembling in their usual roosts. Few nests were built; few young appeared. The pattern was repeated with monotonous regularity in succeeding springs. The sprayed area had become a lethal trap in which each wave of migrating robins would be eliminated in about a week. Then new arrivals would come in, only to add to the numbers of doomed birds seen on the campus in the agonized tremors that precede death.

"The campus is serving as a graveyard for most of the robins that attempt to take up residence in the spring," said Dr. Wallace. But why? At first he suspected some disease of the nervous system, but soon it became evident that "in spite of the assurances of the insecticide people that their sprays were "harmless to birds" the robins were really dying of insecticidal poisoning; they exhibited the well-known symptoms of loss of balance, followed by tremors, convulsions, and death."

Several facts suggested that the robins were being poisoned, not so much by direct contact with the insecticides as indirectly, by eating earthworms. Campus earthworms had been fed inadvertently to crayfish in a research project and all the crayfish had promptly died. A snake kept in a laboratory cage had gone into violent tremors after being fed such worms. And earthworms are the principal food of robins in the spring.

A key piece in the jigsaw puzzle of the doomed robins was soon to be supplied by Dr. Roy Barker of the Illinois Natural History Survey at Urbana. Dr. Barker's work, published in 1958, traced the intricate cycle of events by which the robins' fate is linked to the elm trees by way of the earthworms. The trees are sprayed in the spring (usually at the rate of 2 to 5 pounds of DDT per 50-foot tree, which may be the equivalent of as much as 23 pounds per acre where elms are numerous) and often again in July, at about half this concentration. Powerful sprayers direct a stream of poison to all parts of the tallest trees, killing directly not only the target organism, the bark beetle, but other insects, including pollinating species and predatory spiders and beetles. The poison forms a tenacious film over the leaves and bark. Rains do not wash it away. In the autumn the leaves fall to the ground, accumulate in sodden layers, and begin the slow process of becoming one with the soil. In this they are aided by the toil of the earthworms, who feed in the leaf litter, for elm leaves are among their favorite foods. In feeding on the leaves the worms also swallow the insecticide, accumulating and concentrating it in their bodies. Dr. Barker found deposits of DDT throughout the digestive tracts of the worms, their blood vessels, nerves, and body wall. Undoubtedly some of the earthworms themselves succumb, but others survive to become "biological magnifiers" of the poison. In the spring the robins return to provide another link in the cycle. As few as 11 large earthworms can transfer a lethal dose of DDT to a robin. And 11 worms form a small part of a day's rations to a bird that eats 10 to 12 earthworms in as many minutes.

Not all robins receive a lethal dose, but another consequence may lead to the extinction of their kind as surely as fatal poisoning. The shadow of sterility lies over all the bird studies and indeed lengthens to include all living things within its potential range. There are now only two or three dozen robins to be found each spring on the entire 185-acre campus of Michigan State University, compared with a conservatively estimated 370 adults in this area before spraying. In 1954 every robin nest under observation by Mehner produced young. Toward the end of June, 1957, when at least 370 young birds (the normal replacement of the adult population) would have been foraging over the campus in the years before spraying began, Mehner could find only one young robin. A year later Dr. Wallace was to report: "At no time during the spring or summer [of 1958] did I see a fledgling robin anywhere on the main campus, and so far I have failed to find anyone else who has seen one there."

Part of this failure to produce young is due, of course, to the fact that one or more of a pair of robins dies before the nesting cycle is completed. But Wallace has significant records which point to something more sinister—the actual destruction of the birds' capacity to reproduce. He has, for example, "records of robins and other birds building nests but laying no eggs, and others laying eggs and incubating them but not hatching them. We have one record of a robin that sat on its eggs faithfully for 21 days and they did not hatch. The normal incubation period is 13 days... Our analyses are showing high concentrations of DDT in the testes and ovaries of breeding birds," he told a congressional committee in 1960. "Ten males had amounts ranging from 30 to 109 parts per million in the testes, and two females had 151 and 211 parts per million respectively in the egg follicles in their ovaries."

Soon studies in other areas began to develop findings equally dismal. Professor Joseph Hickey and his students at the University of Wisconsin, after careful comparative studies of sprayed and unsprayed areas, reported the robin mortality to be at least 86 to 88 per cent. The Cranbrook Institute of Science at Bloomfield Hills, Michigan, in an effort to assess the extent of bird loss caused by the spraying of the elms, asked in 1956 that all birds thought to be victims of DDT poisoning be turned in to the institute for examination. The request had a response beyond all expectations. Within a few weeks the deep-freeze facilities of the institute were taxed to capacity, so that other specimens had to be refused. By 1959 a thousand poisoned birds from this single community had been turned in or reported. Although the robin was the chief victim (one woman calling the institute reported 12 robins lying dead on her lawn as she spoke), 63 different species were included among the specimens examined at the institute.

The robins, then, are only one part of the chain of devastation linked to the spraying of the elms, even as the elm program is only one of the multitudinous spray programs that cover our land with poisons. Heavy mortality has occurred among about 90 species of birds, including those most familiar to suburbanites and amateur naturalists. The populations of nesting birds in general have declined as much as 90 per cent in some of the sprayed towns. As we shall see, all the various types of birds are affected—ground feeders, treetop feeders, bark feeders, predators.

It is only reasonable to suppose that all birds and mammals heavily dependent on earthworms or other soil organisms for food are threatened by the robins' fate. Some 45 species of birds include earthworms in their diet. Among them is the woodcock[8], a species that winters in southern areas recently heavily sprayed with heptachlor. Two significant discoveries have now been made about the woodcock. Production of young birds on the New Brunswick breeding grounds is definitely reduced, and adult birds that have been analyzed contain large residues of DDT and heptachlor.

Already there are disturbing records of heavy mortality among more than 20 other species of ground-feeding birds whose food—worms, ants, grubs, or other soil organisms—has been poisoned. These include three of the thrushes whose songs are among the most exquisite of bird voices, the olive-backed, the wood, and the hermit. And the sparrows that flit through the shrubby understory of the woodlands and forage with rustling sounds amid the fallen leaves—the song sparrow and the white-throat—these, too, have been found among the victims of the elm sprays.

Mammals, also, may easily be involved in the cycle, directly or indirectly. Earthworms are important among the various foods of the raccoon[8], and are eaten in the spring and fall by opossums[8]. Such subterranean tunnelers as shrews and moles capture them in numbers, and then perhaps pass on the poison to predators such as screech owls and barn owls. Several dying screech owls were picked up in Wisconsin following heavy rains in spring, perhaps poisoned by feeding on earthworms. Hawks and owls have been found in convulsions—great horned owls, screech owls, red-shouldered hawks, sparrow hawks, marsh hawks. These may be cases of secondary poisoning, caused by eating birds or mice that have accumulated insecticides in their livers or other organs.

Nor is it only the creatures that forage on the ground or those who prey on them that are endangered by the foliar spraying of the elms. All of the treetop feeders, the birds that glean their insect food from the leaves, have disappeared from heavily sprayed areas, among them those woodland sprites the kinglets, both ruby-crowned and golden-crowned, the tiny gnatcatchers, and many of the warblers, whose migrating hordes flow through the trees in spring in a multicolored tide of life. In 1956, a late spring delayed spraying so that it coincided with the arrival of an exceptionally heavy wave of warbler migration. Nearly all species of warblers present in the area were represented in the heavy kill that followed. In Whitefish Bay, Wisconsin, at least a thousand myrtle warblers could be seen in migration during former years; in 1958, after the spraying of the elms, observers could find only two. So, with additions from other communities, the list grows, and the warblers killed by the spray include those that most charm and fascinate all who are aware of them: the black-and-white, the yellow, the magnolia, and the Cape May; the ovenbird, whose call throbs in the Maytime woods; the Blackburnian, whose wings are touched with flame; the chestnut-sided, the Canadian, and the black-throated green. These treetop feeders are affected either directly by eating poisoned insects or indirectly by a shortage of food.

The loss of food has also struck hard at the swallows that cruise the skies, straining out the aerial insects as herring strain the plankton of the sea. A Wisconsin naturalist reported: "Swallows have been hard hit. Everyone complains of how few they have compared to four or five years ago. Our sky overhead was full of them only four years ago.

Now we seldom see any.... This could be both lack of insects because of spray, or poisoned insects."

 注释

1. ornithologist：鸟类学家。
2. cardinals, chickadees, downies and nuthatches：分别是：主红雀、美洲山雀、丘陵雀、五子雀。
3. DDT：二氯二苯三氯乙烷，当时使用最广泛的杀虫剂。
4. robins and starlings：知更鸟和八哥。
5. jay：松鸦；wren：鹪鹩。
6. elm：榆树。
7. fungus：真菌，菌类。
8. raccoon：浣熊：北美食肉类哺乳动物；opossum：负鼠：一种夜间行动的杂食性树栖种袋鼠。

 作品导读

  春天是万物复苏的季节。在春天的田野中，本来应该看到一幅百花齐放、百鸟齐鸣的充满生机的画面。然而在不知不觉中，我们发现原本应该非常热闹的春天突然变得十分寂静，田间再也听不到鸟儿的歌唱。一些人开始去寻找这种奇怪现象发生的缘由。
  DDT 是二氯二苯三氯乙烷的简称，是一种人工合成的化学物质。瑞士科学家保罗·米勒发现了这种物质在杀灭蚊子和农业害虫上的独特效力，于 1948 年获得诺贝尔奖。DDT 也作为农业杀虫剂被广泛使用。然而这种杀虫剂的毁灭性力量却未被人完全了解。DDT 的毒性在杀灭害虫后并不会消失，而是沉积在害虫体内。由于大自然里的所有生物都处于一条完整的食物链上面，每一种生物都是食物链上方更高一级生物的食物，害虫也不例外。由于害虫体内沉积了大量 DDT 的毒素，当它们成为其他动物，主要是各种鸟类的食物以后，体内毒素转移到鸟类身体中，从而直接将鸟类杀死。这便是本应该生机勃勃的春天变得如此寂静的原因。
  当然，DDT 伤害的绝不仅仅只是鸟类。大自然是一个严密的整体系统，每一种生物都和其他物种之间有着严谨的关系。如果其中一个环节被破坏，将导致整个链状关系以及系统的崩溃。人类也是大自然系统中的一个部分。如果大自然系统遭到严重破坏，那么人类自身的利益也将受到损失。卡森的《寂静的春天》正是用一个个鲜活的事例向人们证明大自然的破坏所带来的严重后果，同时也讨论了这些破坏发生的深层次原因。
  大自然是一个有机的整体，每一个生态物种都是这个系统不可缺少的一部分，发挥着重要作用。《寂静的春天》反映的是一种生态整体主义思想。在卡森看来，人类把自己看做是万物中心，世上其他一切有生命或无生命的物质都是为人类而生的这种思想是极其错误的，在这种人类中心主义的思想支配下的对大自然肆意的改造和破坏行为是十分危险的。作为

一名生物学家的卡森用大量的科学事实向人们证明了自己的观点。人们为了保护榆树而大量喷洒DDT,虽然杀灭了害虫,但同时也破坏了大自然食物链的完整性。由于害虫体内的毒素进入了以害虫为食的鸟类体内,大量鸟类绝迹。同时受到影响的还有许多哺乳动物。与此同时,残留的毒素还进入土壤和河流之中,从而影响土地上生长的各种作物和河流里的鱼类。这种毒素的沉积和传递最终也将会伤害到自身也处于生态系统中的人类。因此人类必须意识到,自己是大自然的一部分;而不是万物的"中心",不能完全按照自己的意志去彻底消灭某一种生物或者不顾一切地去扶持另一种生物。只有把大自然看作是一个整体,尊重大自然的规律以及自然界中的每一个物种,人类才能够得到长久的生存和发展。

思考题

1. How did the pesticides kill birds like robins?
2. In what way were mammals influenced by the spraying of pesticides?
3. What, according to the writer, can people do to fight against the Dutch elm disease, rather than the spraying of pesticides?

推荐阅读

Carson, Rachel. *Silent Spring*. Mifflin, 1962.

Lear, Linda. *Rachel Carson: Witness for Nature*. Henry Holt, 1997.

Lytle, Mark Hamilton. *The Gentle Subversive: Rachel Carson, Silent Spring, and the Rise of the Environmental Movement*. Oxford University Press, 2007.

Moore, Kathleen Dean & Lisa H. Sideris, *Rachel Carson: Legacy and Challenge*. SUNY Press, 2008.

Murphy, Priscilla Coit. *What a Book Can Do: The Publication and Reception of Silent Spring*. University of Massachusetts Press, 2005.

Montrie, Chad. *The Myth of Silent Spring: Rethinking the Origins of American Environmentalism*. University of California Press, 2018.

Stein, Karen F. *Rachel Carson: Challenging Authors*. Sense Publishers, 2012.

Spears, Ellen. *Rethinking the American Environmental Movement post-1945*. Routledge, 2020.

奥尔多·利奥波德(Aldo Leopold)

【作者简介】

奥尔多·利奥波德(1887—1948),美国著名理论家、科学家和环境保护主义者,被誉为"美国野生生物管理之父"和"美国的先知"。利奥波德出生于爱荷华州伯灵顿,父亲是一位桃木家具制造商,祖父是一位受过良好教育的园林技艺师。他从小在密西西比河岸边长大,与大自然结下了不解之缘。在上大学期间,利奥波德始终保持着对鸟类学和自然科学历史的浓厚兴趣。他在日志中把观察到的东西都记录下来,并终生保持着这一习惯。1909年7月,他从耶鲁大学毕业获得森林学硕士学位后,加入了新成立的美国国家森林局,并被派往亚利桑那州和新墨西哥州工作。他很快获得了大量的工作经验,并得到提升,在1912年成为新墨西哥北部卡森国家森林局的局长。1915年,他被任命负责管理森林局西南部地区的渔猎活动。1924年,森林局采纳了他的建议,将新墨西哥州的大毒蜥地区开辟为野生自然保护区。1933年他成为威斯康星大学的一名教师,教授野生动植物课程。1948年4月24日,利奥波德死于心脏病。

利奥波德长期从事林学和猎物管理研究,在帮助创建林学和野生动物管理学这两个20世纪才出现在美国的新兴专业方面卓有建树。他一生共出版了三本书和大约500篇文章,大部分都是有关科学和技术的题目。《沙乡年鉴》(*A Sand County Almanac*, 1949)是他最著名的作品。这是一本随笔和哲学论文集,是他一生观察、经历和思考的结晶。

以下片段选自《沙乡年鉴》第二篇《随笔——这儿和那儿》中"亚利桑那和新墨西哥"一节,标题为"像大山那样思考"。

Thinking Like a Mountain

A deep chesty bawl echoes from rimrock to rimrock, rolls down the mountain, and fades into the far blackness of the night. It is an outburst of wild defiant sorrow, and of contempt for all the adversities of the world.

Every living thing (and perhaps many a dead one as well) pays heed to[1] that call. To the deer it is a reminder of the way of all flesh, to the pine a forecast of midnight scuffles and of blood upon the snow, to the coyote a promise of gleanings to come, to the cowman a threat of red ink at the bank, to the hunter a challenge of fang against bullet.[2] Yet behind these obvious and immediate hopes and fears there lies a deeper meaning, known only to the mountain itself. Only the mountain has lived long enough to listen objectively to the howl of a wolf.

Those unable to decipher the hidden meaning know nevertheless that it is there, for it is felt in all wolf country, and distinguishes that country from all other land. It tingles in the spine of all who hear wolves by night, or who scan their tracks by day. Even without sight or sound of wolf, it is implicit in a hundred small events: the midnight whinny of a pack horse, the rattle of rolling rocks, the sound of a fleeing deer, the way shadows lie under the spruces. Only the ineducable tyro[3] can fail to sense the presence or absence of wolves, or the fact that mountains have a secret opinion about them.

My own conviction on this score dates from the day I saw a wolf die. We were eating lunch on a high rimrock, at the foot of which a turbulent river elbowed its way.[4] We saw

what we thought was a doe[5] fording the torrent, her breast awash in white water. When she climbed the bank toward us and shook out her tail, we realized our error: it was a wolf. A half-dozen others, evidently grown pups, sprang from the willows and all joined in a welcoming mêlée[6] of wagging tails and playful maulings. What was literally a pile of wolves writhed and tumbled in the center of an open flat at the foot of our rimrock. In those days we had never heard of passing up a chance to kill a wolf. In a second we were pumping lead into the pack, but with more excitement than accuracy: how to aim a steep downhill shot is always confusing. When our rifles were empty, the old wolf was down, and a pup was dragging a leg into impassable slide-rocks.

We reached the old wolf in time to watch a fierce green fire dying in her eyes. I realized then, and have known ever since, that there was something new to me in those eyes—something known only to her and to the mountain. I was young then, and full of trigger-itch;[7] I thought that because fewer wolves meant more deer, that no wolves would mean hunters' paradise. But after seeing the green fire die, I sensed that neither the wolf nor the mountain agreed with such a view. Since then I have lived to see state after state extirpate its wolves. I have watched the face of many a newly wolfless mountain, and seen the south-facing slopes wrinkle with a maze of new deer trails. I have seen every edible bush and seedling browsed, first to anaemic desuetude, and then to death. I have seen every edible tree defoliated to the height of a saddlehorn. Such a mountain looks as if someone had given God a new pruning shears, and forbidden Him all other exercise. In the end the starved bones of the hoped-for deer herd, dead of its own too-much, bleach with the bones of the dead sage, or molder under the high-lined junipers.

I now suspect that just as a deer herd lives in mortal fear of its wolves, so does a mountain live in mortal fear of its deer. And perhaps with better cause, for while a buck pulled down by wolves can be replaced in two or three years, a range pulled down by too many deer may fail of replacement in as many decades. So also with cows. The cowman who cleans his range of wolves does not realize that he is taking over the wolf's job of trimming the herd to fit the range. He has not learned to think like a mountain. Hence we have dustbowls, and rivers washing the future into the sea.

We all strive for safety, prosperity, comfort, long life, and dullness. The deer strives with his supple legs, the cowman with trap and poison, the statesman with pen, the most of us with machines, votes, and dollars, but it all comes to the same thing: peace in our time. A measure of success in this is all well enough, and perhaps is a requisite to objective thinking, but too much safety seems to yield only danger in the long run. Perhaps this is behind Thoreau's dictum: In wildness is the salvation of the world. Perhaps this is the hidden meaning in the howl of the wolf, long known among mountains, but seldom perceived among men.

注释

1. pay heed to:注意到,留意到。

2. 此处使用了一系列的排比句,用来强调狼的嗥叫在山谷中产生的巨大影响力。在英文中使用排比句时,一般只需在主句中给出完整的句型结构,后面的句子则可以采用省略句的形式。在此句中,"a reminder of the way of all flesh"意指狼的嗥叫提示鹿警惕自己可能会变成肉食的下场;"gleaning"原意为"拾穗"或者"收集情报",此处意指狼捕食之后,郊狼这类食腐动物会前去捡拾狼剩下的食物;"red ink"意为赤字;"fang"意为犬科动物尖利的牙齿。

全句可被译为:对鹿来说,它是死亡的警告;对松林来说,它是半夜里在雪地上混战和流血的预言;对郊狼来说,是就要来临的拾遗的允诺;对牧牛人来说,是银行里赤字的坏兆头;对猎人来说,是狼牙抵制弹丸的挑战。(侯文蕙译,1997年)

3. ineducable:adj.不堪教育的。tyro:n.初学者,新手,与novice意义相仿。

4. elbow one's way:原意指从拥挤的地方开辟道路前进,此处指河流蜿蜒流过。

5. doe:许多雌性哺乳动物的特定称谓,与之相对应的雄性哺乳动物称为buck。在通常情况下此词专指母鹿。

6. mêlée:(法文)混战。

7. trigger-itch:打枪的冲动(不动扳机就手痒)。

作品导读

《沙乡年鉴》的第一篇章是对一个荒弃的沙乡农场上一年十二个月中不同景象的追述,利奥波德和他的一家人曾在这个农场亲手进行过恢复生态完整性的探索。第二篇章进一步就资源保护主义方面的问题陈述了利奥波德在美国其他地方的某些经历。第三篇章则集合了数篇有关人与环境的关系、美学和伦理学思考的文章。在全书中,第三篇章中的《土地伦理》是他最有代表性的文章,它把土地看成一个由相互依赖的各个部分组成的共同体,而人

只是共同体中的一个普通成员和公民。这一概念成为几个全国性环境保护组织和政府机构行动宗旨的基础。《沙乡年鉴》从1941年起就开始寻求出版,但直到1949年作者去世后才问世。当时正值战后经济复苏时期,人们都在充满信心地征服和利用自然,生态学的意识和概念对人们来说还十分陌生,所以这本书的出版在当时并没有引起很大的影响。书中利奥波德把本来用于人与人之间的伦理扩展到人与自然之间,要求人们改变观念,遵循生态规律。到了20世纪60年代,人们终于发现了环境问题的严重性,发现了利奥波德学说的指导意义。利奥波德被尊为新自然保护运动浪潮的领袖,《沙乡年鉴》也被称为"美国资源保护运动的圣书"。

所选章节取材于利奥波德的真实经历,他在年轻的时候随朋友一起在山中射杀了一头母狼;在目睹了母狼临死前双眼发出的无望幽光之后,他对自己的猎杀行为进行了反思。利奥波德的反思触及的是环境保护运动当中"保护生物多样性"这一议题。在人类中心主义的影响下,许多人曾经认为应当保护对人类有益的物种,消灭对人类有害的。即使是在生态主义日渐壮大的今天,仍然有许多人从自己的角度出发,倾向于优先保护那些看上去更加可爱的物种(例如熊猫和海豚),而对那些并不可爱的物种(例如毒蛇和蜘蛛)的命运不甚关心。无数的科学实践已经证明,在地球这个庞大的生态系统内部,任何物种都不可能独立存在,而是互相依赖、同生共存,对一个物种的伤害甚至消灭就等于伤害甚至消灭整个生态系统。正如利奥波德在所选章节之后继续写道的,由于猎人不断捕杀狼群,狼的数量日益减少,缺乏天敌的鹿群和牛群于是开始大量繁衍,随即对森林和草地造成了严重的破坏,生态环境失衡了。利奥波德将这一小节的题目定为"像大山那样思考",就是为了警示读者放弃以人类的利益需求为中心和准绳的方式,真正从自然的角度出发,为维系生态平衡贡献力量。

思考题

1. Why is the mountain the only one to "listen objectively" to the howl of a wolf?
2. What is the impression left by wolves on human beings?
3. Why does the narrator say "after seeing the green fire die, I sensed that neither the wolf nor the mountain agreed with such a view"? What view do you think the wolf and the mountain would agree with then?

推荐阅读

Barash, David, ed. *Approaches to Peace: A Reader in Peace Studies*. Oxford University Press, 2000.

Curtin, Deane. *Environmental Ethics for a Postcolonial World*. Rowman & Littlefield Publishers, 2005.

Knight, Richard L. and Suzanne Riedel, eds. *Aldo Leopold and the Ecological Conscience*. Oxford University Press, 2002.

McKibben, Bill, ed. *American Earth: Environmental Writing since Thoreau*. Penguin Putnam, 2008.

Meine, Curt and Richard L. Knight, eds. *The Essential Aldo Leopold: Quotations and Commentaries*. University of Wisconsin Press, 1999.

傅华:《生态伦理学探究》,华夏出版社,2002年。

何怀宏:《生态伦理——精神资源与哲学基础》,河北大学出版社,2002年。

贾丁斯:《环境伦理学——环境哲学导论》,林官明等译,北京大学出版社,2002年。

爱德华·艾比(Edward Abbey)

【作者简介】

爱德华·艾比(1927—1989)是美国著名生态主义作家和评论家,被称为"美国西部的梭罗"。他于1927年1月生于宾夕法尼亚州的印第安纳,1989年3月因病逝世。按照他的遗愿,他的遗体被安葬在亚利桑那州的荒野中。艾比以其对环境问题的热切关注以及无政府主义的政治立场而闻名。他的代表作品包括小说《有意破坏帮》(*The Monkey Wrench Gang*)以及散文集《沙漠独居者》(*Desert Solitaire*)。

艾比的生态思想影响很大。其中比较著名的是生态防卫观,即为了保护生态而对破坏生态的行为进行有意破坏。在其代表作《有意破坏帮》里,这种激进的生态主义思想就得以体现。小说里,主人公为了保护生态环境的原貌,向修建巨型水坝等破坏生态环境、扭曲自然规律的行为进行了有意的"生态性的破坏"(eco-sabotage)。艾比通过自己的行为以及作品对美国民众的思想产生了巨大影响,唤醒了人们的生态意识,并激发起许多人为保护生态家园而行动。

下文来自于他的散文集《回家的旅程》(*The Journey Home*)中的一篇文章。

Shadows from the Big Woods

The idea of wilderness needs no defense. It only needs more defenders.

In childhood the wilds seemed infinite. Along Crooked Creek in the Allegheny Mountains of western Pennsylvania there was a tract of forest we called the Big Woods. The hemlock, beech, poplar, red oak, white oak, maple, and shagbark hickory[1] grew on slopes so steep they had never been logged. Vine of wild grape trailed from the limbs of ancient druidical oaks—dark glens of mystery and shamanism[2]. My brothers and I, simple-minded farm boys, knew nothing of such mythologies, but we were aware, all the same, of the magic residing among and within those trees. We knew that the Indians had once been here, Seneca and Shawnee, following the same deeper paths that wound through fern, moss, yarrow, and mayapple[3] among the massive trunks in the green-gold light of autumn, from spring to stream and marsh. Those passionate warriors had disappeared a century before we were born, but their spirits lingered, their shades still informed the spirit of the place. We knew they were there. The vanished Indians were reincarnated, for a few transcendent summers, in our bones, within our pale Caucasian skins, in our idolatrous mimicry. We knew all about moccasins and feathers, arrows and bows, the thrill of sneaking naked through the underbrush, taking care to tread on not a single dry twig. Our lore came from boy's books, but it was the forest that made it real.

My brother Howard could talk to trees. Johnny knew how to start a fire without matches, skin a squirrel, and spot the eye of a sitting rabbit. I was an expert on listening to mourning doves, though not on interpretation, and could feel pleasure in the clapperclaw of crows. The wolf was long gone from those woods, and also the puma, but there were still plenty of deer, as well as bobcat and raccoon and gray fox; sometimes a black bear, or the rumor of one, passed through the hills. That was good country then, the country of boyhood, and the woods, the forest, that sultry massed deepness of transpiring green, formed the theater of our play. We invented our boyhood as we grew along; but the forest—in which it was possible to get authentically lost—sustained our sense of awe and terror in ways that fantasy cannot.

Now I would not care to revisit those faraway scenes. That forest which seemed so vast to us was only a small thing after all, as the bulldozers, earth movers, and dragline shovels have proved. The woods we thought eternal have been logged by methods formerly considered too destructive, and the very mountainside on which the forest grew has been butchered by the strip miners into a shape of crude symmetry, with spoil banks and head walls and right-angled escarpments where even the running blackberry has a hard time finding a roothold. Stagnant water fills the raw gulches, and the creek below runs sulfur-yellow all year long.

Something like a shadow has fallen between present and past, an abyss wide as war that cannot be bridged by any tangible connection, so that memory is undermined and the image of our beginnings betrayed, dissolved, rendered not mythical but illusory. We have connived in the number of our own origins. Little wonder that those who travel nowhere but in their own heads, reducing all existence to the space of one skull, maintain dreamily that only the pinpoint tip of the moment is real. They are right: A fanatical greed, an arrogant stupidity, has robbed them of the past and transformed their future into a nightmare. They deny the world because the only world they know has denied them.

Our cancerous industrialism, reducing all ideological differences to epiphenomena, has generated its own breed of witch doctor. There are men with a genius for control and organization, and the lust to administrate. They propose first to shrink our world to the dimensions of a global village, over which some technological crackpot will erect a geodesic dome to regulate air and light; at the same time the planetary superintendent of schools will feed our children via endless belt into reinforcement-training boxes where they will be conditioned for their functions in the anthill arcology[4] of the future. The ideal robot, after all, is simply a properly processed human being.

The administrators laying out the blueprints for the technological totalitarianism of tomorrow like to think of the earth as a big space capsule, a machine for living. They are wrong: the earth is not a mechanism but an organism, a being with its own life and its own reasons, where the support and sustenance of the human animal is incidental. If man in his newfound power and vanity persists in the attempt to remake the planet in his own image, he will succeed only in destroying himself—not the planet. The earth will survive our most ingenious folly.

Meanwhile, though, the Big Woods is gone—or going fast. And the mountains, the rivers, the canyons, the seashores, the swamps, and the deserts. Even our own, the farms, the towns, the cities, all seem to lie helpless before the advance of the techno-industrial juggernaut. We have created an iron monster with which we wage war, not only on small peasant nations over the sea, but even on ourselves—a war against all forms of life, against life itself. In the name of Power and Growth. But the war is only beginning.

The Machine may seem omnipotent, but it is not. Human bodies and human wit, active here, there, everywhere, united in purpose, independent in actions, can still face that machine and stop it and take it apart and reassemble it—if we wish—on lines entirely new. There is, after all, a better way to live. The poets and the prophets have been trying to tell us about it for three thousand years.

 注释

1. hemlock, beech, poplar, red oak, white oak, maple, and shagbark hickory:这些植物分别是:铁杉、山毛榉、白杨、红橡木、白栎木、枫树、山胡桃树。
2. shamanism:萨满教,黄教,亚洲北部某些民族的泛神宗教。
3. yarrow, and mayapple:西洋蓍草和盾叶鬼臼。
4. arcology:这个词是 architecture 和 ecology 组成的合成词,指的是有极高人口密度的综合性建筑。

 作品导读

"荒野的概念不需要防御,它仅仅需要防御者。"(The idea of wilderness needs no defense. It only needs more defenders.)就像这开头的第一句话一样,这篇文章的语言看似简单平淡、朴实无华,但所讲述的内容却十分震撼、发人深省。

作者在宾夕法尼亚州的山区中的一个农场长大。他小时候有许多机会接触最原生态的大自然。正是在大自然中的各种体验让作者能够获得许多知识,并能够深刻地感悟自然。对于他来说,大自然就是良师益友。然而若干年过去以后,作为成年人的作者却发现自己曾经那么熟悉地叫做"Big Woods"的地方已经面目全非。自己小时候曾经十分崇敬的充满了神秘力量的大自然在代表着工业文明的力量的推土机、挖掘机面前显得是那么软弱无力。以前那个充满生机活力、地貌复杂的树林已经被冷冰冰的机械改造成单调、死板的对称图形。不仅仅是 Big Woods,其他的山川、河流、沙漠、海滩、沼泽等一切的自然地貌形态都在遭受着或者早已遭受了相同或类似的命运。大自然正在被充满了统治欲望的人类改造成一个单调的机械系统。

然而我们不能忘记,我们赖以生存的地球并不是一个机械系统,而是一个有机体系统。就像作者在该书第一页所说的那样,这个有机体系统"属于每一个人,同时不属于任何人"。人类对自然肆意改造的最终结果便是让人类自身卷入了一场可怕的战争:一切生命形式和机械文明之间的战争。这场战争的结果或许现在还不得而知。但可以肯定的是,这场战争绝对没有最后的赢家。

思考题

1. What did the "Big Woods" mean to the author's childhood?
2. What is the culprit, according to the author, for the destruction of the "Big Woods," as well as other forms of nature?
3. What do the "shadows" in the title of the essay refer to?
4. What does the author call for in the end of the essay?

推荐阅读

Cahalan, James M. *Edward Abbey: A Life*. University of Arizona Press, 2003.

Foreman, Dave. *Confessions of an Eco-Warrior*. Crown Publishing, 1992.

Knott, John Ray. "Edward Abbey and the Romance of the Wilderness". *Imagining Wild America*. University of Michigan, 2002.

Lynch, Tom. *Xerophilia: Ecocritical Explorations in Southwestern Literature*. Texas Tech University Press, 2008.

Meyer, Kurt A. *Edward Abbey: Freedom Fighter, Freedom writer*. University of Wyoming Press, 1987.

Quigley, Peter. Ed. *Coyote in the Maze: Tracking Edward Abbey in a World of Words*. University of Utah Press, 1998.

加里·斯耐德(Gary Snyder)

【作者简介】

加里·斯耐德(1930—　)是20世纪美国著名的诗人、评论家和环保主义者。他于1930年出生于美国旧金山。1953年他进入加州大学伯克利分校学习东方语言和文化,在此期间他加入了"垮掉的一代"(Beat Generation)诗歌运动,后来成为该派别的代表性人物。1975年,凭借诗歌集《龟岛》(*Turtle Island*),斯耐德获得该年度普利策诗歌奖。1985年他成为加州大学戴维斯分校教授,同时继续广泛地游历和讲学,并致力于环境保护运动。他受到东方文化和佛家思想的影响,因此作品常常反映出一种沉浸于大自然的思考。

1990年,斯耐德出版了文集《荒野的实践》(*The Practice of the Wild*)。该书共收录9篇散文,这些文章展示了作者对大自然世界的广博的学识以及深刻的理解。通过这些文章,读者可以深刻地了解到斯耐德的生态和环保思想。本书选录了其中的一篇的一部分。

Good, Wild, Sacred

My family and I have been living for twenty years now on land in the Sierra Nevada range of northern California. These ridges and slopes are somewhat "wild" and not particularly "good." The original people here, the Nisenan (or Southern Maidu) were almost entirely displaced or destroyed during the first few decades of the gold rush. It seems there is no one left to teach us which places in this landscape were once felt to be "sacred"—though with time and attention, I think we will be able to feel and find them again.

Wild land, good land, sacred land. At home working on our mountain farmstead, in town at political meetings, and farther afield studying the problems of indigenous peoples, I hear such terms emerging. By examining these three categories perhaps we can get some insights into the problems of rural habitation, subsistence living, wilderness preservation, and Third and Fourth World resistance to the appetites of industrial civilization.

Our idea of Good Land comes from agriculture. Here "good" (as in good soil) is narrowed to mean land productive of a small range of favored cultivars, and thus it favors the opposite of "wild": the cultivated. To raise a crop you fight the bugs, shoo the birds, and pull the weeds. The wild that keeps flying, creeping, burrowing in—is sheer frustration. Yet wild nature cannot be called unproductive, and no plant in the almost endless mosaics of micro and macro communities is ever out of place. For hunting and gathering peoples for whom that whole spread of richness, the wild natural system, is also their economy, a cultivated patch of land might seem bizarre and definitely not good, at least at first. Gathering people draw on the whole field, ranging widely daily. Agricultural people live by a map constructed of highly productive nodes (cleared fields) connected by lines (trails through the scary forest)—a beginning of "linear."

For pre-agricultural people the sites considered sacred and given special care were of course wild. In early agrarian civilizations, ritually cultivated land or special temple fields were sometimes considered sacred. The fertility religions of those rimes were not necessarily rejoicing in the fertility of fall nature, but were focusing on their own harvest. The idea of cultivation was conceptually extended to describe a kind of training in social forms that guarantees membership in an elite class. By the metaphor of "spiritual cultivation" a holy man has weeded out the wild from his nature. This is agrarian theology. But weeding out the wild from the natures of members of the Bos and Sus clans—cattle and pigs—gradually changed animals which are intelligent and alert in the wild into sluggish meat-making machines.

Certain groves from the original forest lingered on into classical times as "shrines." They were viewed with much ambivalence by the rulers from the metropole. They survived because the people who worked the land still half-heard the call of the old ways, and lore that predated agriculture was still whispered around. The kings of Israel began to cut down the sacred groves, and the Christians finished the job. The idea that "wild" might also be "sacred" returned to the Occident only with the Romantic movement. This nineteenth-century rediscovery of wild nature is a complex European phenomenon—a reaction against formalistic rationalism and enlightened despotism that invoked feeling, instinct, new nationalisms, and a sentimentalized folk culture. It is only from very old place-centered cultures! That we hear of sacred groves, sacred land, in a context of genuine belief and practice; Part of that context is the tradition of the commons: "good" land becomes private property; the wild and the sacred are shared.

Throughout the world the original inhabitants of desert, jungle, and forest are facing relentless waves of incursions into their remotest territories. These lands, whether by treaty or by default, were left in their use because the dominant society thought the arctic tundra or and desert or jungle forest "no good." Native people everywhere are now conducting an underprivileged and underfunded fight against unimaginably wealthy corporations to resist logging or oil exploration or uranium mining on their own land. They persist in these struggles not just because it has always been their home, bur also because some places in it are sacred to them. This last aspect makes them struggle desperately to resist the powerful temptation to sell out—to take the cash and accept relocation. And sometimes the temptations and confusion are too great, and they do surrender and leave.

Thus some very cogent and current political questions surround the traditional religious use of certain spots. I was at the University of Montana in the spring of 1982 on a program with Russell Means, the American Indian Movement founder and activist, who was trying to get support for the Yellow Thunder Camp of Lakota and other Indian people of the Black Hills. Thunder Camp was on traditional tribal land that was under Forest Service jurisdiction at the time. These people wanted to block further expansion of mining into the Black Hills. Their argument was that the particular place they were reoccupying is not only ancestral but sacred.

During his term in office California Governor Jerry Brown created the Native American Heritage Commission specifically for California Indians, and a number of elders were charged with the task of locating and protecting sacred sites and native graves in California. This was done partly to head off confrontations between native people versus landowners or public land managers who start developments on what is now considered their property. The trouble often involves traditional grave sites. It was a sensitive move, and though barely comprehensible to the white voters, it sent a ripple of appreciation through all the native communities. Although the white Christian founders of the United States were probably not considering American Indian beliefs when they guaranteed freedom of religion, some court decisions over the years have given support to certain Native American churches. The connection of religion to land, however, has been resisted by the dominant culture and the courts. This ancient aspect of religious worship remains virtually incomprehensible to Euro-Americans. Indeed it might: if even some small bits of land are considered sacred, then they are forever nor for sale and not for taxing. This is a deep threat to the assumptions of an endlessly expansive materialist economy.

Waterholes

In the hunting and gathering way of life, the whole territory of a given group is fairly equally experienced by everyone. Those wild and sacred spots have many uses. There are places where women go for seclusion, places where the bodies of the dead are taken, and spots where young men and women are called for special instruction. Such places are numinous, loaded with meaning and power. The memories of such spots are very long. Nanao Sakaki, John Stokes, and I were in Australia in the fall of 1981 at the invitation of the Aboriginal Arts Board doing some teaching, poetry readings, and workshops with both aboriginal leaders and children. Much of the time we were in the central Australian desert south and west of Alice Springs, first into Pitjantjara tribal territory and then three hundred miles northwest into Pintubi lands. The aboriginal people in the central desert all still speak their languages. Their religion is fairly intact, and most young men are still initiated at fourteen, even the ones who go to high school at Alice Springs. They leave the high school for a year and are taken into the bush to learn bush ways on foot, to master the lore of landscapes and plants and animals, and finally to undergo initiation.

We were traveling by truck over dirt track west from Alice Springs in the company of a Pintubi elder named Jimmy Tjungurrayi. As we rolled along the dusty road, sitting back in the bed of a pickup, he began to speak very rapidly to me. He was talking about a mountain over there, telling me a story about some wallabies that came to that mountain in the dreamtime and got into some kind of mischief with some lizard girls. He had hardly finished that and he started in on another story about another hill over here and another story over there, I couldn't keep up. I realized after about half an hour of this that these were tales to be told while walking, and that I was experiencing a speeded-up version of what might be leisurely told over several days of foot travel. Mr. Tjungurrayi felt graciously compelled to share a body of lore with me by virtue of the simple fact that I was there.

So remember a time when you journeyed on foot over hundreds of miles, walking fast and often traveling at night, traveling nightlong and napping in the acacia shade during the day, and these stories were told to you as you went. In your travels with an older person you were given a map you could memorize, full of lore and song, and also practical information. Off by yourself you could sing those songs to bring yourself back. And you could maybe travel to a place that you'd never been, steering only by songs you had learned.

We made camp at a waterhole called Ilpili and rendezvoused with a number of Pintubi people from the surrounding desert country. The Ilpili waterhole is about a yard across, six inches deep, in a little swale of bush full of finch. People camp a quarter mile away. It's the only waterhole that stays full through drought years in tens of thousands of square miles. A place kept by custom open to all. Until late at night Jimmy and the other old men sac around a small thornbrush fire and sang a cycle of journey songs, walking through a space of desert in imagination and music. They kept a steady rhythmic beat to the song by clapping two boomerangs together. They stopped between songs and would hum a phrase or two and then argue a bit about the words and then start again. One would defer to another and let him start. Jimmy explained to me that they have so many cycles of journey songs they can't quite remember them all, and they have to be constantly rehearsing.

Each night they'd start the evening saying, "What will we sing?" and get a reply like "Let's sing the walk up to Darwin." They'd start out and argue and sing and clap their way along through it. It was during the full moon period: a few clouds would sail and trail in the cool light and mild desert wind. I had learned that the elders liked black tea, and several times a night I'd make a pot right at the fire, with lots of white sugar, the way they wanted it. The singers would stop when they felt like it. I'd ask Jimmy, "How far did you get tonight?" He'd say, "Well, we got two-thirds of the way to Darwin." This can be seen as one example of the many ways landscape, myth, and information were braided together in preliterate societies.

One day driving near Ilpili we stopped the truck and Jimmy and the three other elderly gentlemen got out and he said, "We'll take you to see a sacred place here. I guess you're old enough." They turned to the boys and told them to stay behind. As we climbed the bedrock hill these ordinarily cheery and loud-talking aboriginal men began to drop their voices. As we got higher up they were speaking whispers and their whole manner changed. One said almost inaudibly, "Now we are coming close." Then they got on their hands and knees and crawled. We crawled up the last two hundred feet, then over a little rise into a small basin of broken and oddly shaped rocks. They whispered to us with respect and awe of what was there. Then we all backed away. We got back down the hill and at a certain point stood and walked. At another point voices rose. Back at the truck, everybody was talking loud again and no more mention was made of the sacred place. Very powerful. Very much in mind. We learned later that it was indeed a place where young men were taken for ceremony.

I traveled by pickup truck along hundreds of miles of rough dirt tracks and hiked into the mountainous and rocky country where the roads stopped. I was being led to special places. There were large unique boulders, each face and facet a surprise. There was the sudden opening out of a hidden steep defile where two cliffs meet with just a little sandbed between, and some green bushes, some parrots calling. We dropped down cliffs off a mesa into a waterhole you wouldn't guess was there, where a thirty-foot blade of rock stands on end, balancing. Each of these spots was out of the ordinary, fantastic even, and sometimes rich with life. Often there were pictographs in the vicinity. They were described as teaching spots and some were "dreaming spots" for certain totem ancestors, well established in song and story over tens of thousands of square miles.

"Dreaming" or "dreamtime" refers to a time of fluidity, shape-shifting, interspecies conversation and intersexuality, radically creative moves, whole landscapes being altered. It is often taken to be a "mythical past," but it is not really any time. We might as well say it is right now. It is the mode of the eternal moment of creating, of being, as contrasted with the mode of cause and effect in time. Time is the realm where people mainly live and within which history, evolution, and progress are imagined to take place. Dogen gave a difficult and playful talk on the resolution of these two modes early in the winter of 1240. It is called "Time/Being."

In Australian lore the totem dreaming place is first of all special to the people of that totem, who sometimes make pilgrimages there. Second, it is sacred (say) to the honey-ants which actually live there—there are hundreds of thousands of them. Third, it's like a little Platonic cave of ideal honey-antness, maybe the creation spot for all honey-ants. It mysteriously connects the essence of honey-antness with the archetypes of the human psyche and makes bridges between humanity, the ants, and the desert. The honey-ant place is in stories, dances, songs, and it is a real place which also happens to be optimum habitat for a world of ants. Or take a green parrot dreaming place: the stories will tell of the cracks of the ancestors going across the landscape and stopping at that dreaming place, and it is truly a perfect place for parrots. All this is a radically different way of expressing what science says, as well as another set of metaphors for the teachings of the Hua-yen or the Avatamsaka Sutra.

This sacredness implies a sense of optimal habitat for certain kinfolk that we have out there—the wallabies, red kangaroo, bush turkeys, lizards. Geoffrey Blainey (1976, 202) says, "The land itself was their chapel and their shrines were hills and creeks and their religious relics were animals, plants, and birds. Thus the migrations of aboriginals, though spurred by economic need, were also always pilgrimages. "Good (productive of much life), wild (naturally), and sacred were one."

This way of life, frail and battered as it is, still exists. Now it is threatened by Japanese and other uranium mining projects, large-scale copper mining, and petroleum exploration. The issue of sacredness has become very political—so much so that the Australian Bureau of Aboriginal Affairs has hired some bilingual anthropologists and bush people to work with elders of the different tribes to try and identify sacred sites and map them. There has been much hope that the Australian government would act in good faith and declare certain areas off-limits before any exploratory team even gets near them. This effort is spurred by the fact that there have already been some confrontations in the Kimberly region over oil exploration, as at Nincoomba. The local native people stood their ground, making human lines in front of bulldozers and drilling rigs, and the media coverage of this resistance won over some of the Australian public. Since in Australia a landowner's mineral rights are always reserved to "The Crown," even somebody's ranch might be subject to mining. So to consider sacred land a special category, even in theory, is an advanced move. But it's shaky. A "registered site" near Alice Springs was bulldozed supposedly on the instructions of a government land minister, and this was in the relatively benign federal jurisdiction!

作品导读

人类自从进入农业社会以来,就开始了对大自然的征服和改造。这些对自然的开发在人类进步的历程中起到了至关重要的作用。因此长久以来,大自然(或是说"荒野")便被人类看做了待开发、征服以及改造的对象。如果用二元论的思维来看,以荒蛮、贫瘠、无序为特点的荒野便站在了文明、肥沃、有序的人类"文明"社会的对立面。这种观点在人类社会的进程中持续了很久,直到20世纪随着生态思想的崛起,才开始慢慢遭到质疑。作为生态主义者的诗人斯耐德的这篇散文,也表达了对这种思想的不认同。

什么样的土地算是"好的"土地?从农耕的角度来看,只有肥沃的、能够产出大量作物的土地才是"好的"土地。而纵观人类的农业文明史,人类对大自然的征服和改造正是从把那些"荒野"土地开垦、最后变为"高产"的土地开始的。在开垦、种植的过程中,为了让作物丰收,人类需要除草、杀虫、赶走野鸟,从而获得所需的资源,并且让土地变得"肥沃"。然而在诗人看来,荒野(大自然)中没有哪一块土地是"不肥沃"的,因为土地总是要遵循自然法则,产生出各种生命所需的资源。而那些杂草、野鸟、昆虫,甚至生活在原始部落中的人群,无一不是遵循着一定的自然法则,有规律地从土地以及大自然的其他方面汲取所需资源的。因此一块"开垦过"的土地(以及背后所代表的人类"文明")只不过是人类改变了自然法则、破坏了生物圈中已有的、平衡的食物链的产物罢了。

斯耐德认为，当今社会的人类对自然的过度开采完全是出于私欲，是不断膨胀的自我中心在作怪。人们应该立即停止对大自然的破坏行为。与此同时，诗人并没有走到另一个极端，而是非常理性地指出，人类和自然其实是融为一体的。人不是不可以利用大自然，但应该首先尊敬大自然。作者用自己在澳大利亚和当地原始部落一起生活的短暂经历，向我们展现了当地土著人是如何崇敬自然、和自然过着和谐相处的生活的。作者并不否认人类文明在过去所取得的进步对人类社会自身所做出的巨大贡献，同时也毫不留情地指出现代文明的荒谬观点以及对自然的破坏。在他看来，人类需要做的便是摒弃自我中心的错误观点，重新理性地、客观地审视自然，最终和自然融为一体、和谐相处，就像他在文中所勾勒出的那一幅乌托邦式的画面一样：在一片"完全未被损坏、完全不非自然"（never totally ruined, never completely unnatural）的土地上，大量的人们生活在其中；当我们在街道上漫步时，灰熊与我们同行，鲑鱼在我们身旁畅游。

思考题

1. What land, according to the poet, is "sacred"? And what is "good"?
2. Is the wilderness chaotic? Why, or why not?
3. How do the Aboriginal people in Australia worship their sacred land?

推荐阅读

Buell, Lawrence. *The Future of Environmental Criticism: Environmental Crisis and Literary Imagination*. Blackwell, 2005.

Kyger, Joanne. *Strange Big Moon: The Japan and India Journals: 1960 — 1964*. North Atlantic Books, 2000.

Murphy, Patrick D. *Understanding Gary Snyder*. University of South Carolina Press, 1992.

Snyder, Gary. *The Practice of the Wild*. North Point Press, 1990.

Snyder, Gary. *The Real Work: Interviews & Talks 1964 — 1979*. New Directions, 1980

Snyder, Gary. *Turtle Island*. New Directions, 1974.

Snyder, Gary. *Left Out in the Rain*. Shoe-maker & Hoard, 2005.

温德尔·贝里(Wendell Berry)

【作者简介】

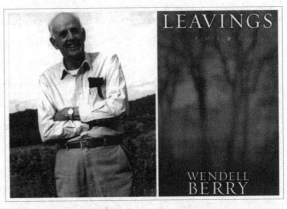

温德尔·贝里(1934—),美国诗人、学者和经济学家。贝里出生在美国肯塔基州亨利郡附近的一个乡村,这也是他的祖辈们生活和务农的地方。在他的骨子里,有着一种对土地与生俱来的亲近感。他曾先后在肯塔基大学和斯坦福大学学习,获得文学硕士学位,后来又任教于纽约大学和肯塔基大学。1965年,贝里携妻子和两个孩子回到出生地亨利郡附近的乡村定居。贝里现在依旧住在肯塔基的乡下,用最传统的耕种方式务农,拒绝使用电脑、电视等一切现代设备。由于他在文学领域的卓越表现,他不仅获得了古根海姆基金(Guggenheim Fellowship)和洛克菲勒基金(Rockefeller Fellowship)的支持,还荣获美国国家人文奖章(the National Humanities Medal),并被选为南方作家研究会(Fellowship of Southern Writers)的成员。除此之外,贝里还是一位社会活动家。从20世纪60年代至今,他参与了大大小小的社会活动,为反对越战、修建核电装置、死刑以及"911事件"之后的美国外交政策四处奔走、大声疾呼。

贝里是一位涉猎广泛、著作颇丰的作家,他不仅创作诗歌,还写下了许多十分有影响力的长篇小说、短篇小说和散文,并为他所积极参与的社会活动撰写了许多宣传材料。他的主要作品有:长篇小说《回忆老杰克》(The Memory of Old Jack, 1974)与《汉娜·考尔特》(Hannah Coulter, 2004),诗歌选集《破土而出》(The Broken Ground, 1964)、《一九六三年十一月二十六日》(November twenty six nineteen hundred sixty three, 1964)、《在家旅行》(Traveling at Home, 1989)与《木材唱诗班:1979—1997 安息日诗歌集锦》(A Timbered Choir: The Sabbath Poems 1979—1997, 1998)等。

以下诗歌选自《木材唱诗班:1979—1997 安息日诗歌集锦》,是该诗集的题名诗歌。第二篇诗歌评论《漫长沉默后的言说》选自《塞沃尼评论》[The Sewanee Review, Vol. 104, No. 1 (Winter, 1996), pp. 108—110]。

A Timbered Choir

Even while I dreamed I prayed that what I saw was only fear and no foretelling,
for I saw the last known landscape destroyed for the sake
of the objective, the soil bludgeoned,[1] the rock blasted.
Those who had wanted to go home would never get there now.

I visited the offices where for the sake of the objective the planners planned
at blank desks set in rows. I visited the loud factories
where the machines were made that would drive ever forward
toward the objective. I saw the forest reduced to stumps and gullies; I saw
the poisoned river, the mountain cast into the valley;
I came to the city that nobody recognized because it looked like every other city.
I saw the passages worn by the unnumbered[2]
footfalls of those whose eyes were fixed upon the objective.

Their passing had obliterated the graves and the monuments
of those who had died in pursuit of the objective
and who had long ago forever been forgotten, according
to the inevitable rule that those who have forgotten forget
that they have forgotten. Men, women, and children now pursued the objective
as if nobody ever had pursued it before.
The races and the sexes now intermingled perfectly in pursuit of the objective.
the once-enslaved, the once-oppressed were now free
to sell themselves to the highest bidder
and to enter the best paying prisons
in pursuit of the objective, which was the destruction of all enemies,
which was the destruction of all obstacles,
which was the destruction of all objects,
which was to clear the way to victory,
which was to clear the way to promotion, to salvation, to progress,
to the completed sale, to the signature
on the contract, which was to clear the way
to self-realization, to self-creation,
from which nobody who ever wanted to go home
would ever get there now, for every remembered place
had been displaced;
the signposts had been bent to the ground and covered over.

Every place had been displaced, every love
unloved, every vow unsworn, every word unmeant[3]
to make way for the passage[4] of the crowd
of the individuated, the autonomous, the self-actuated,[5] the homeless
with their many eyes opened toward the objective
which they did not yet perceive in the far distance,

having never known where they were going,
having never known where they came from.

Speech After Long Silence

I first heard John Haines read his poems one evening in the Jones Room of the old library at Stanford University. That was in 1969—twenty-five years ago—and I still remember clearly the almost incommunicable[6] impression I carried away[7] from that reading. I had heard the poems, the words; but I had also received from them or through them a sense of the condition of mind that had allowed them to be written—though at the time I knew little of the circumstances in which they had been written or the character of the man who had written them. The explainers of the language of poetry will be forever embarrassed, I hope, by the experience of readers of poetry: poems tell more than they say. They convey, as if mutely, the condition of the mind that made them, and this is a large part of their meaning and their worth.

Mr. Haines's poems, as I heard them that evening, told that they were the work of a mind that had taught itself to be quiet for a long time. His lines were qualified unremittingly by a silence that they came from and were going toward, that they for a moment broke. One felt that the words had come down onto the page one at a time, like slow drops from a dripping eave[8], making their assured small sounds, the sounds accumulating. The poems seemed to have been made with a patience like that with which rivers freeze or lichens cover stones. Within the condition of long accepted silence, each line had been acutely listened for, and then acutely listened to.[9]

The poem I remembered particularly from that evening was "The Traveler," which speaks of a lamp whose "light came as though from far off/through the yellow skin of a tent," and which ends: We were away for a long time. The footsteps of a man walking alone on the frozen road from Asia crunched in the darkness and were gone. Another mystery of reading, or of consciousness itself, is the way an image will return not by intention or even by remembering, but as if by its own power and volition[10]. This image of an anonymous traveler or searcher on a road, since I first heard it, has often returned to me in that way, as apparently it has often returned to the poet, who records it again in "The Forest Without Leaves," a much later poem: Snow is falling, the sun is late and someone has gone with a lantern to search the roads. And the same image ends his beautiful memoir, The Stars, the Snow, the Fire. The attendant silence thus becomes the enabling condition both of a kind of language and a kind of knowledge.

John Haines homesteaded in Alaska in 1947, when he was twenty-three. He went there, he says, "to see the shadows waver and leap, listen to water, birds in their sleep, the tremor in old men's voices." Only a few perhaps are able to choose so resolutely such ordinary wonders; Harlan Hubbard of the Ohio Valley was another. This requires a certain constancy and austerity, and an unusual sort of curiosity. One would like to see what the world has to offer more or less on its own—if, say, one will not go too far in search or in pursuit; if one will wait, perhaps for a long time. The land gave up its meaning slowly, as the sun finds day by day a deeper place in the mountain. And then, finally, one begins to know, or perhaps realizes that one some how already knows, how "Old ladders shorten, pulled down/in the sod." Or one sees images of travelers, solitary individuals or whole nations, passing over the face of the country, passing over the snow, leaving no more sound in the land than a handful of berries tumbled in a miner's pail images that have the power to unite experience, history, and dream, constituting "another episode of the myth-journey of humankind." The land gives up its meaning slowly, and it is that given-up meaning, patiently waited for, that has moved Mr. Haines's poems, which honor it by a just and frugal[11] speech. How much to his honor it is that, in an age of easy art, he never has been glib[12]!

Hearing this poet read his poems aloud, or reading them quietly for yourself, you imagine how little "originality" has mattered to him—how little worry he has expended on the latter day poetical business of "finding his own voice." You must even ask if the voice of the poems is in fact his, and then, when you read *Living Off the Country*, his book of critical essays, you find that the poet himself has addressed this question: "What counts finally in a work are not novel[13] and interesting things, though these can be important, but the absolutely authentic. I think that there is a spirit of place, a presence asking to be expressed; and sometimes when we are lucky as writers, and quiet in a way few of us want to be anymore, a voice enters our own."

And he says: "I have come to feel that there is here in North America a hidden place obscured by what we have built upon it, and that whenever we penetrate the surface of the life around us that place and its spirit can be found." He therefore speaks of our need for literature "as a matter of practical necessity." And thus his work is far removed from "self-expression" or the "originality" of the personal voice, as is all work that is skilled enough and humbly enough submitted to inspiration. This, of course, comes of an unabashed[14] love of country—an authentic patriotism—which opens a way beyond our superficial doctrines of self liberation, self-expression, the modern, and the new. Once a place and its spirit have become not just subjects but standards of a writer's work, then the connections between art and community, art and tradition, art and thought become necessary and clear; and Mr. Haines has been, of understood necessity, a defender of these things.

As a critic he has opposed "the cultivation of disorder, the random association of images, the breakup of syntax[15], the dismissal of intellect, of reason, the continual seeking after new thrills.' "He has done so, I think, because he opposes the shrinkage of the world to the limits of the isolated, displaced, desiring and despairing self, the self that ultimately knows nothing and can say nothing: you will always be waiting for what you do not know, knowing that when at last it appears you will not know it. How valuable John Haines's work might be to the still preponderant[16] majority for whom the issues of place have been eclipsed by issues of self and career, I cannot say. Of its value, and its potential value, to the increasingly competent minority who long for an authentic settlement of our country, I have no doubt. I acknowledge here my own debt and my gratitude.

注释

1. bludgeon：*v.* 重击，重创，给予深刻的影响。

2. unnumbered：*adj* 有双重意义，一是"数之不尽的"(innumerable)，二是"搞不清数目的"。

3. 此节运用了英文中一种常见的构词法，即为原词加上否定前缀以构成否定词。尤其在文学作品当中，使用这种构词法构成的否定词与使用原词的反义词往往会造成颇为不同的效果。

4. 本诗的第 11 行也出现了 passage 一词，但与此处的意义是不同的。前者意为具体的"人行道路"(the passage way)，后者意为抽象的"通过"(passing)。

5. self-actuated：*adj.* 自我驱动的。

6. incommunicable：*adj.* 不能传达的。

7. carry away the impression：带走……的印象。

8. slow drops from a dripping eave：从屋檐缓慢滴落的水珠。作者用此句比喻诗句的质感，与唐代诗人白居易在长诗《琵琶行》中以"幽咽泉流冰下难"喻音乐有异曲同工之妙。

9. each line had been acutely listened for, and then acutely listened to：每一句诗行都被热切地期待着，然后被敏锐地聆听着。

10. volition：*n.* 决定；自主；意志力。

11. frugal：*adj.* 节俭的；省钱的。此处意为"惜字如金的"。

12. glib：*adj.* 能说善道的；圆滑的。

13. novel：*adj.* 新奇的。

14. unabashed：*adj.* 不畏惧的；不害躁的；满不在乎的。

15. syntax：*n.* 句法。

16. preponderant：*n.* 优势，大多数。

作品导读

温德尔·贝里的诗歌常常被人们称为"现代牧歌"。他延续了从维吉尔、贺拉斯一直传承至罗伯特·弗罗斯特(Robert Frost)的西方田园诗歌传统。他从一位农夫和实践家的角度而不是从一位文人的角度创作，他的诗歌不以繁复绚烂的意象或者宏大深邃的思想取胜，而是用明白晓畅的语言记录他对自然与人类社会的观察和思考。因此，他的诗歌立足当下、贴近现实，因其通俗易懂而受到大众的欢迎。

在二十余年的时间当中，贝里一直保持着在周日早晨散步冥想的生活习惯。他将自己在冥想过程中产生的思索和领悟写成诗歌，并且定期结集出版。由于周日是基督教的安息日，这些诗集被命名为"安息日诗歌"；从 1987 年到 2009 年，贝里一共出版了五部安息日诗集，它们成为贝里的诗歌之中一股不可忽视的力量。因为这些诗歌是在安息日的冥想过程

中写下的,它们不可避免地带上了静谧而深沉的特点。所选诗歌即为安息日诗歌中的一首,它表达了诗人对现代社会中人们急功近利、欲望膨胀的批判。诗中不断提到"objective"一词,既有目的之意亦有客体之意,意指现代人孜孜以求的物质财富。在贝里看来,对物质的过分追求不仅造成了森林被毁、河流污染这些环境问题,更毁灭了现代人的精神世界。对物质的贪婪令人们忘记历史、爱和誓言,哪怕他们中的一些人曾经为反抗压迫而勇敢地抗争过,现在也都屈服于物质的主宰,争相向"出价最高的人"(the highest bidder)售卖自己。诗歌采用自由韵体,语言通俗易懂,读之朗朗上口,引人深思。

评论文章《漫长沉默后的言说》是贝里对约翰·海恩斯(John Haines)诗歌的评论。约翰·海恩斯(又译约翰·海内斯)是美国当代著名诗人,属于新超现实主义的代表人物。他于1924年生于弗吉尼亚州的诺福克(Nolfork),曾在美国国家艺术学院修习艺术。他在阿拉斯加建有一个牧场,隐居四十余年并在阿拉斯加费尔班克斯大学教授英语。著有《来自冰川的讯息:1960—1980 诗选》《新诗:1980—1988》《为世纪末而作:1990—1999 诗选》等诗集。贝里在这篇评论中借海恩斯的诗歌探讨了诗歌艺术与自然的关系。他认为,好的诗歌并不是以新奇有趣的内容取胜,而是因为表达了真实,而这种真实正是自然投注在诗歌当中的。诗人的工作是表达自然的表达,用文字艺术的形式将真实的自然呈现在读者眼前。将贝里本人的诗歌与这篇评论结合来读,可以体会到他的创作理念是如何融入到创作实践当中去的。

思考题

1. How do you understand "Their passing had obliterated the graves and the monuments"? Whose passing are they? Why are the graves and the monuments obliterated? What is "the inevitable rule"?

2. What do those phrases beginning with "which was the destruction of" imply?

3. What does the image that "the signposts had been bent to the ground and covered over" imply?

推荐阅读

Aloi, Giovanni, ed. *Why Look at Plants? The Botanical Emergence in Contemporary Art*. Brill, 2019.

Armstrong, Rebecca. *Vergil's Green Thoughts: Plants, Humans, and the Divine*. Oxford University Press, 2019.

Nancy Goldfarb. *Reverence for Nature: Trees in the Poetry of W. S. Merwin and Others*. Palgrave Macmillan, 2023.

Meeker, Natania, and Antónia Szabari. *Radical Botany: Plants and Speculative Fiction*. Fordham University Press, 2019.

Parker, Elizabeth. *The Forest and the EcoGothic: The Deep Dark Woods in the Popular Imagination*. Palgrave Macmillan, 2020.

Branch, Michael P. ed. *Reading the Roots: American Nature Writing before Walden*. University of Georgia Press, 2004.

Clark, Timothy. *The Cambridge Introduction to Literature and the Environment*. Cambridge University Press, 2011.

Finch, Robert and John Elder. *Nature Writing: The Tradition in English*. Norton, 2002.

Moore, Bryan L. *Ecology and Literature: Eco-centric Personification from Antiquity to the Twenty-first Century*. Palgrave Macmillan, 2008.

海德格尔:《人、诗意地栖居——海德格尔语要》,郜元宝译,张汝伦校,上海远东出版社,1995年。

黄秉生:《生态美学探索》,民族出版社,2005年。

瑟帕玛:《环境之美》,武小西等译,湖南科学技术出版社,2006年。

徐恒醇:《生态美学》,陕西人民教育出版社,2000年。

曾繁仁:《生态存在论美学论稿》,吉林人民出版社,2003年。

章海荣编著:《生态伦理与生态美学》,复旦大学出版社,2005年。

多丽丝·莱辛(Doris Lessing)

【作者简介】

多丽丝·莱辛(1919—2013),英国女作家,被誉为继弗吉尼亚·伍尔夫之后最伟大的女性作家。2007年10月11日,诺贝尔奖委员会宣布将2007年度诺贝尔文学奖授予这位英国女作家,她是迄今为止获奖时最年长的女性诺贝尔奖获得者,也是历史上第三十四位女性诺贝尔奖得主。她获奖的理由是"她以怀疑主义、激情和想像力审视一个分裂的文明,登上了这方面女性体验的史诗巅峰"。

莱辛1919年10月22日生于伊朗,父母是英国人。莱辛的童年时期家境贫困,她青年时期积极投身反对殖民主义的左翼政治运动,曾参加共产党。莱辛是一位多产作家,除了长篇小说以外,还著有诗歌、散文和剧本,短篇小说中也有不少佳作。她的主要作品有:《青草在歌唱》(Grass Is Singing,1950)、《金色笔记本》(Golden Notebook,1962),五部曲《暴力的孩子们》(The Children of Violence,1952—1969)以及《好恐怖分子》(The Good Terrorist,1985)等。进入21世纪以后,莱辛仍然笔耕不辍,其重要作品有《最甜蜜的梦》(The Sweetest Dream,2001)和《裂缝》(The Cleft,2007)等。

以下片段选自长篇小说《裂缝》的结尾部分。

The Cleft (excerpt)

Meanwhile he looked out over the top of the trees—he was on a little hill—and he gazed at The Cleft,[1] which looked so different from this angle, and he saw white clouds coming out of The Cleft, and heard the thud-thudding[2] of several explosions. He knew at once what had happened. Those mad men, his brave young men, had been unable to resist throwing a boulder or two down into the pit.

And now groups of the hunters, of those who could not keep out of the caves, came running to Horsa, and, too, the boys who had been rescued from the well in the cave.[3] They stood around Horsa, looking at him, waiting for his anger, his recriminations, but all he said was, "And now it is time we went to the women."

Slowly, at first, they all set off, but Horsa could not keep up and soon he was far behind, with the rescued boys. "Will Maronna be angry with us?" they asked, and he said, "Well, what do you think?" The further they went, the more they could see the damage that was done by the explosions. White lay ever more thickly over the trees and then, when they reached it, the rocky shore where the women would be waiting for them.

The powdered bones of so many generations were making a thick layer from where drifts of white went off into the air as the breezes blew.[4] And then there were the women, in the distance, and the boys set up a howl, because they feared those white ghosts who were wailing and crying.

In front of Horsa had pressed the young males, but they were hanging back now, afraid of the women.[5] They were close together, for protection. The sea breezes lifting the white powder from the women made them look as if they were smoking. The Cleft that had dominated all that landscape was half its size, and it shed little avalanches of yet more white dust. The sea had a white crust and the waves lifted it, crinkling against the beach. The white looked solid enough to walk on. Some women trying to rid themselves of the white powder at the edge of the sea found themselves even more crusted thick and they were trying to rub the stuff off them, crying out in horror and rage. Yet a little further the sea was clear.

When Maronna saw Horsa, at first she did not recognise this limping man, and then she went for him, screaming, "Why did you do it? The Cleft! You've killed The Cleft. Why?" She knew the men were responsible, and that meant Horsa was responsible. Her accusations were hysterical, her ugly screams distorted her white-streaked face.

"It's our place, you've destroyed our place."

"But Maronna, there are better places. I keep telling you. There is a much better place a little further along. We've just passed it."

"We've been here always, always. We are born here. You were born here. You were born in that cave up there." And now she began to sob pitifully, her rage abating,[6] and he loosely held her, and thought that he would never understand females. Why had Maronna, or some previous Maronna, not moved long ago?

This shore had always been cramped and crowded. And if they moved just a little way... it was a good thing The Cleft had been blown up if that meant the women would at last have a decent beach.

"Come on, Maronna, you can't stay here," and he summoned his young men by pointing along the shore behind him. They understood him, because they had all many times discussed how foolish the women were not to move to a more spacious shore.

With his arm round Maronna, Horsa led the company, quite a large one we have to deduce, of the mateable women, who would soon be mothers again, and just behind them were the little boys rescued from the cave, as close to Maronna as they could get; they had forgotten, in all those months of being so much with men, that women did mean comfort, warmth, kindness. Behind them came the three girls who had run here from the forest; they had not told Maronna about the bad things on the trip. All the women wept and looked back at their desecrated[7] shore. Then they were not looking back; the sea was no longer white, but blue with a white film, and then it was itself, its own colour. They had left the world of powdered bone behind. At once all the women plunged into the sea, their element,[8] their mother—at least so some of them believed—and they emerged glistening like healthy seals. And here we have another little clue as to how they looked. "They stood wringing out their long hair." The males stood watching, and then at once began the long-awaited mating. Maronna and Horsa went ahead down the beach. For how long? For how far? "It was quite a distance" is what we have. And, "A comfortable walk for healthy women."

Horsa pulled Maronna to stand with him on rocks so similar to the ones they had left behind-for ever. Rocks, and rock pools and lively splashing waves and beyond them a long shining beach of clean white sand: there was no beach at the women's old shore.

"And look," said Horsa, pointing up at the cliffs that overshadowed this beach. "Caves. Just as good as the ones you used."

Maronna, who after all had all the qualities that enabled her to rule the women, stood silent, looking at the beach: she understood very well what advantages were there.

The rescued little boys, having washed themselves, came running up to Maronna and Horsa.

But, as we know, there were few of them.

Maronna stepped back from the shelter of his arms and said, "Where are the other boys? When are they coming?"

And here it was, the dreaded moment. Horsa stood in front of his accuser, head bowed, his arms loose at his sides, palms towards her—and this posture told her what she would hear. Horsa trembled as he stood, and his crutch, the stick, shook too.

Maronna was already tearing her wet hair with both hands. Remember, she usually had hair "piled on top of her head". Now it flowed down, excepting for[9] where the white powder clogged it. She tugged and tore at it, trying to make this pain bad enough to still the anguish[10] she felt.

"Where are they, Horsa, where?"

He shook his head and she screamed, "They are dead, then? You have killed our little boys. Oh, I might have known. What did I expect, really? You are so careless, you don't care..." And so they stood, facing each other, on the edge of the splendid beach which would soon house all the women and the children and the visiting men too. She was so full of anger, while he stood there, limp, guilty, in the wrong.[11] Maronna screamed and went on screaming, and at last her voice went hoarse, and she stood silent, looking, but really looking at him. He was trembling, he was limp with the grief he now genuinely did feel, because her agony of grief was telling him what an enormity[12] he had committed. And she saw this, understood it. She saw, and really took in that pitiful leg, the shrivelled, twisted leg.

Tenderness is not a quality we associate easily with young men. Life has to beat it into us, beat us softer and more malleable than our early pride allows. Horsa saw Maronna, as he had not before. Perhaps he had felt her more than seen her, as an always accusing critical presence. He saw this trembling girl, still streaked with the white powder, though her face was washed with tears. She was in such distress, so helpless: he grew up in that moment, and stood forward to take her in his arms as she opened her arms to him. "Poor child," she was whispering. "Poor boy," she crooned,[13] and now he broke down and wept and the great Horsa was a little boy again. It was sweet, yes, I am sure I may safely say that. To become a little child in your mother's arms, petted and forgiven... and for all we know, or they knew, Maronna was Horsa's mother.

The greater the capitulation[14] to the female, the greater there will be the recoil: and I have to write this, too. Who has not seen it, known it, understood?

There, in Maronna's arms, loved and forgiven, somewhere in Horsa's restless mind had started the thought: Tell her about the wonderful place I found, yes I will. She'll want to see it too, I am sure of it. She will understand, yes, she'll come with me, we'll go together, I'll make a ship better than any we've made, and we'll land together on that shore and...

I had not expected to say any more on this subject, for one thing I am old now, and the scholarly life is not easy for me. But the eruption of Vesuvius[15] has made me think again about The Cleft, and its comparatively modest explosion. Vesuvius killed people at a great distance from it, as far away as Pompeii[16], and it seems a noxious powder was the cause. Nothing survives its touch. But The Cleft too had poisonous fumes, and its outburst of whitish powder killed no one. Yet The Cleft was quite close to the shore where the women and children were. This in itself must surely provoke questions? There is a great deal it seems we do not know, though we Romans like to behave as if we know everything. Pliny, my old friend, was in pursuit of knowledge—and died for his efforts. For some days the sea near the women's shore washed in waves crusted with bone dust, on rocks that acquired a hard patina[17] which did not disappear, so the records say. And a little further down the coast the sea ran in blue and clean. A pretty minor affair, the destruction of The Cleft—and yet it leaves questions that in their own way are as difficult as the ones we ask over the great volcano, which we must assume will one day blow again.

The white rocks near The Cleft looked as if they had been covered with guano[18], and it occurs to me now to wonder if a careful search around all the coasts of the islands of our sea might reveal once whitened rocks that we would agree were the site of that old story, Clefts and Monsters. But the outburst of Vesuvius tells us we may not assume permanence for the coastlines of islands or even the islands themselves. And suppose we did decide that this set of bleached rocks was what we were after—this would be of only a sentimental interest. Those historians—and they called themselves so, seeing themselves as the recorders of the very long ago—wrote from their villages in the forests as of chronicles of events that had their end when The Cleft exploded. (Villages—how many? Where? Of how many people?) The village historians wrote with charcoal sticks on the inside of bark. They no longer spoke their stories into receiving ears. None of these old bark records remain, but what followed them, marks on reed scrolls, still remain—a few. The explosion of The Cleft is both the end of a tale and the beginning of the next. Historians who wrote long ages before me agreed on that-and so let it be.[19]

注释

1. 裂缝这一意象有着双重意义：第一，它指的是岩石上的一道裂缝，就在小说的主要人物"裂缝人"世代居住的洞穴附近；第二，它隐喻女性的生殖器外观，仿佛一道裂缝。
2. thud：v. 击打；n. 沉闷的响声。
3. 在之前的章节中，老女人们为了消灭男孩，将他们中的许多人诱骗至裂缝附近，随后将他们推入井中。
4. 裂缝中埋葬的是世世代代死去的裂缝人，因此白色粉末是骨骸长期累积的结果。
5. 此句的前半分句为部分倒装句，正常语序应当是"The young males had pressed in front of Horsa"。press 在此意为"to force or push one's way"，有打前阵的意思。整句话的中文意思为：那些年轻男人原本走在霍沙的前面，现在却落在后面，因为他们害怕女人们。
6. abate：v. 缓和，消散。
7. desecrate：v. 亵渎；使……失去神圣。反义词 consecrate。
8. element：原意指古代哲学中组成世界的四大元素：空气，水，火和土。后引申为组成或支持某事物的基本要素。
9. excepting for＝except for：with the exclusion of
10. still the anguish：令痛苦平息。
11. in the wrong：犯了错。
12. enormity：n. 暴行。
13. croon：v. 低吟。
14. capitulation：n. 投降，妥协。
15. Vesuvius：维苏威火山，全世界最著名的火山之一。是意大利南部活火山，位于坎帕尼亚平原的那不勒斯湾畔。自罗马时代以来，它已经爆发过五十多次，摧毁了周围所有的城镇。公元 79 年，它毁灭了庞贝城和赫克雷尼亚城，将企图逃离火山盛怒的居民当场活埋。
16. Pompeii：庞贝古城，或译庞培城，为古罗马城市之一，位于意大利南部那不勒斯附近，那不勒斯湾的岸边，维苏威火山西南脚下 10 公里处。得名于古罗马政治及军事家格奈乌斯·庞培。庞贝古城于公元 79 年 8 月 24 日被维苏威火山爆发时的火山灰覆盖。
17. patina：n. 铜绿；光泽；神情。
18. guano：海鸟粪。
19. 小说在以第三人称讲述裂缝人与喷射族的故事的过程中，时常穿插第一人称叙述的片段，叙述者是一位古罗马的历史学家。这一叙述提供了一种男性的、历史的叙事视角，与裂缝人故事中女性的、自然的叙事视角相映成趣。

作品导读

多丽丝·莱辛在《裂缝》的序言中写道，她是从一篇科学论文中获得灵感，进而创作了这部小说，该论文认为人类的始祖是女人，男人则是漫长进化过程的产物。作者于是提出这样

一个疑问：现代社会中的两性差异与矛盾是不是自然选择的结果？（Is Nature trying something out?）《裂缝》可以被视作一部以科幻小说的手法写成的关于人类起源的小说：在广阔的大海边居住着"裂缝人"（the Clefts），也就是女性。她们是世界上最早的并且是唯一的人类，仅仅依靠与自然的交流就能够怀孕生产。然而有一天，某一个裂缝人生下了一个怪物——书中称为"喷射族"（the Squirts），也就是男性。怪物的出现打破了女性世界的平衡，老女人（the Old Females/the Old Shes）代表的女性权威主张将男性婴儿丢弃或者阉割，不少年轻女性却为男性所吸引，女性与男性之间从此出现了一系列的冲突与融合。小说在裂缝人与喷射族的故事线索之外还增加了一条线索，让一位古罗马的男性历史学家充当了第一人称叙述者，这为小说提供了一个"喷射族"的视角。所选章节的背景是裂缝人与喷射族均已发展壮大之时，双方都有了自己的头领；裂缝人的头领是马罗娜（Maronna），喷射族的头领是霍沙（Horsa）。霍沙带领男孩毁掉了女人们长久以来视为圣地的裂缝，劝说马罗娜与女孩们和他们一起迁徙到更好的地方去。这激起了马罗娜的不满，她与霍沙发生了激烈的争执，但两人最终达成了和解，霍沙开始畅想与马罗娜在新家园的幸福生活。

尽管莱辛本人并不承认自己是一位女性主义作家，但是《裂缝》在很大程度上对女性主义批评的新分支——生态女性主义（Eco-feminism）作出了回应。生态女性主义是生态主义与女性主义两股现代思潮相结合的产物，它认为人类对自然的压迫是与男性对女性的压迫联系在一起的，都是人类中心论（anthropocentrism）和男性中心论（androcentrism）作祟的结果。在人统治自然的思想与人统治人的思想之中，如果能够消除一种，必定有助于另一种的消除。生态女性主义往往将自然与女性相联系，认为她们互为隐喻，都是父权制二元对立体系中受到压制的一方。《裂缝》为我们审视生态女性主义提供了一个有趣的视角：诚然，女性与自然之间的关系的确十分紧密，在男性出现之前，她们仅靠与自然的交流就能够受孕；故事的发展也证明男性的确对女性的生活造成了一定的破坏，他们炸毁了裂缝，切断了女性与祖先的联系。然而与此同时，读者也能从小说中读出，男性同样也是自然的孩子，鹰和母鹿抚养他们长大，而女性也对他们造成了一定的压迫，许多男孩是被老女人杀死的。小说并未谴责男性与女性之中的任何一方，而是对两性都既有赞美又有批评。生态女性主义的理想是建立一个两性和谐共存、人类与自然和谐共存的大同世界，《裂缝》最终展现了这样的世界，却并不是通过批判某一性别或某一群体来达到的。

思考题

1. What do you think is the symbolic meaning of the Cleft and its explosion?
2. What kind of person is Horsa, and what is Maronna?
3. Why do you think Maronna forgives Horsa in the end? Why is Maronna Horsa's mother?
4. What do the sea, the beach and the cave symbolize?

推荐阅读

Christina Nelson. "Ecofeminism vs. Deep Ecology." In *Comparative Philosophy*

Today and Tomorrow: Proceedings from the 2007 Uehiro Conference. Eds. Geoff Ashton, Joshua P. Kimber and Sarah A. Mattice. Cambridge Scholar Publishing, 2009.

Frederick, Suresh. *Ecocriticism: Paradigms and Praxis*. NCBH, 2019.

Marks, Peter, Jennifer A. Wagner-Lawlor and Fátima Vieria. Eds. *The Palgrave Handbook of Utopian and Dystopian Literatures*. Palgrave Macmillan, 2022.

Singh, Java. *Feminist Literary and Cultural Criticism*. Springer, 2022.

Vint, Sherryl, and Sümeyra Buran. *Technologies of Feminist Speculative Fiction*. Palgrave Macmillan, 2022.

Andrew, Barbra. Ed. *Feminist Interventions in Ethics and Politics: Feminist Ethics and Social Theory*. Rowman & Littlefield Publishers, 2005.

Gaard, Greta Claire. *Eco-feminism: Women, Animals, Nature*. Temple University Press, 1993.

Gaard, Greta. Ed. *Ecofeminist Literary Criticism: Theory, Interpretation, Pedagogy*. University of Illinois Press, 1998.

Howell, Nancy, R. *A Feminist Cosmology: Ecology, Solidarity, and Metaphysics*. Humanity Books, 2000.

Plant, Judith. Ed. *Healing the Wounds: The Promise of Ecofeminism*. New Society Publishers, 1989.

Merchant, Carolyn. *Earthcare: Women and the Environment*. Routledge, 1996.

Warren, Karen J. *Eco-feminist Philosophy: A Western Perspective on What It Is and Why It Matters*. Rowman & Little Field Publishers, 2000.

第五编　反思自然——21世纪英美生态文学

背景介绍

　　2000年,为了引起人类对于大气污染、气候变化等环境问题的关注,诺贝尔化学奖得主保罗·克鲁岑(Paul Crutzen)首次提出"人类世"(Anthropocene)概念,认为地球已经进入以气候变化为表征的新地质历史时期。2021年,克鲁岑辞世,他在20多年前使用的"人类世"概念已经被现实中的气候变化危机所印证。而且,和20年前相比,全球生态系统益发显得脆弱,生物多样性丧失、极端气候导致灾害事件等频见新闻头条。和克鲁岑"人类世"概念有着类似的环境史研究重要节点意义的是劳伦斯·布伊尔(Lawrence Buell)的《为濒危的世界写作》(*Writing for an Endangered World: Literature, Culture, and Environment in the U.S. and Beyond*)。在这部环境文学批评经典著作中,布伊尔将荒野环境拓展至城市环境,从陆地延伸到海洋,标志着21世纪以来人类对于环境、自然的反思迈入了一个新的阶段。不过,不断拓展生态批评疆界的劳伦斯·布伊尔估计也会很惊讶自2010年以来人工智能、数字环境对于人类生活的颠覆性改变。快速发展的高新技术日渐将人类拉入现实与虚拟交互的"元宇宙"世界中。2020年以来,环境危机叠加气候危机给人类生存带来巨大风险,环境危机演变为深刻而广泛的经济、政治、文化问题。现实中的环境危机、伦理危机乃至生存危机也促使人类进一步思考危机,反思自然。

　　危机语境为文学创作孕育了丰厚土壤,催生了21世纪以来生态文学创作的新趋势。21世纪英美作家通过丰富多元的文学创作反思助推环境危机、给自然带来毁灭性灾难的深层思想根源,构筑了21世纪外国生态文学创作的新景观。而所谓"新景观",不但指涉大量以现实环境危机为题材的文学作品的涌现,如重述2005年卡特里娜飓风的《拯救骨头》(*Salvage the Bones*, 2011)、回顾1927年密西西比河大洪水的《倾斜的世界》(*The Tilted World*, 2013)以及关于2004年印度洋海啸的回忆录《浪》(*Wave*, 2013)等,还表现为对传统文学创作体裁的突破和更新,如将科幻创作和环境危机话语巧妙融合的科幻生态叙事作品的日渐增多等。值得特别指出的是,受21世纪愈演愈烈的生态危机影响,各种聚焦生态危机、反思自然的文学作品的数量急剧增多,并且在经过不断扩容和沉淀后,逐渐又生成若干具有独特审美格调的文学创作类型,如气候变化小说、能源危机小说、人工智能科幻小说等。

　　21世纪以来的气候变化小说创作热潮当属当代外国生态文学创作最显著的增长点。全球变暖加剧、冰川融化、海平面上升、异常天气现象增多(厄尔尼诺和拉尼娜现象)等气候变化实例让人类逐渐意识到人类世无法逃避的各种危机。与此同时,以美国前总统特朗普为代表的部分精英政客否认全球气候变暖是由人为活动引起,这种气候变化怀疑论调无疑阻碍了全人类应对气候变暖的行动。以罗伯特·麦克法兰(Robert Macfarlane)为代表的英美学者呼吁在文学创作中回应气候变化的迫切问题,以便"气候变化的原因和后果能够被讨论、被感知、被传达"①。因此,进入21世纪后,气候变化小说(Cli-Fi)作为一个新兴文类开始蓬勃发展,其中既包括玛格丽特·阿特伍德(Margaret Atwood)、芭芭拉·金索沃(Barbara Kingsolver)、伊恩·麦克尤恩(Ian McEwan)等文坛老将的作品,也涌现出保罗·巴奇加卢皮(Paolo Bacigalupi)、纳撒尼尔·里奇(Nathaniel Rich)等新人新作。这些作品往往以末世或后末世书写为特征,以科幻体裁形式想象气候变化对于未来的影响,通过"未来已来"的环境危机警示唤起公众气候危机意识。气候变化小说这一独特的文类创作吸引了国内外生态学者的广泛关注,批评家们从人类世批评话语、生态世界主义、"超客体"、空间理论、记忆理论等多个角度呈现气候危机本身以及气候变化背后"涉及生物多样性、种群发展、资源利用、城市空间布局、能源经济发展、人际关系变革、心理创伤治疗等方方面面"的系统性问题②,为这些问题的解决寻找出路。

除了气候变化小说创作,能源污染小说也是21世纪以来生态文学创作的重要组成部分。虽然能源为人类生存与发展提供了重要的物质基础,但随着化石能源的过度消耗,人类也越来越意识到其中的弊端,与煤炭、石油、天然气的开采、加工和使用直接相关的地表水土流失、水污染、有毒气体排放、全球气候变暖等环境危机已经成为人类必须应对的重要问题。以美国南方为例,阿巴拉契亚山脉也遭受因煤矿业开采相关的山巅移除计划带来的"慢暴力";众多石化企业导致美国南部某些地区"癌症发病率是全国平均水平的18倍"③。由于美国南方不但是历史上著名的蓄奴地带,而且也是很多印第安部落的聚集地,南方贫穷白人、黑人或印第安部落居住的地区常常为了全国经济的发展被迫付出环境代价,沦为著名的"污染地带"(sacrifice zone)。美国核电站所在的区域往往也是黑人人口最多的社区;有色人种等弱势群体的居住区域更容易成为有毒废物处理厂或垃圾填埋地。这些现实使得美国南方环境危机与南方阶级、种族政治之间产生错综复杂的关系,也赋予了能源污染小说浓厚的环境正义思想。以安·潘凯克为代表的美国作家以阿巴拉契亚山脉山巅移除采矿计划带来的深重环境灾难为背景,将煤炭开采带来的山洪爆发、森林面积锐减、物种多样性减少等具体环境事件镶嵌在复杂的叙事线索中,通过被裹挟其中的人物命运的悲剧性呈现和传递人与自然相互依存的生态理念。能源污染小说中对于能源与政治、能源与历史、能源与阶级的多维呈现,使得能源污染小说不但是生态小说重要构成,也是能源人文的重要组成部分。加拿大学者伊姆雷·史泽曼(Imre Szeman)和美国学者多米尼克·博伊(Dominic Boyer)立足环境人文学,在2014年首次使用"能源人文"(energy

---

① Macfarlane, Robert. "The Burning Question." *The Guardian*. September 24, 2005. https://www.theguardian.com/books/2005/sep/24/featuresreviews.guardianreview29.

② 袁源:"人类纪的气候危机书写——兼评《气候变化小说:美国文学中的全球变暖表征》",《外国文学》2020(03):165—172。

③ Beverly H., Wright, Pat Bryant, and Robert D. Bullard. "Coping with Poisons in Cancer Alley." *Unequal Protection: Environmental Justice and Communities of Color*. Ed., Robert D. Bullard. Sierra Club Books, 1994.

humanities)概念,指出"人类的能源和环境困境根本上而言是伦理、习惯、价值观、制度、信仰和权力的问题——涉及人文学科和人文社会科学的所有专业领域"①,仅仅依靠自然科学并不能彻底解决能源带来的环境问题,也不能充分实现可持续发展。可见,能源污染小说传递的生态警示与教训对于我国当前生态文明建设具有积极的借鉴意义。

如果说气候变化小说、能源污染小说所聚焦的环境危机主要源自人与自然环境的关系失衡,近年来呈快速上升趋势的人工智能题材小说所折射的则是技术文明和人类文明关系失衡的危机。21世纪以来,"赛博格"、仿生人等新物种开始参与并介入人类的情感和家庭,这些曾经仅在科幻小说中出现的情形已经渐渐成为难以抵挡的现实,引发人类对何为身体的界限、何为人类主体性的思考和担忧。此外,生物科学的发展突飞猛进,生物技术能够进行基因治疗、显微手术、辅助生殖技术,能够制造仿生假肢装置、药物情绪和行为调节器,以及完成克隆、转基因作物培育和基因杂交。如果说人工智能是让机器模拟并延伸人的智能,那么基因生物技术就是直接改造人类身体,从而开启一个"后人类"时代。唐娜·哈拉维(Donna Haraway)在1987年发表文章《赛博格宣言》("Manifesto for Cyborgs: Science, Technology, and Socialist Feminism in the 1980s"),将这种"人机合一"的身体称为"赛博格"——"一个控制机体,一个机器和有机体的混合物,一个社会现实的创造物,同时也是虚构的产物";她更是在当时就指出"赛博格就是我们的本体"。哈拉维的说法在今天得到了印证,义肢、人工晶状体、心脏起搏器等植入人体以帮助残疾躯体恢复正常功能的工具在医疗领域得到广泛使用,除此之外,互联网的高速发展让几乎每个人都以虚拟的数字形式在网络空间出现,人类比以往任何时候都更接近哈拉维所说的"我们都是赛博格"的状态——并且这一趋势还将不断加强。在这种情况下,赛博格不再是具有他性的想象客体,而成为拥有某种主体性的人类经过改造后的形态,因此,后人类主义一定程度上削弱了人类于自然、于世界的主宰者地位,人类身体也被理解为一个开放的系统,与周围的环境形成复杂互动。然而,生物科技在创造赛博格、颠覆人类中心主义思想的同时,也会不可避免地产生社会伦理价值方面的风险。这些主题在21世纪以来英美科幻小说创作中得到了充分体现。以石黑一雄(Kazuo Ishiguro)、伊恩·麦克尤恩、科马克·麦卡锡(Cormac McCarthy)、杰夫·范德米尔(Jeff VanderMeer)为代表的当代英美小说家积极拓展小说体裁边界,借助新的表现手法和表意方式回应、参与或批判资本逻辑支配下的科技伦理失范和秩序失衡危机。麦卡锡在小说《路》(The Road)中将科幻书写和反乌托邦叙事相结合,这种末日式叙事策略不但启发我们关注科幻小说与环境话语之间的交集,也迫使我们重新定义人类、自然和科技之间的多重关系。而新怪谭科幻作家杰夫·范德米尔则在"遗落的南境"三部曲"博恩"等系列小说中以融科幻、南方哥特、环境危机为一体的新怪谭科幻体裁创作塑造后人类时代人与物质世界混溶共生的新形态,进而实现科幻恐怖与

---

① Szeman, Imre. "Conjectures on World Energy Literature: Or, What Is Petroculture?" *Journal of Postcolonial Writing*, 2017, 53(3): 277—288.

环境伦理之间的有机结合。此外,文坛老将石黑一雄创作的《别让我走》(*Never Let Me Go*, 2005)、麦克尤恩的《我这样的机器》(*Machines Like Me*, 2019)都直击仿生人伦理问题,其中对于智能合成生命的塑造不但对人的概念发出挑战,也催生对其伦理责任的拷问,对于读者审视人类中心主义,思考人与自然边界何在有着重要的意义。

当今世界正经历百年未有之大变局。当代英美作家敏锐捕捉时代的脉搏,通过充满审美异质性的环境书写介入生态危机日渐凸显的现实,体现了作家群体勇于肩负缓解环境危机、匡扶环境正义使命的创作情怀。作家叙事策略更加多元化,对科技文明的审视、对历史的反思与拟写、对政治事件影响的写照等构筑了21世纪生态文学主题的新景观,是读者审视环境与人文复杂关系的重要媒介。值得补充的是,在品鉴、挖掘当代外国生态文学中所蕴含的深刻环境伦理时,读者们还应该坚持中国立场进行异文化观照,与西方同行展开积极对话,实现东西方文明的互利互鉴。

罗伯特·麦克法兰(Robert Macfarlane)

【作者简介】

罗伯特·麦克法兰(1976—),年轻有为的英国学者、作家和文学批评家。麦克法兰生于英国的牛津,在剑桥和牛津都接受过教育,其创作以旅行文学和自然写作为主题。他的第一部著作《心灵的群山》(*Mountains of the Mind*, 2003)即为他赢得了一系列奖项,包括《卫报》图书处女作奖(Guardian First Book Award)、毛姆奖(Somerset Maugham Award)等。他在书中用第一人称叙事的方式讲述历史,探寻人类为何被群山所吸引,不顾危险也要奋力攀登的原因。麦克法兰的第二部著作是一部文学批评专著《原著:十九世纪文学的剽窃和原创》(*Original Copy: Plagiarism and Originality in Nineteenth-Century Literature*, 2007)。在他的第三部著作《荒野之地》(*The Wild Places*, 2007)中,麦克法兰又回归自然写作,在书中记述了他在英国和爱尔兰的数次旅行,他的足迹遍布森林、沼泽、盐碱地和岛屿。该书聚焦于"荒野"这一概念,力图从地理和精神两个层面阐释人类眼中之荒野的内涵和意义。《荒野之地》问世后又获得了众多奖项,并一度成为英国的畅销书。

麦克法兰现任剑桥大学伊曼纽尔学院研究员,已经就英美文学、20世纪诗歌及20世纪英美两国的自然写作发表了百余篇文章和书评,是《〈泰晤士报〉文学副刊》《伦敦书评》《观察家报》等报刊的长期撰稿人。他被视作自然写作在21世纪的继承人,他接续了约翰·缪尔(John Muir)、理查德·杰弗里斯(Richard Jefferies)和威廉·柯柏特(William Cobbet)发扬光大的自然写作传统,并将其带入了由新媒体主宰的全球化世界。

以下片段选自《荒野之地》中的一节。

The Wild Places (excerpt)

At last light, near the tip of Enlli's[1] southern arm, I walked through a field of dead sea-pink, the compact plant that grows so well in the saline conditions of coastal margins. The crisp heads of the flowers, on their stiff stalks, vibrated in the breeze, so that in the twilight it seemed as though the ground were shivering. On water to the south, I could hear the clatter of a cormorant taking off. I could see the glimmer of the cabin lights of John's boat, swaying in the bay, and briefly wished I was there with them: hot food, a glass of whisky, good company.

I glanced back towards the mainland. It was visible only as a line in the dusk, wire-thin. The monks would have launched their boats from the coves of the peninsula. The crossing is difficult even now. In summer, if the weather is poor, it can be two to three days before it becomes possible to reach the island. When the winter storms set in, Enlli can be isolated for weeks at a time.

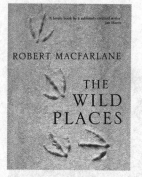

The monks would have gauged their timing carefully. The long wait for flat weather. The watching of tides. Then the launch, feet crunching in the pebbles, splashing in the water. The boats bobbing and bucking even in the swell of the coves, and then tacking out into the open waters of the Sound, the currents stacked in descending storeys beneath them.

How exposed they must have felt, I thought. Yet perhaps they did not, perhaps their faith was so absolute that it resembled fatalism[2], which is a type of fearlessness. Certainly, many of them—nameless, unchronicled—died there in the Sound, drowned by wave and current. "There is an island there is no going to / but in a small boat," wrote the priest-poet R. S. Thomas, whose little parish of Aberdaron looked out onto Enlli:

The way
the saints went, travelling the gallery
of the frightened faces of
the long-drowned, munching the gravel
of its beaches. . . .

We can know little for certain about the *peregrini*[3]. We know few of their names. Yet, reading the accounts of their journeys, and of their experiences on places like Enlli, I had encountered a dignity of motive and attitude that I found salutary. These men were in search not of material gain, but of a hallowed[4] landscape: one that would sharpen their faith to its utmost point. They were, in the phrasing of their own theology, exiles looking for the *Terra Repromissionis Sanctorum*—the Promised Land of Saints.

A long Christian tradition exists that considers all individuals as *peregrini*, in that all human life is seen as an exile. This idea was perpetrated in the "Salve Regina[5]", the chant often recited as a last night-prayer. *Post hoc exilium*, the prayer declares; all will be resolved after this exile. The chant, when sung, sounds ancient and disquieting. It is unmistakably music about wildness, an ancient vision of wildness, and it still has the capacity to move us.

Much of what we know of the life of the monks of Enlli, and places like it, is inferred from the rich literature which they left behind them. Their poems speak eloquently of a passionate and precise relationship with nature, and of the blend of receptivity and detachment which characterised their interactions with it. Some of the poems read like jotted lists, or field-notes: "Swarms of bees, beetles, soft music of the world, a gentle humming; brent geese, barnacle geese,[6] shortly before All Hallows, music of the dark wild torrent." Others record single beautiful instants: a blackbird calling from a gorse branch near Belfast Loch, foxes at play in a glade. Marban, a ninth-century hermit who lived in a hut in a fir-grove near Druim Rolach, wrote of the "wind's voice against a branchy wood on a day of grey cloud." A nameless monk, responsible for dry-stone walling on the island of North Rona in the ninth century, stopped his work to write a poem that spoke of the delight he felt at standing on a "clear headland[7]," looking over the "smooth strand" to the "calm sea," and hearing the calls of "the wondrous birds." A tenth-century copyist, working in an island monastery, paused long enough to scribble a note in Gaelic[8] beside his Latin text. "Pleasant to me is the glittering of the sun today upon these margins."

Gleanings such as these give us glimpses of the nature of faith of the *peregrini*. They are recorded instants which carry purely over the long distances of history, as certain sounds carry with unusual clarity within water or across frozen land. For these writers, attention was a form of devotion and noticing continuous with worship. The art they left behind them is among the earliest testimonies to a human love for the wild.

Ideas, like waves, have fetches. They arrive with us having travelled vast distances, and their pasts are often invisible, or barely imaginable. "Wildness" is such an idea: it has moved immensely through time. And in that time, two great and conflicting stories have been told about it. According to the first of these, wildness is a quality to be vanquished; according to the second, it is a quality to be cherished.

The etymology[9] of the word "wild" is vexed and subtle, but the most persuasive past proposed for it involves the Old High German[10] *wildi*, and the Old Norse *willr*, as well as the pre-Teutonic[11] *ghweltijos*. All three of these terms carry implications of disorder and irregularity, and as Roderick Nash has written, they bequeathed to the English word "a descriptive meaning of wilful, or uncontrollable." Wildness, according to this etymology, is an expression of independence from human direction, and wild land is *self-willed* land. Land that proceeds according to its own laws and principles, land whose habits—the growth of its trees, the movements of its creatures, the free descent of its streams through its rocks—are of the its own devising and own execution. Land that, as the contemporary definition of wild continues, "acts or moves freely without restraint; is unconfined, unrestricted."

This basic definition of wildness has remained largely constant since those first appearances. The values ascribed to this quality, however, have diverged dramatically.

On the one hand, wildness has been perceived as a dangerous force, that confounds the order-bringing pursuits of human culture and agriculture. Wildness, according to this story, is cognate with wastefulness. Wild places resist conversion to human use, and they must therefore be destroyed or overcome. Examples of hostility to the wild are ubiquitous in cultures ancient and modern, Eastern and Western. "Except for the true civilisation builders," hallelujahed the American preacher and writer James Stalker in 1881, "the very land in which we live would still be an undiscovered wilderness! These men see teeming cities, and thriving factories upon the desert, where others see only sage brush and alkali plains... these men have tunnelled our mountains, have spanned our great rivers, and opened our mines of wealth!" The Old English epic poem *Beowulf* is filled with what the poet calls *wildéor*, or savage creatures. In the poem, these monstrous dragon-like beings inhabit a landscape of wolf-haunted forests, deep lakes, windswept cliffs and treacherous mist-bound marshes. It is against these wild places and *wildéor* that the civilisation of Beowulf's tribe, the Geats—with their warm and well-lit mead halls, their hierarchical warrior culture—sets itself.

Parallel to this history of a hatred of the wild, though, has run an alternative story: one that tells of wildness as an energy both exemplary and exquisite, and of wild places as realms of miracle, diversity and abundance. At the same time that the Beowulf-poet was writing his parable of the conquest of the wild, the monks of Enlli, Rona, the Skelligs and elsewhere were praising its beauty and its riotous fecundity.

Even earlier than the *peregrini*, indeed, evidence can be found of a love for the wild. It is there in the Chinese artistic tradition known as *shan-shui* or "rivers-and-mountains." *Shan-shui* originated in the early fifth-century BC, and endured for two thousand years. Its practitioners—T'ao Chi'en[12], Li Po, Du Fu, Lu Yu[13]—were usually wanderers or self-exiles who lived in the mountain-lands of China, and wrote about the wild world around them. Their art, like that of the early Christian monks, sought to articulate the wondrous processes of the world, its continuous coming-into-being. To this quality of aliveness, the *shan-shui* artists gave the name *zi-ran*, which might be translated as "self-ablazeness[14]," "self-thusness," or "wildness."

Pilgrims and walkers, they explored their mountains in what they called the "dragon-suns" of summer, and in the long winds of winter and the blossom-storms of late spring. They wrote of the cool mist that settled into valleys at dawn, of bamboo groves into which green light fell, and of how thousands of snowy egrets[15] would take off from lakes like lifting blizzards. They observed the way winter light fell upon drifted snow, and how shadows hung from cold branches, and wrote that such sights moved them to a "bright clear joy." Night was especially marvellous to them, because of the clean luminous presence of the moon, and its ability to silver the world into strangeness. Beauty did not always connote benignity: Li Po so loved the moon, it is said, that he drowned while trying to embrace its reflection in a river. Nevertheless, reading the poems and viewing the paintings of the *shan-shui* tradition, you encounter an art in which almost no divide exists between nature and the human. Form imposes itself on content so absolutely that these artefacts do not represent the world's marvels, but partake of them.

 注释

1. Enlli:巴德西岛(Bardsey Island),在威尔士语中称作"Ynys Enlli",是威尔士境内的一个小岛,位于利恩(Lleyn)半岛尖端外,面积1.8平方千米。隔海峡与威尔士本土相望,海峡宽3千米,潮水湍急。6世纪初,凯尔特人圣卡德范(St. Cadfan)在这座天然隐密的小岛上建立了威尔士第一座圣所,后被一座奥古斯丁会修道院取代。中世纪该地成为朝圣地,

后成为海盗出没之所。现为英国重要的天然资源和鸟类保护区。

2. fatalism：*n.* 宿命论。

3. *peregrini*：(拉丁文)外来的人,云游客。在英文中,以此词为词源衍生出的 peregrine 做名词讲时意为"隼(一种飞翔速度极快的猛禽)",做形容词讲时意为"外来的,移住的,云游不定的"。

4. hallowed：*adj.* 神圣的。hallow 意指祖先、圣人,例如 All Hallows (Halloween)意为 All Saints' Day。

5. Salve Regina：《又圣母经》,是一首赞颂圣母玛利亚的轮唱赞美诗。

6. brent geese, barnacle geese：分别为布伦特鹅和黑雁。

7. headland：*n.* 延伸至水域的一块高的陆地。

8. Gaelic：盖尔语,英国及爱尔兰地区的古老语言。一般来说,盖尔语包括苏格兰的盖尔语和爱尔兰的盖尔语。苏格兰盖尔语是苏格兰最古老的语言,3 世纪前后首先出现于苏格兰。5 世纪罗马结束对英国统治后,盖尔语已成为苏格兰大多数人使用的语言,直至 19 到 20 世纪盖尔语逐渐被排斥出苏格兰学校教育和公众生活领域。爱尔兰的盖尔语则是凯尔特语的一种。

9. etymology：*n.* 词源学。

10. Old High German：古高地德語(800—1100 年间南德所用)。

11. Teutonic：*n.* 条顿语;日耳曼语。

12. T'ao Chi'en：陶潜,陶渊明(约 365—427),字元亮,(又一说名潜,字渊明)号五柳先生,私谥靖节,东晋末期南朝宋初期诗人、文学家、辞赋家、散文家。汉族,东晋浔阳柴桑人。曾做过几年小官,后辞官回家,从此隐居,田园生活是陶渊明诗的主要题材,相关作品有《饮酒》《归园田居》《桃花源记》《五柳先生传》《归去来兮辞》等。

13. Li Po：李白。

Du Fu：杜甫。

Lu Yu：陆羽(733—804),字鸿渐;汉族,唐朝复州竟陵(今湖北天门市)人,一生嗜茶,精于茶道,以著世界第一部茶叶专著——《茶经》闻名于世,对中国茶业和世界茶业发展作出了卓越贡献,被誉为"茶仙",尊为"茶圣",祀为"茶神"。他也很善于写诗,但其诗作目前世上存留的并不多。

14. ablazeness：闪耀;兴奋。

15. egret：*n.* 白鹭。

作品导读

为了寻找英国和爱尔兰地区残存的荒野之地,罗伯特·麦克法兰踏上了旅程。他白天徒步旅行、跋山涉水,夜晚就在山顶上或树林里露宿。他将旅行的热情与细致的观察结合起来,注入自己掌握的深厚历史、文学和文化知识,成就了《荒野之地》这本大受欢迎的旅游著作。《荒野之地》之所以成功,除了缘于作者亲力亲为造成的逼真亲切的效果之外,还要归功于自然景物描写之中浸淫的人文思索。例如,当麦克法兰在湖区的山上过夜时,他仰望布满繁星的夜空,感叹现代社会的人们远离大自然深沉的黑暗是多么大的损失;当他穿越沼泽地时,又为沼泽的广阔而赞叹不已,深觉语言在壮美的自然面前苍白无力。因此,这本书并不仅仅引领读者游览了自然景观,而是带着他们经历了一段思想上的旅程。

所选章节讲述了麦克法兰在威尔士境内的巴德西岛上旅行的经历。该岛不仅风光优美、景色迷人,而且历史悠久,是威尔士地区的宗教圣地。像其他章节一样,这一段文字除了景物描写,也蕴含着作者的观察和思考。麦克法兰认为,居住在小岛上的修士以宗教的虔诚敬仰着自然,他们是人类对自然之爱的最早见证人。在某种意义上,这一思索回应了20世纪后半叶兴起的一股思潮——生态神学(Ecological Theology)。顾名思义,生态神学是生态主义进入宗教(主要是基督教)领域而形成的神学运动,是对日益严重的生态问题的一种基督教觉醒和回应。这种对生态的关怀不仅是对某一特定神学课题的强调,更是让生态关怀主导整个神学方向,将很多传统的神学课题放在生态关怀的视域中予以重新诠释。

思考题

1. Why do you think the author narrates in such a thorough way about how the monks go across the water (3rd paragraph)? What does the narration imply about the monks?

2. What does the word "*peregrini*" mean, both literarily and symbolically?

3. Why is the art left by the monks "the earliest testimonies to a human love for the wild"?

推荐阅读

Schneider-Mayerson, Matthew; von Mossner, Alexa Weik; Małecki, W. P. "Empirical Ecocriticism: Environmental Texts and Empirical Methods." *Interdisciplinary Studies in Literature and Environment*, 2020, 27 (2).

Wohlleben, Peter. *The Secret Wisdom of Nature: Trees, Animals and the Extraordinary Balance of All Living Things*. Translated by Jane Billinghurst. Greystone Books, 2019.

Cain, Clifford Chalmers. *An Ecological Theology: Reunderstanding Our Relation to Nature*. Edwin Mellen Press, 2009.

Dalton, Anne Marie and Henry C. Simmons. *Ecotheology and the Practice of Hope*. State University of New York Press, 2010.

Horrell, David G. *The Bible and the Environment: Towards a Critical Ecological Biblical Theology*. Equinox Publishing. Ltd., 2010.

莫尔特曼:《创造中的上帝,生态的创造论》,隗仁莲等译,生活·读书·新知三联书店,2002年。

萨克塞:《生态哲学》,文韬等译,东方出版社,1991年。

佘正荣:《中国生态伦理传统的诠释与重建》,人民出版社,2002年。

王茜:《生态文化的审美之维》,上海世纪出版集团,2007年。

余谋昌:《生态哲学》,陕西人民教育出版社,2000年。

伊恩·麦克尤恩(Ian McEwan)

【作者简介】

伊恩·罗素·麦克尤恩（1948— ）是当代英国最著名的作家之一。2008年，《泰晤士报》将他列入"1945年以来50位伟大的英国作家"名单。麦克尤恩于1948年出生于英格兰。1975年，他的第一部作品——短篇小说集《先爱后礼》(*First Love, Last Rites*)出版，并凭借此作品在次年获得毛姆奖。1998年，他的小说《阿姆斯特丹》(*Amsterdam*)获得英语文坛最高奖之一的布克奖。随后，《赎罪》(*Atonement*, 2001)、《星期六》(*Saturday*, 2005)《在瑟切尔海滩上》(*On Chesil Beach*, 2007)等几部作品也获得布克奖提名，但最终均未能如愿获奖。

《日光》(*Solar*，又译作《太阳能》)是麦克尤恩2010年的作品。该小说用讽刺的语调讲述在全球变暖的大背景下，一个曾经获得过诺贝尔奖、但私生活无比混乱的物理学家麦克·比尔德（Michael Beard）试图利用太阳能来解决气候变化的故事。全书大体上按照时间顺序编排，以2000年、2005年以及2009年为坐标，分为三个部分。在第一部分，即"2000"，已经是53岁的比尔德在一个研究中心工作，而他获得诺贝尔奖则是二十多年前的事了。此时的比尔德对科学研究已毫无兴趣，只是顶着诺贝尔奖得主的光环混日子。当研究中心一个名叫奥德斯（Tom Aldous）的博士后向他提议进行"人工光合作用"课题时，他的反应也仅仅是嗤之以鼻。于此同时，他的妻子帕特里斯（Patrice）无法忍受丈夫的出轨，于是作为报复，和建筑工塔平（Tarpin）发生了婚外恋。比尔德得知消息以后，决定去北极进行"科考"，作为对此事的回应。但当他从北极回来以后，发现自己的妻子竟然又和年轻的奥德斯有不正当关系。在一次和比尔德的争执中，奥德斯不慎丧命。比尔德则伪造现场，嫁祸给塔平。最终塔平被判入狱16年，比尔德也和妻子离婚。第一部分到此结束。

在第二部分"2005"里，比尔德由于家庭丑闻，被迫离开所在的研究中心。但他盗用了奥德斯的研究成果，四处寻找资本为他的"人工光合作用"基地进行投资。此时他又有了新的女朋友梅丽莎（Melissa）。梅丽莎非常希望能有一个孩子，尽管比尔德害怕尽父亲的责任，一再拒绝，但最终梅丽莎还是如愿以偿地怀孕了。得知消息的比尔德无比愤恨，认为自己成了被欺骗的受害者。

到全书的第三部分"2009"的时候，比尔德已经62岁，并且体态臃肿，健康状况很糟糕。他在美国的光合作用基地即将建成，并且他又结交了另一位女友——女服务生达林（Darlene）。达林非常爱比尔德，并希望嫁给他。但此时比尔德和梅丽莎的女儿都已经3岁多了。就在他的事业即将大功告成时，所有的麻烦都接踵而至。他在英国研究所的同事布莱比（Brabby）向媒体揭发他剽窃奥德斯的研究成果；梅丽莎带着女儿来美国找他，希望他能回心转意;当年被他陷害而锒铛入狱的塔平已经出狱;曾资助他进行太阳能基地建设的生意伙伴在这个节骨眼上抛弃他。当梅丽莎带着女儿,和达林同时来到比尔德面前对峙时,小说便就此结尾。

下面的节选来自于第一部分,讲述了比尔德在得知妻子帕特里斯出轨后,去北极进行"科学考察"的经历。

Solar (excerpt)

It turned out that Beard was the only scientist among a committed band of artists. The entire world and all its follies, one of which was to warm up the planet, was to their south, which seemed to be in every direction. Before dinner that night in the mess room[1], the convenor, Barry Pickett, a benign and wizened fellow, who had rowed across the Atlantic single-handed before he devoted his life to recording the music of nature (the rustling of leaves, the crashing of waves), addressed the gathering of the Eighty Degrees North Seminar.

"We are a social species," he began, with the kind of biological flourish that Beard generally distrusted, "and we cannot survive without some basic rules. Up here, in these conditions, they are even more important. The first concerns the boot room."

It was simple enough. Below the wheelhouse was a cramped, underlit changing room. All coming on board must stop there and remove and hang up their outer layers. On no account was wet, snowy or iced-up clothing to be brought into the living quarters. Prohibited items included helmets, goggles, balaclavas, gloves, boots, wet socks and snowmobile suits. Wet, snowy, icy or dry, they were to remain in the boot room. Penalty for infringement was certain death. There was forgiving laughter from the good-natured artists, pink-faced, sensible folk in chunky sweaters and work shirts. Beard, squashed in a corner with his fifth glass of Libyan vin de pays, dosed up on painkillers and in pain, constitutionally hostile to groups, feigned a smile. He did not like to be part of a group, but he did not want the group to know. There were other rules and housekeeping items, and his attention was drifting. From behind Pickett, from the galley on the other side of an oak-veneered wall, came the smell of frying meat and garlic, and the sounds of spoons against saucepans and the hectoring growl of the international chef chivvying an underling. Hard to ignore the kitchen when it was already eight twenty and there had been nothing to eat for hours. Not being able to eat when he chose was one of the freedoms Beard had left behind in the foolish south.

...

Finally it had been hunger and the need for a drink that drove him from his cabin. After Pickett's speech, Beard was not able to move out of his corner in time to sit next to Stella Polkinghorne and instead found himself wedged between the bulkhead and a famous ice sculptor from Mallorca called Jesus, an elderly man with a mournful face and curved yellowish-white moustache who smelled richly of cigars, and had a wheezing, honking sound in his voice like a teddy bear's growl. After they had introduced themselves, Beard suggested that such a profession might be difficult to pursue in the Balearics. Jesus explained that back in the old days, the ice houses in the mountains kept the fishmongers of Palma supplied with giant blocks of ice in summer, and this was how his grandfather learned the skills he passed on to his son, who passed them on to his. Jesus had won many ice-carving competitions in cities around the world—a recent triumph was in Riyadh—and his speciality was penguins. He imported whisky when he was not carving, had four sons and five daughters, and had founded twenty years ago a school for blind children outside the port of Andratx. His wife and two of the sons ran his olive and vineyard estate in the Tramuntana, high on the sea cliffs fifteen kilometres south of Pollensa, not so far from the famous Cova de ses Bruixes, the Witches Cave. Beard's pain was lifting, the painkillers had a strong euphoric effect. He had never enjoyed anything quite so good as the steak, French fries, green salad and red wine before him. And Jesus—he had never met anyone with this name, even though he knew it was common in Spain—seemed to him the most interesting man he had met in years.

In reply to the reciprocal question, Beard said he was a theoretical physicist. It always sounded like a lie. The sculptor paused, perhaps to rehearse mentally his English, then asked a surprising question. Señor Beard was to excuse an uneducated man's naïvety and ignorance, but was the strange reality described by quantum mechanics a description of the actual world, or was it simply a system that happened to work? Infected by the Mallorcan's courtly style, Beard complimented him on the question. He could not have phrased it better himself, for there was no better interrogation of quantum theory than this. It was a matter that had dominated years of Einstein's life and led him to insist that the theory was correct but incomplete. Intuitively, he just could not accept that there was no reality without an observer, or that this reality was defined by the observer, as Bohr and the rest seemed to be saying. In Einstein's memorable phrase, there was out there a "real factual situation." "When a mouse observes," he had once asked, "does that change the state of the universe?" Quantum mechanics seemed to imply that a measurement of the state of one particle could instantaneously determine the state of another, even if it was far away. But this was "spiritualistic" in Einstein's view, it was "spooky action at a distance," for nothing could move faster than the speed of light. Beard the realist was sympathetic to Einstein's extended, failing battle with the brilliant coterie of quantum pioneers, but it had to be faced: the experimental proof suggested that there really could be long-range spooky correlations, and that the texture of reality at the small and large scale really did defy common sense. Einstein was also convinced that the mathematics needed to describe the universe would ultimately be shown to be elegant and relatively simple. But even in his lifetime, two new fundamental forces had been found, and ever since, the view had been complicated by a messy array of new particles and antiparticles, as well as various imaginary dimensions and all kinds of untidy accommodations. But Beard still clung to the hope that as yet more was revealed, a genius would arise to propose an overarching theory binding all in a formulation of astounding beauty. After many years (this was his little joke as he placed a confiding hand on Jesus's frail arm), he had finally given up hopes of being the mortal chosen to find this grail.

He said all this over the rising din of twenty climate-change artists settling down to the wine as the plates were cleared away. Jesus failed or refused to detect the self-irony and pronounced solemnly, turning his sad, drooping face to gaze about the crowded quarters, that it was a mistake to abandon hope at any stage of life. All his best penguins, the ones truest to life and most expressive of pure form, had been carved in the last two years, and recently he had started on polar bears, creatures much threatened by rising temperatures and, at one time, well beyond the reach of his artistic powers. In his humble view, it was important never to lose faith in the possibility of profound inner change. Clearly, a scientist like Señor[2] Beard should strive for this theory, for this beauty, for what was life without the highest ambitions? How could Beard confide to Jesus that he had done no serious science in years, and that he did not believe in profound inner change? Only slow inner and outer decay. He was returning the conversation to the safer ground of penguin as compared to polar-bear ice carving, but as he did so he felt his spirits sinking back. The painkillers were wearing off, the wine, this same wine, now tasted thin and sharp, the cheerfulness around him was reminding him that his marriage was over. He felt weary, and too cynical for the company. His liveliness in conversation was revealed as a fake, a product of shock, drugs and drink.

He brought the conversation to an end and said goodnight to Jesus and, muttering apologies, squeezed along the packed rows to the aisle. All the conversations he passed through were of art and climate change. At the next table a choreographer, a woman he had not seen before, sleek and beautiful and brimming with goodwill, was describing through a French accent a geometric dance she had planned to take place on the ice. He could not stand it, the optimism was crushing him. Everyone but Beard was worried about global warming and was merry, and he was uniquely morose. He cared only for darkness and silence. He lay a long while on his bunk in the airless cabin, kept awake by the throbbing in his groin—his heartbeat seemed to have migrated down there—and listening to voices and laughter, and wondering if his misanthropy would last all week. The helicopter idea he now saw was absurd. Coming away from his life in remote Belsize Park to this lifeless wilderness had confronted him with the idiocy of his existence. Patrice, Tarpin, the Centre and all the other pseudo-work he did to mask his irrelevance. What was life without the highest ambitions? The answer was exactly this, another night of unmemorable insomnia.

Two hours later he was on the edge of sleep when there came the sound of the guitar being tuned and he groaned and turned angrily on his side. But it was not strumming and singing he heard through the woodwork, but a tenderly played melody that sounded Spanish, reflective, with a touch of lightness and precision, like something of Mozart's. In the morning he would learn that it was a study by Fernando Sor. Lying in total darkness on his narrow bed he did not doubt that it was Jesus who played, as if to him, and it was to this melancholy air that at last he fell asleep.

It was late in the morning, the sun was up and shining heroically at a slant across the brilliant fjord, while Beard moved effortfully through the dimness of the boot room, trying to find his stuff. He was standing opposite peg number eighteen, on which, the day before, he knew this for a fact, he had hung his snowmobile suit. Directly below the peg was a wire basket where he had stowed his goggles, helmet and smaller items, and below that, under a slatted bench, was the compartment in which he had placed his boots. Even from down here, directly beneath the wheelhouse, he could hear the roar of many snowmobiles—getting them started in the morning was, apparently, an ordeal. A party of six, plus Jan armed with a rifle, was about to set off up the fjord to investigate the glacier. Five and the guide were already out on the ice, stamping their feet and flapping their arms to keep warm, and Beard as always was last. Someone had taken his gear, or some of it. His suit was not on its peg, his wire basket had been shoved along to position nineteen, only his boots—if they were his boots—were in the correct position. His undesirable cracked goggles were lying on the floor.

He took a suit—it was probably his anyway-from peg seventeen. It turned out to be at least two sizes too big, but once it was on he was not inclined to remove it. The boots, however, were a size too small. Among the smaller items in the basket only a glove liner was missing, and he made it up by taking a spare liner from number twenty-three, and promised himself to return it. The crack in his goggles no longer troubled him. He stepped out on deck to ironic applause from the group waiting below on the ice and, wanting to get in the spirit of group life, he made a bow. Even in his hurry, he had time to take in the scene from the top of the shallow ramp of the gangplank. There were many figures scattered on the ice around the ship. The helmets transformed the proportions of their heads, the snowmobile suits swelled their rumps, so that from a distance they resembled infants in a nursery playground. The choreographer and three friends were marking out her geometric dance; two figures were building what looked like a snowman or a statue; a lone person, probably Pickett, was rigging a microphone between two cones of ice; a person with a chainsaw was helping another, surely Jesus, load four ice blocks onto a sledge; someone was kneeling to polish a lens of ice a metre across. Another figure was going about in circles with a red flag and a whistle for the benefit of a movie camera on a tripod.

He had amazed himself by volunteering so soon for another snowmobile ride. Claustrophobia had driven him out, and the tawny light across the fjord as seen from the mess windows, and the fact that it was not permitted to go anywhere without a guide and his gun. He sat astride the last machine and the group set off in single file across the ice in an easterly direction, deeper into the fjord. It should have been fun, to be skimming down a wide corridor of ice and snow, with mountains rising sheer on both sides. But once again, the wind cut through every layer, the cracked goggles fogged up and froze within minutes and Beard could make out no more than a greyish blob of the machine in front. He was directly in the wash of six exhausts. For ten kilometres Jan kept up a wild speed,

Where the winds had stripped the snow away, the surface of the fjord was like ridged iron and the snowmobiles rattled and bucked.

Twenty minutes later they were standing in sudden silence a hundred metres from the glacier's terminus, a broken blue wall that stretched for fifteen kilometres across the valley. The impression was of a ruined city, grubby and dissolute, with rubble, broken towers and giant fissures. At minus twenty-eight, it was too cold today, Jan explained, for displays of ice shearing away in the cause of polar warming. They passed an hour taking photographs and walking up and down. Then someone saw a print in the snow. They huddled round it, and stepped back to allow their guide, whose rifle was over his shoulder, to display his expertise. A polar bear's print, of course, and very new. The snow was thin where they stood, and it was not easy to find another impression. Jan used his binoculars to scan the horizon.

"Ah," he said quietly. "I think we leave now." He pointed and at first they saw nothing. But when it moved, it was clear enough. At a distance of a mile or so, a bear was ambling towards them.

"He's hungry," Jan said forgivingly. "Time for skidoos[3]."

Even with the prospect of being eaten alive, dignity prevailed and they only half ran to the machines. As he reached his, Beard knew what to expect. Everything about this trip had conspired to reduce him. Why would his luck change now? He pushed the button. Nothing. Fine. So let his sinews be stripped from his bones. He tried again, then again. Around him, clouds of blue smoke, and high-pitched roars, the proper expression at last of full-throated panic. Already, half the party was shooting away in the direction of the ship. It was every-man-for-himself. Beard wasted no energy cursing. He pulled out the choke lever, though he knew it was a mistake, for the engine was still warm. He tried again. And again, nothing. He smelled petrol. He had flooded the engine and he deserved to die. Now all the others had gone, along with the guide, whose dereliction of duty Beard resolved to report to Pickett, or the King of Norway. His agitation was steaming up his goggles, and, as usual, the steam froze. Pointless then, to look back, but he did it all the same, and saw frozen steam fringed with a glimpse of the fjord's ice. It was reasonable to assume the bear was still coming, but he had clearly underestimated its speed over the ground, because at that moment his shoulder was struck a heavy blow.

Rather than turn and have his face ripped away, he hunched his shoulders in expectation of the worst. His last thought—that in his carelessly unchanged will he had left everything to Patrice for Tarpin's use[4]—would have been a dismal one, but what he heard was the guide's voice.

"Let me do it." The Nobel laureate had been pressing the headlight switch.

The machine came to life at first touch.

"Go," Jan said. "I'm behind you."

Despite the danger he was in, Beard glanced back again, hoping to catch sight, for anecdote's sake, of the animal he was about to outpace. In the narrow perimeter of semi-clarity that surrounded the goggle's frozen fog patch there was movement, but it may have been the guide's hand or a corner of his own balaclava. In the account he would give for the rest of his life, the one that became his true memory, a polar bear with open jaws was twenty metres distant and running at him when his snowmobile started forward, not because, or not only because, he was a liar, but because he instinctively knew it was wrong to dishonour a good story.

Racing away across the rackety ice, he gave out a whoop of joy that was lost to the icy hurricane in his face. How liberating to discover in the modern age that he, a city-dweller, an indoors man who lived by the keyboard and screen, could be tracked and ravaged and be an entire meal, a source of nourishment to others.

Perhaps that was the best moment of his week. They were back at their base within minutes, it seemed. Already, at one forty-five, there was a deeper chill in the air, and orange evening light illuminated the few artists who had not yet retreated into the ship. His groin was so tender that he waited until the others had gone inside, then he walked backwards up the gangplank. It hurt less that way. He paused in the entrance of the boot room, waiting for his eyes to adjust to the poor light, and soon it was clear enough-someone had hung all his stuff at Beard's station. In a constructive spirit, he removed the lot, boots and all, to a vacant spot in a corner. When he took off his woollen balaclava, it slipped to the floor with a clunk and seemed to stare up at him in open-mouthed disbelief. What was he doing here? He put his gear away, then he went to the mess room, said a round of hellos to the half-dozen people there, and took a hot drink to his cabin and lay on the bunk.

It was an accident of cartography that placed the South Pole under the North, but he could not dispel the impression that he was near the top of the world and that everybody else, Patrice included, was below him. He had an overview then, and they became a feature of his week, these afternoons in the Arctic dusk, when he reminded himself over the cocoa that his life was about to empty out and that he must begin again, take himself in hand, lose weight, get fit, live in a simple, organised style. And get serious at last about work, though he had no idea what work he could do that was not detached from or eased by his peculiar fame. Must he give forever the same lecture series about his one small contribution, sit on committees, be a Presence? He had no answers, but the musing was comforting and often he fell asleep in the darkness of three o'clock and woke hungry, with renewed appetite for the vin de pays.

After his deliverance from the jaws of a polar bear, he did nothing adventurous all week. Bolder types went off with a guide to hike in the mountains, or make a snow cave, or explored on snowmobiles a steep valley that rose through rocky outcrops on the far side of the fjord. Each day he spent two or three hours outside the ship, pottering about with the others. He was taken on as an assistant, holding an end of a piece of string, cutting blocks of ice for Jesus, helping with Pickett's microphones, joining in the dance. This involved being filmed walking in single file at a measured pace behind a dozen others for two hundred yards in a straight line, before making a right-angled turn and walking the same distance before the next turn. It was soothing, he was content to think of nothing and be told what to do. In a warmer climate, with better health, he might have tried his chances with the choreographer, slender Elodie, from Montpellier, especially if she had come away without her husband, a bullet-headed photographer who had once played rugby for France. Stella Polkinghorne also had a husband-the convenor, Barry Pickett.

  Beard's life, then, was simplified. Caring little for art or climate change, and even less for art about climate change, he kept his thoughts to himself and was affable, and was surprised to find himself faintly popular. His mind emptied as he went about the ice on his errands. One lunchtime he carried out from the ship cups of tomato soup, which froze as he reached the bottom of the gangplank. They were incorporated into a sculpture. His spirits rose, or ceased to sink. He thought about his fitness again. Only ten or twelve years before, he had played a plausible game of tennis, compensating for his height with a vicious, stabbing little forehand volley at the net. And he had once skied with near competence. Eight years ago he could still touch his toes. Surely, it was not inevitable that he should get heavier by the month until he dropped dead? He arranged to take a daily hike on the fjord, a two-mile circuit around the ship, escorted by Jan carrying a gun. After the second excursion, lying on his bunk in the afternoon with aching legs, he made a mental list of the food he would no longer touch. He was fifteen pounds overweight. Act now, or die early. He swore off all the usual things—dairy produce, red meat, fried food, cakes, salted nuts. And crisps, for which he had a particular weakness. There were other items, but he was asleep before the list was complete. During the last three days of his stay he kept to the new regime.

  From the second day, the disorder in the boot room was noticeable, even to Beard. He suspected that he never wore the same boots on consecutive days. Even though he wrapped his goggles (these ones were undamaged) in his inner balaclava on the third day, they were gone by the fourth, and the balaclava was on the floor, soaking up water. That morning he saw several snowmobile suits, also on the floor. They had a trampled appearance, and he decided, without looking too closely, that none could be his. Pickett admitted to him, while they were out recording the sound of the wind in the ship's rigging, that for two days he had been wearing two left boots. But he was a hardy sort who did not seem to mind. Beard did mind. He was not a communally-spirited person, but there were certain decencies he took for granted-in himself, and therefore in others. He always put his stuff on and below the same peg, number seventeen, and was disappointed to note that others had trouble observing such simple procedures. Gloves were a particular problem, for it was impossible to go outside without them. As a precaution, he stuffed his inside his boots, along with the glove liners. The next day the boots were gone.

  He liked the evenings. By the time they started gathering in the mess room before dinner, it had been dark for five hours. There was two hours' drinking before the first course. The wine was from a neglected region of Libya. He generally started on the white, drank the red until he sickened and returned to the white, and there was generally enough time to switch back before bedtime. After dinner, there was, of course, only one topic. Mostly, Beard listened. Never before had he encountered idealists in such concentration and he was by turns intrigued, embarrassed, constrained. When Pickett asked him on the third night to talk about his work, he stood up to speak. He described the Centre and the quadruple-helix rooftop wind turbine, plausibly claiming it as his own initiative. It was a revolutionary design, he told the room, and he made a sketch to be passed around. It would cut household bills by eighty-five per cent, a saving that would be the equivalent of building—not quite drunk, he summoned a number—twenty-three medium-sized power stations. There were respectful questions, and he answered them judiciously, lucidly. He was among scientific illiterates and could have said anything. There was an impassioned statement of support from Stella Polkinghorne. She said that Beard was the only one here doing something "real," at which the whole room warmed to him and applauded loudly. He had never cared much what others thought, but now-how lowering-he was touched and could not conceal it, to be, for just a few minutes, the darling of the ship.

Otherwise, he listened and drank. After two or three glasses of the white, the red went down painlessly, like water, at least at first. There were themes—some were canonic and chased each other crazily, others were fugal and ran concurrently, as disappointment did with bitterness: the century had ended and climate change remained a marginal concern, Bush had torn up Clinton's modest proposals, the United States would turn its back on Kyoto, Blair showed no grip on the subject, the long-ago hopes of Rio were lost. Canonically pursuing then overtaking disappointment was alarm. The Gulf Stream would vanish, Europeans would freeze to death in their beds, the Amazon would be a desert, some continents would catch fire, others would drown, and by 2085 the Arctic summer ice would be gone and the polar bears with it. Beard had heard these predictions before and believed none of them. And if he had, he would not have been alarmed. A childless man of a certain age at the end of his fifth marriage could afford a touch of nihilism. The earth could do without Patrice and Michael Beard. And if it shrugged off all the other humans, the biosphere would soldier on, and in a mere ten million years teem with strange new forms, perhaps none of them clever in an apeish way. Then who would regret that no one remembered Shakespeare, Bach, Einstein, or the Beard-Einstein Conflation[5]?

While dark and even greater cold enveloped the ship in the lonely frozen fjord, and the brave yellow gleam from its portholes was the only light, the only sign of life for a hundred miles across the crackling icy wastes, other themes flourished symphonically: what was to be done, what treaties were to be made between the quarrelsome nations, what concessions, what gifts should the rich world self-interestedly make to the poor? In the mess room's humid after-dinner warmth, it seemed to the owners of full stomachs sealed with wine that it was only reason that could prevail against short-term interests and greed, only rationality could draw, by way of warning, the indistinct cartoon of a calamitous future in which all must bake, shiver or drown.

The statehood-and-treaty talk was worldly in comparison with another leitmotiv that summoned a cooling measure of austere plainsong, a puritanical air from the old conservation days, distrustful of technological fixes, determined that what was required was a different way of life for everyone, a lighter tread on the precious filigree of ecosystems, a near-religious regard for new rules of human fulfilment in order to flourish beyond supermarkets, airports, concrete, traffic, even power stations—a minority view, but heard with guilty respect by all who had steered a stinking snowmobile across the pristine land.

Listening, as he usually did, with Jesus at his side from their corner of the mess room, Beard interjected only once, on the last evening when a gangling novelist called Meredith, appearing to forget there was a physicist present, said that Heisenberg's Uncertainty Principle, which stipulated that the more one knew of a particle's position, the less one knew of its velocity, and vice versa, encapsulated for our time the loss of a "moral compass," the difficulty of absolute judgements. Beard was peevish in his interruption. It was worthwhile to be correct, he told this crop-haired fellow with rimless glasses. What was at issue was not velocity but momentum, in other words, mass times velocity. At such hairsplitting there were muted groans. Beard said that the principle had no application to the moral sphere. On the contrary, quantum mechanics was a superb predictor of the statistical probability of physical states. The novelist blushed but would not give way. Did he not know who he was talking to? Fine, yes, OK, statistical probability, he insisted, but that was not certainty. And Beard, just finishing his eighth glass of wine and feeling nose and upper lip elevate in contempt for an ignorant trespasser on his field, said loudly that the principle was not incompatible with knowing precisely the state of, say, a photon, so long as one could observe it repeatedly. The analogy in the moral sphere might be to reexamine a moral problem a number of times before arriving at a conclusion. But this was the point-Heisenberg's Principle would only have application if the sum of right plus wrong divided by the square root of two had any meaning. The silence in the room was not so much stunned as embarrassed. Meredith stared helplessly as Beard brought his fist down hard on the table. "So come on. Tell me. Let's hear you apply Heisenberg to ethics. Right plus wrong over the square root of two. What the hell does it mean? Nothing!"

Barry Pickett intervened to move the discussion on.

That was an isolated discordant note. What was memorable and surprising came every evening, usually late on, in the bright tones of a marching brass band, or the sound of massed voices in unison, elated in common purpose and obliterating for a while all disappointment, all bitterness. Beard would not have believed it possible that he would be in a room drinking with so many seized by the same particular assumption, that it was art in its highest forms, poetry, sculpture, dance, abstract music, conceptual art, that would lift climate change as a subject, gild it, palpate it, reveal all the horror and lost beauty and awesome threat, and inspire the public to take thought, take action, or demand it of others. He sat in silent wonder. Idealism was so alien to his nature that he could not raise an objection. He was in new territory, among a friendly tribe of exotics. Those sentinel snowmen guarding the foot of the gangplank, the recorded sound of the wind moaning through the rigging, the disc of polished ice that refracted the day-long setting sun, Jesus's penguins, thirty of them, and three polar bears, marching along the ice beyond the ship's bow, the harsh, impenetrable fragment of a novel punctuated with expletives that Meredith read, or shouted, aloud one evening—all these demonstrations, like prayers, like totem-pole dances, were fashioned to deflect the course of a catastrophe.

Such was the music and magic of ship-bound climate-change talk. Meanwhile, on the other side of the wall he had learned to call a bulkhead, the boot room continued to deteriorate. By midweek four helmets were missing along with three of the heavy snowmobile suits and many smaller items. It was no longer possible for more than two thirds of the company to be outside at the same time. To go out was to steal. The state of the boot room, the gathering entropy, became a subject of Barry Pickett's evening announcements. And Beard, oblivious to his own vital role, his generous assistance in setting the initial conditions, could not help reflecting expansively on this post-lapsarian state. Four days ago the room had started out in orderly condition, with all gear hanging on or stowed below the numbered pegs. Finite resources, equally shared, in the golden age of not so long ago. Now it was a ruin. Even harder to impose order once the room was strewn with backpacks and stuff-bags and supermarket plastic bags half filled with extra gloves and scarves and chocolate bars. No one, he thought, admiring his own generosity, had behaved badly, everyone, in the immediate circumstances, wanting to get out on the ice, had been entirely rational in "discovering" their missing balaclava or glove in an unexpected spot. It was perverse or cynical of him to take pleasure in the thought, but he could not help himself. How were they to save the earth—assuming it needed saving, which he doubted—when it was so much larger than the boot room?

On the last morning they ate their breakfast to the din of the entire snowmobile fleet warming up outside. They went out onto the ice, many of them missing pieces of their equipment. Beard was without a helmet. While he waited for the signal to leave, he warmed his goggles on the engine, and wound a scarf round his head. The low orange sun was unhindered, there would be a useful tailwind, and it looked like the journey back to Longyearbyen might even be pleasant, if one were fully clothed. There was a shout from the deck. Between them, Barry Pickett and one of the crew were manhandling down the gangplank a huge plastic and fibre sack of the sort that builders use to store sand in. Lost property. They gathered around the treasure and poked about in it. Beard found a helmet that fitted and knew it must be his. No one was ashamed, or even faintly embarrassed. Here was their stuff. Where had it been hiding all this time? They said their goodbyes to the crew, and set off in loud and poisonous single file across the fjord towards Longyearbyen, keeping to a stately twenty-five kilometres per hour to avoid the cutting headwind. Hunched low over his machine, trying to draw a little of its heat onto his face,

Beard found himself in a mellow state-an unfamiliar cast of mind for the morning. He was not even hung-over. On the frozen shores of the fjord they slowed to walking pace to navigate deep ruts, trenches, in the ice. He could not remember them from the outward journey. But of course, he had been asleep behind Jan's back. Then they were on a long straight snowy track, passing a hut where, the guides had told them, a great eccentric once lived a lonely life.

If, Beard thought, he ever travelled by spaceship to another galaxy, he would soon be fatally homesick for these, his brothers and sisters up ahead of him, for everyone, ex-wives included. He was suffused with the pleasant illusion of liking people. Entirely forgivable, all of them. And somewhat cooperative, somewhat selfish, sometimes cruel, above all, funny. The snowmobiles were passing through the narrow, high-sided gully, scene of his shame, a moment best buried. He preferred to recall his cool escape from a murderous bear. But yes, he felt unusually warm towards humankind. He even thought that it could warm to him. Everyone, all of us, individually facing oblivion, as a matter of course, and no one complaining much. As a species, not the best imaginable, but certainly the best, no, the most interesting there was. But what about the general disgrace that was the boot room? Evidently, a matter of human nature. And how were we ever going to learn about that? Science of course was fine, and who knew, art was too, but perhaps self-knowledge was beside the point. Boot rooms needed good systems so that flawed creatures could use them properly. Leave nothing, Beard decided, to science or art, or idealism. Only good laws would save the boot room. And citizens who respected the law.

注释

1. mess room：船上的餐厅，后文中的 boot room 指的是船上的更衣室。
2. Señor：西班牙语，"先生"之意。
3. skidoo：走开，离开。
4. ...in his carelessly unchanged will he had left everything to Patrice for Tarpin's use：比尔德去北极之前已经发现妻子 Patrice 和建筑工人 Tarpin 有外遇，因此他认为自己如果死掉，根据之前并未修改的遗嘱，自己的所有财产就最终落到妻子以及 Tarpin 手里。
5. Beard-Einstein Conflation：比尔德三十多岁时正是凭借"Beard-Einstein Conflation"获得诺贝尔物理学奖。

作品导读

《日光》涉及一个当今社会的热门话题：全球变暖以及人类对这一严峻情况的应对。面对地球能源的枯竭、人类生存环境的不断恶化，人类社会的生态意识和环境保护意识被大大提升，人们越来越意识到维护生态平衡对于人类自身生存和发展的重要性，并且也在采取各种手段来应对所面临的环境问题。在人类解决环境问题的进程中,科学技术一直扮演了极其重要的角色,甚至可以说,科技就是人类和环境恶化做斗争的有力武器。但是这个武器本身该如何正确使用?人类在使用过程中有没有犯过任何错误?麦克尤恩的小说引起了读者对上述问题的思考。

  小说的主人公是一位曾获得过诺贝尔奖的科学家。一般来讲,科学家可以被看做是人类精英的代表,他们掌握着最先进的科学技术,并且是新学科领域的探索者和带路人。但是小说里的比尔德却完全打破了这一形象。虽然三十多岁就获得诺贝尔奖,但在此后的岁月里他在科研上毫无建树,顶着诺奖的光环不劳而获。他不但自己不思进取,而且无情打压后来人。在小说的第一部分,由于自己的错误判断,他让整个研究中心去搞毫无价值的"风力制动"项目。当年轻的研究人员奥德斯向他提出"人工光合作用"概念时,他毫不理睬;然而后来他却剽窃了奥德斯的研究成果,决定进行太阳能基地建设,但他进行该项目的动机并不是为了通过科学研究来应对人类的生态危机,而仅仅是这个项目有巨大的经济利益,能够拉到大量的投资。可以看出,作为一个科技工作者,比尔德的价值观和道德观是扭曲的。除此以外,他在个人生活上也是一团糟。他一次又一次地背叛自己的婚姻和感情,完全没有尽到并且也十分害怕尽到作为丈夫和父亲的责任。总的来说,他的形象特点可以用贪婪和懒惰两个词来概括。而贪婪和懒惰又恰恰是我们人类最本质的弱点。从这个意义来讲,比尔德可以看作是人性丑恶的一面的代言人。必须承认,当下所面临的生态恶化的困境其实正是人类由于自身永远无法满足的贪欲,对地球环境肆无忌惮的破坏所造成的恶果。现在,人类已经认识到了环境问题的严峻性,并且着手应对这一困境。但是如果人类依然无法控制自己贪婪的欲望的话,无论科技有多么发达,在与环境恶化的斗争中也将很难取得胜利。作者在小说中为比尔德安排的结局表达了作者对人类最终命运的隐约担忧。

  该小说最显著的特点便是情节荒诞离奇,语言幽默风趣。本书所节选的比尔德在北极的经历可以算是小说这一特点的集中体现。比尔德去北极的路上碰到了一群自称去北极寻找关于生态方面创作灵感的艺术工作者,于是和他们结伴同行。而他们在北极的经历却滑稽荒诞并且引人深思。这群由科学家、艺术家组成的文化精英团队在一次野外旅途中遇到了北极熊的威胁,于是大家仓皇逃命,最终化险为夷。事后他们却对这段经历夸夸其谈,把它当成自我炫耀的资本。从这个细节可以看出,这些文化精英虽然总是把生态保护挂在嘴边,但他们的生态价值观却是有问题的。一方面,他们把动物视为一种对人类安全的威胁;另一方面,他们成功"逃离"后的自我吹嘘表明,这种"威胁"是一种潜在的、可以被征服的对象,对它们的征服因此成为值得炫耀的胜利。这说明在他们看来,人类和动物、自然界处于一种二元对立的关系,后者是人类征服的对象。如果连这些文化精英都依然持有这种扭曲的生态观点,那么我们人类社会正在进行着的保护生态环境的事业最终将走向何方?

  在北极科考过程中,发生在更衣室里的故事值得我们注意。考察队员住所的更衣室是用来堆放外出所需装备的地方。起初更衣室的物件堆放地井然有序。但很快人们便随意乱放,以至于外出时找不到自己的装备,只能拿别人的去用。这个情况的最大受害者便是比尔德。他每天外出时戴的护目镜、头盔等装备都是不一样的,并且不符合自己的尺寸。到了第四天,等他到更衣室时,甚至发现已经没有足够的装备,于是只能不戴头盔外出。愤怒的他只能感慨:"只有完善的法律才能拯救这个更衣室,以及遵守法律的人。"从某种意义上来讲,更衣室可以看作是我们生存的星球的缩影。地球也是一个密闭的空间。在人类文明高速发展以前,地球上的生物也井然有序地生活着,遵守着大自然的生存法则。然而自从近代以来,人类为了满足自身不断增长的欲求,开始违背自然法则,大肆破坏生态环境。最终的结果便是环境的不断恶化,犹如那个杂乱无章的更衣室。难怪比尔德自己也开始质疑:"他们将如何拯救地球?(假设地球需要拯救的话,当然这一点他自己是怀疑的。)地球可比更衣室大多了。"但我们不能忘记的是,在更衣室经历中,比尔德虽然是受害者,并且提出了许多代表"正义"的批评以及思考,但是他自己也和其他所有人一样,内心充满了对物质永远无法满足的欲望。小说作者的这种自相矛盾的安排确实发人深思。

思考题

1. What is the name of the ice sculptor from Mallorca? What does his name imply?
2. What do the band of artists as well as Beard do for the most of time on the ship in the Arctic?
3. How does the writer describe the deterioration of the boot room?

推荐阅读

Byrnes, Christina. *The Work of Ian McEwan: A Psychodynamic Approach*. Paupers' Press, 2002.

Childs, Peter. Ed. *The Fiction of Ian McEwan (Readers' Guides to Essential Criticism)*. Palgrave Macmillan, 2005.

Dodou, Katherina. *Childhood Without Children: Ian McEwan and the Critical Study of the Child*. Uppsala University, 2009.

Malcolm, David. *Understanding Ian McEwan*. University of South Carolina, 2002.

Reynolds, Margaret & Jonathan Noakes. *Ian McEwan: The Essential Guide*. Vintage, 2002.

Roberts, Ryan. *Conversations with Ian McEwan*. University Press of Mississippi, 2010.

石黑一雄(Kazuo Ishiguro)

【作者简介】

石黑一雄(1954—),著名日裔英国小说家,出生于日本长崎,1960 年随家人移民英国。曾就学于东安格里亚大学(University of East Anglia)和肯特大学(University of Kent)。石黑一雄年轻时即享誉世界文坛,与塞尔曼·拉什迪(Salman Rushdie)和维苏·奈保尔(V. S. Naipaul)并称为"英国文坛移民三雄"。1989 年,石黑一雄获得了在英语文学界享有盛誉的布克奖。他的文体以细腻优美著称,几乎每部小说都被提名或得奖,其作品已被翻译成 28 种语言。虽然石黑一雄拥有东西方双重的文化背景,他却并不以民族认同作为小说的唯一题材。对他而言,在这个日益全球化的现代世界中,不计文化背景的人类共同命运才是他在小说创作中力图探寻和表达的主题。

石黑一雄的主要作品有:《群山淡景》(*A Pale View of Hills*, 1982),获得英国皇家学会奖(Royal Society of Literature)与温尼弗雷德·霍尔比奖(Winifred Holtby Prize);《浮世画家》(*An Artist of the Floating World*, 1986)获得英国及爱尔兰图书协会颁发的惠特布莱德年度最佳小说奖(Whitbread Book of the Year Award),并第一次获得布克奖的提名;《长日将尽》(*The Remains of the Day*, 1989)获得布克奖;《无法安慰》(*The Unconsoled*, 1995)获得契尔特纳姆文学艺术奖(Cheltenham Prize);《我辈孤雏》(*When We Were Orphans*, 2000)再次获得布克奖提名;《别让我走》(又译《千万别丢下我》,*Never Let Me Go*, 2005),又一次获得布克奖提名。2017 年 10 月,石黑一雄获得诺贝尔文学奖。

以下片段选自长篇小说《别让我走》第七章中的一节。

Never Let Me Go (excerpt)

We were fifteen by then, already into our last year at Hailsham[1]. We'd been in the pavilion getting ready for a game of rounders[2]. The boys were going through a phase of "enjoying" rounders in order to flirt with us, so there were over thirty of us that afternoon. The downpour had started while we were changing, and we found ourselves gathering on the veranda—which was sheltered by the pavilion roof—while we waited for it to stop. But the rain kept going, and when the last of us had emerged, the veranda was pretty crowded, with everyone milling around[3] restlessly. I remember Laura was demonstrating to me an especially disgusting way of blowing your nose for when you really wanted to put off[4] a boy.

Miss Lucy was the only guardian present. She was leaning over the rail at the front, peering into the rain like she was trying to see right across the playing field. I was watching her as carefully as ever in those days, and even as I was laughing at Laura, I was stealing glances at Miss Lucy's back. I remember wondering if there wasn't something a bit odd about her posture, the way her head was bent down just a little too far so she looked like a crouching animal waiting to pounce.

And the way she was leaning forward over the rail meant drops from the overhanging gutter were only just missing her—but she seemed to show no sign of caring. I remember actually convincing myself there was nothing unusual in all this—that she was simply anxious for the rain to stop—and turning my attention back to what Laura was saying. Then a few minutes later, when I'd forgotten all about Miss Lucy and was laughing my head off at something, I suddenly realised things had gone quiet around us, and that Miss Lucy was speaking.

She was standing at the same spot as before, but she'd turned to face us now, so her back was against the rail, and the rainy sky behind her.

"No, no, I'm sorry, I'm going to have to interrupt you," she was saying, and I could see she was talking to two boys sitting on the benches immediately in front of her. Her voice wasn't exactly strange, but she was speaking very loudly, in the sort of voice she'd use to announce something to the lot of us, and that was why we'd all gone quiet. "No, Peter, I'm going to have to stop you. I can't listen to you any more and keep silent." Then she raised her gaze to include the rest of us and took a deep breath. "All right, you can hear this, it's for all of you. It's time someone spelt it out[5]."

We waited while she kept staring at us. Later, some people said they'd thought she was going to give us a big telling-off[6]; others that she was about to announce a new rule on how we played rounders. But I knew before she said another word it would be something more.

"Boys, you must forgive me for listening. But you were right behind me, so I couldn't help it. Peter, why don't you tell the others what you were saying to Gordon just now?" Peter J. looked bewildered and I could see him getting ready his injured innocence face. But then Miss Lucy said again, this time much more gently:

"Peter, go on. Please tell the others what you were just saying."

Peter shrugged. "We were just talking about what it would feel like if we became actors. What sort of life it would be."

"Yes," Miss Lucy said, "and you were saying to Gordon you'd have to go to America to stand the best chance[7]."

Peter J. shrugged again and muttered quietly: "Yes, Miss Lucy."

But Miss Lucy was now moving her gaze over the lot of us. "I know you don't mean any harm. But there's just too much talk like this. I hear it all the time, it's been allowed to go on, and it's not right." I could see more drops coming off the gutter and landing on her shoulder, but she didn't seem to notice. "If no one else will talk to you," she continued, "then I will. The problem, as I see it, is that you've been told and not told. You've been told, but none of you really understand, and I dare say, some people are quite happy to leave it that way. But I'm not. If you're going to have decent lives, then you've got to know and know properly. None of you will go to America, none of you will be film stars. And none of you will be working in supermarkets as I heard some of you planning the other day. Your lives are set out for you. You'll become adults, then before you're old, before you're even middle-aged, you'll start to donate your vital organs. That's what each of you was created to do. You're not like the actors you watch on your videos, you're not even like me. You were brought into this world for a purpose, and your futures, all of them, have been decided. So you're not to talk that way any more. You'll be leaving Hailsham before long, and it's not so far off, the day you'll be preparing for your first donations. You need to remember that. If you're to have decent lives, you have to know who you are and what lies ahead of you, every one of you."

Then she went silent, but my impression was that she was continuing to say things inside her head, because for some time her gaze kept roving over us, going from face to face just as if she were still speaking to us. We were all pretty relieved when she turned to look out over the playing field again.

"It's not so bad now," she said, even though the rain was as steady as ever. "Let's just go out there. Then maybe the sun will come out too." I think that was all she said. When I was discussing it with Ruth a few years ago at the centre in Dover, she claimed Miss Lucy had told us a lot more; that she'd explained how before donations we'd all spend some time first as carers, about the usual sequence of the donations, the recovery centres and so on—but I'm pretty sure she didn't. Okay, she probably intended to when she began talking. But my guess is once she'd set off[8], once she'd seen the puzzled, uncomfortable faces in front of her, she realised the impossibility of completing what she'd started.

It's hard to say clearly what sort of impact Miss Lucy's outburst at the pavilion made. Word got round[9] fast enough, but the talk mostly focused on Miss Lucy herself rather than on what she'd been trying to tell us. Some students thought she'd lost her marbles[10] for a moment; others that she'd been asked to say what she had by Miss Emily and the other guardians; there were even some who'd actually been there and who thought Miss Lucy had been telling us off for being too rowdy on the veranda. But as I say there was surprisingly little discussion about what she'd said. If it did come up, people tended to say: "Well so what? We already knew all that."

But that had been Miss Lucy's point exactly. We'd been "told and not told," as she'd put it. A few years ago, when Tommy and I were going over it all again, and I reminded him of Miss Lucy's "told and not told" idea, he came up with a theory. Tommy thought it possible the guardians had, throughout all our years at Hailsham, timed very carefully and deliberately everything they told us, so that we were always just too young to understand properly the latest piece of information. But of course we'd take it in[11] at some level, so that before long all this stuff was there in our heads without us ever having examined it properly.

It's a bit too much like a conspiracy theory for me—I don't think our guardians were that crafty—but there's probably something in it. Certainly, it feels like I *always* knew about donations in some vague way, even as early as six or seven. And it's curious, when we were older and the guardians were giving us those talks, nothing came as a complete surprise. It *was* like we'd heard everything somewhere before.

One thing that occurs to me now is that when the guardians first started giving us proper lectures about sex, they tended to run them together with talk about the donations. At that age—again, I'm talking of around thirteen—we were all pretty worried and excited about sex, and naturally would have pushed the other stuff into the background[12]. In other words, it's possible the guardians managed to smuggle[13] into our heads a lot of the basic facts about our futures.

Now to be fair, it was probably natural to run these two subjects together. If, say, they were telling us how we'd have to be very careful to avoid diseases when we had sex, it would have been odd not to mention how much more important this was for us than for normal people outside. And that, of course, would bring us onto the donations.

Then there was the whole business about our not being able to have babies. Miss Emily used to give a lot of the sex lectures herself, and I remember once, she brought in a life-size skeleton from the biology class to demonstrate how it was done. We watched in complete astonishment as she put the skeleton through various contortions[14], thrusting her pointer around without the slightest self-consciousness. She was going through all the nuts and bolts[15] of how you did it, what went in where, the different variations, like this was still Geography. Then suddenly, with the skeleton in an obscene heap on the desktop, she turned away and began telling us how we had to be careful *who* we had sex with. Not just because of the diseases, but because, she said, "sex affects emotions in ways you'd never expect." We had to be extremely careful about having sex in the outside world, especially with people who weren't students, because out there sex meant all sorts of things. Out there people were even fighting and killing each other over who had sex with whom. And the reason it meant so much—so much more than, say, dancing or table-tennis—was because the people out there were different from us students: they could have babies from sex. That was why it was so important to them, this question of who did it with whom. And even though, as we knew, it was completely impossible for any of us to have babies, out there, we had to behave like them. We had to respect the rules and treat sex as something pretty special.

Miss Emily's lecture that day was typical of what I'm talking about. We'd be focusing on sex, and then the other stuff would creep in. I suppose that was all part of how we came to be "told and not told." I think in the end we must have absorbed quite a lot of information, because I remember, around that age, a marked change in the way we approached the whole territory surrounding the donations. Until then, as I've said, we'd done everything to avoid the subject; we'd backed off at the first sign we were entering that ground, and there'd been severe punishment for any idiot—like Marge that time—who got careless. But from when we were thirteen, like I say, things started to change. We still didn't discuss the donations and all that went with them; we still found the whole area awkward enough. But it became something we made jokes about, in much the way we joked about sex. Looking back now, I'd say the rule about not discussing the donations openly was still there, as strong as ever. But now it was okay, almost required, every now and then, to make some jokey allusion to these things that lay in front of us.

A good example is what happened the time Tommy got the gash on his elbow. It must have been just before my talk with him by the pond; a time, I suppose, when Tommy was still coming out of that phase of being teased and taunted.

注释

1. Hailsham:小说主要人物凯西、汤米、露丝与其他孩子居住的克隆人寄宿学校。有研究者将这一名称解读为 hail-sham,意为"向虚伪欢呼",或者"欢迎啊,假冒的人"。
2. rounders:孩子们围成圆形进行的一种游戏。
3. mill around:四处乱转。
4. put off:搪塞,敷衍。
5. to spell sth. out:将……解释清楚。
6. telling-off:责骂。tell sb. off:责骂某人。
7. to stand a chance:碰运气。
8. set off:出发;点燃;引起。
9. word got round:消息传开了。
10. lose one's marbles:丧失理智。
11. take in:吸收;接受。
12. pushed the other stuff into the background:把其他的事情往后放放。
13. smuggle: v. 走私;偷运;偷带。
14. contortions:扭曲,弯曲。
15. go through all the nuts and bolts:事无巨细,十分详尽。

作品导读

《别让我走》是石黑一雄的第六部小说,甫一问世就受到极大的关注,并在 2010 年被搬上银幕。小说以第一人称叙述者凯西·H 的倒叙展开,讲述了凯西与朋友们在名叫黑尔舍姆的寄宿学校度过的生活。表面上,这所学校中的孩子过着与其他寄宿学校的孩子相似的生活,他们需要学习各种课程,参加各种活动和游戏。实际上,这些孩子并不是普通人,而是

克隆人。他们没有父母,每个人的姓氏只是一个英文字母,这个字母可能是克隆原型姓氏的缩写,或者只是个代号。他们之所以被创造出来,只是为了能够在成年以后为他们的原型提供器官。也就是说,黑尔舍姆如同圈养动物的农场,这些孩子则是其中的牺畜,他们被精心照料、抚育长大,就是为了将来被屠宰的一天。

所选章节的内容是凯西回忆童年时黑尔舍姆的一位年轻教师露西小姐如何向孩子们揭示了他们的命运。为了让学生长大之后心甘情愿地捐献自己的器官,黑尔舍姆的大多数教师都处心积虑地隐瞒事实,令他们以为自己的人生与正常孩子的人生并无差别。然而,露西小姐是一位有正义感的教师,在听到学生对未来的憧憬和遐想之后,她勇敢地选择揭示他们即将面对的真正未来:黑尔舍姆的克隆人不可能到美国去,不可能成为电影演员,连在超市里工作这样卑微的愿望也不可能实现。露西小姐尖锐地指出:你们是为着一个目的被带到这个世界上来的,你们所有人的未来早已被决定。(You were brought into this world for a purpose, and your futures, all of them, have been decided.)

在科幻小说的表皮之下,《别让我走》体现着对伦理道德的深刻思索。1996 年,以伊恩·威尔穆特(Ian Wilmut)为首的英国科学家创造出世界上第一头克隆羊。自此以后,克隆技术就一直处于伦理道德大讨论的风口浪尖。从动物伦理的角度考察,反对克隆与反对虐待动物一样,皆源自深沉的同理心(empathy),即我们能否将其他的有生命体视作与我们自身拥有同样权利的造物。早在 17 世纪,法国思想家卢梭就在其名著《论人类不平等的起源和基础》一书的序言中阐述过动物权利的概念,他认为动物尽管"缺少智力和自由",但是"它们也有知觉",同样应该享有自然赋予的权利。现代动物权利主义者认为,动物应该被人同等对待,而不仅仅被当作人类的财产或工具。所有(或者至少某些)动物应当享有支配自己生活的权利;动物应当享有一定的精神上的权利;动物的基本权利应当受法律保障。

作为动物当中最为特殊的种群,人在被克隆之后的命运尤其值得关注。尽管这并未成为现实,但是对克隆人引发的伦理问题的思考从未停止过:人类是否有权力制造自身的复制品?如果克隆人存在的理由仅仅是为正常人提供器官、延续生命,那么他们的情感和思想应当如何被对待?像小说中的露西小姐一样,人类会面临不知是否应当令克隆人知晓他们命运的两难处境。

值得注意的是,石黑一雄本人并不愿意读者将这部小说单纯地视作与克隆技术有关的科幻小说,而是认为小说实际上揭示了人类的命运和人性的脆弱。在某种意义上,露西小姐的那一番话并不仅仅针对克隆人,而且适用于现代社会中的每一个普通人——尽管你我对未来充满遐想,我们的美好愿望就一定能够实现吗?我们的未来是否也早已被决定呢?这是另一个阅读该小说的视角。

1. Why was Kathy (the narrator) feeling unusual when she saw Miss Lucy?
2. Do you think it is right for Miss Lucy to tell the students the truth about their lives?
3. Why did the students feel "pretty relieved" when Miss Lucy turned her look over to

the playfield again?

4. The advocates for Cloning Technology believe that it can help people who have serious damages in their vital organs enjoy a much better-off life. Do you think this is a rightful reason for researches on human cloning?

5. What ethical problems can you think of if human beings can be cloned?

6. Would you like to have a clone of yourself?

推荐阅读

Marks, Peter, Jennifer A. Wagner-Lawlor and Fátima Vieria. Eds. *The Palgrave Handbook of Utopian and Dystopian Literatures*. Palgrave Macmillan, 2022.

Borkfelt, Sune and Matthias Stephan. Eds. *Literary Animal Studies and the Climate Crisis*. Palgrave Macmillan, 2022.

Liebermann, Yvonne, Judith Rahn *Nonhuman Agencies in the Twenty-First-Century Anglophone Novel*. Palgrave Macmillan, 2021.

Curry, Patrick. *Ecological Ethics*. Polity Press, 2006.

Goodale, Greg and Jason Edward Black, eds. *Arguments about Animal Ethics*. Lexington Books, 2010.

Ryan, Thomas. *Animals and Social Work: A Moral Introduction*. Palgrave Macmillan, 2011.

彼得·辛格:《动物权利与人类义务》,曾建平、代峰译,北京大学出版社,2010年。

戴维·德格拉齐亚:《动物权利》,杨通进译,外语教学与研究出版社,2007年。

汤姆·雷根:《动物权利研究》,李曦译,北京大学出版社,2010年。

杰夫·范德米尔(Jeff VanderMeer)

【作者简介】

杰夫·范德米尔(1968—)是21世纪美国南方著名作家,以扣人心弦的生态小说著作为人熟知。环境问题常常成为范德米尔作品的关键主题和故事情节,他的作品把科幻、奇特、黑色、恐怖、惊悚与超自然等交织在一起,直面当前人类社会的严重问题,比如气候变化、生物技术、恐怖主义、大规模灭绝、全球性灾难以及科学的拯救和破坏等。

21世纪以来,范德米尔创作了多部以环境危机为背景的"新怪谭"小说(New Weird),如《芬奇》(Finch,2009)、"遗落的南境"三部曲(The Southern Reach Trilogy,2014,包括《湮灭》(Annihilation)、《当权者》(Authority)和《接纳》Acceptance)、《异形博恩》(Borne,2017)、《奇异鸟》(The Strange Bird,2017)、《蜂鸟蝾螈》(Hummingbird Salamander,2021)等。其中《湮灭》荣获科幻文学界重要奖项"星云奖"(Nebula Award)。《纽约客》将这部作品誉为"新怪谭"小说文类的代表作,并称范德米尔为美国当代的"怪谭梭罗"(the weird Thoreau)。

"新怪谭"小说以真实复杂的现实世界为原型,被定义为是一种"融合了幻想、恐怖和科幻小说"特征的文学体裁。该小说描述的世界并不代表一个既定的现实,然而,这些梦幻的领域让读者能够在新的视角下理解人类的思想和历史,将梦幻、边界、气候变化等在面对压倒性证据时的内在非理性而联系起来。范德米尔的"新怪谭"小说所创造的梦幻世界是非人类中心的,实现了一个超越人类社会的可能世界,使地球不仅适合人类的生存,而且适合任何生命的居住。无法解释的事件和梦幻般的物质性贯穿于范德米尔的"新怪谭"小说中,这也是他作品的重要艺术内涵。

作为"新怪谭"小说代表作,《湮灭》主要讲述了四名女性科学家(包括一名生物学家、一名人类学家、一名勘测员和一名心理学家)组成的勘探队深入南部国境边界一处无人区考察的故事。该地区环境若干年前遭到污染后发生变异,具有一种强大的超自然致变因素,能导致生物形态的改变,进而形成一处具有明显后自然特征的"X区域"。小说未明确X区域的具体位置,但从"南部国境"、毗邻海岸、多沼泽河流等文本细节可以推测,X区域大致位于美国南部国境边界。

从第一人称叙事者生物学家的零星讲述看,此处发生了类似生化污染的"特殊事件",政府的解释是由于军事科研实验而导致的局部环境灾变。小说中含糊其词的表述若隐若现地指向了一个环境危机现实:科技公司和权力精英往往是生化类环境污染的罪魁祸首。这些彼此关联的因素使得该小说既可以被理解为作家对全球性生态危机的回应,也可以理解为对美国南方地域环境污染现实的批判。在小说所呈现的后自然世界中,不但华兹华斯笔下可以疗愈人类心灵的自然无处可觅,而且自然在以人类想象不到或者更为恐怖的方式侵袭人类身体；处于后自然世界的人类最终的"湮灭"也是最强有力的环境警示：滥用科技对人类而言无异于自取灭亡、自掘坟墓。

Annihilation (excerpt)

The morning after we discovered the tower we rose early, ate our breakfast, and doused[1] our fire. There was a crisp chill to the air common for the season. The surveyor broke open the weapons stash and gave us each a handgun. She herself continued to hold on to the assault rifle; it had the added benefit of a flashlight under the barrel. We had not expected to have to open that particular container so soon, and although none of us protested, I felt a new tension between us. We knew that members of the second expedition to Area X had committed suicide by gunshot and members of the third had shot each other. Not until several subsequent expeditions had suffered zero casualties had our superiors issued firearms again. We were the twelfth expedition.

So we returned to the tower, all four of us. Sunlight came down dappled[2] through the moss and leaves, created archipelagos[3] of light on the flat surface of the entrance. It remained unremarkable, inert, in no way ominous … and yet it took an act of will to stand there, staring at the entry point. I noticed the anthropologist checking her black box, was relieved to see it did not display a glowing red light. If it had, we would have had to abort our exploration, move on to other things. I did not want that, despite the touch of fear.

"How deep do you think it goes down?" the anthropologist asked.

"Remember that we are to put our faith in your measurements," the psychologist answered, with a slight frown. "The measurements do not lie. This structure is 61.4 feet in diameter. It is raised 7.9 inches from the ground. The stairwell appears to have been positioned at or close to due north, which may tell us something about its creation, eventually. It is made of stone and coquina, not of metal or of bricks. These are facts. That it wasn't on the maps means only that a storm may have uncovered the entrance."

I found the psychologist's faith in measurements and her rationalization for the tower's absence from maps oddly…endearing? Perhaps she meant merely to reassure us, but I would like to believe she was trying to reassure herself. Her position, to lead and possibly to know more than us, must have been difficult and lonely.

"I hope it's only about six feet deep so we can continue mapping," the surveyor said, trying to be lighthearted, but then she, and we, all recognized the term "six feet under" ghosting through her syntax and a silence settled over us.

"I want you to know that I cannot stop thinking of it as a tower," I confessed. "I can't see it as a tunnel." It seemed important to make the distinction before our descent, even if it influenced their evaluation of my mental state. I saw a tower, plunging into the ground. The thought that we stood at its summit made me a little dizzy.

All three stared at me then, as if I were the strange cry at dusk, and after a moment the psychologist said, grudgingly, "If that helps make you more comfortable, then I don't see the harm."

A silence came over us again, there under the canopy[4] of trees. A beetle spiraled up toward the branches, trailing dust motes. I think we all realized that only now had we truly entered Area X.

"I'll go first and see what's down there," the surveyor said, finally, and we were happy to defer to her.

The initial stairwell curved steeply downward and the steps were narrow, so the surveyor would have to back her way into the tower. We used sticks to clear the spiderwebs as she lowered herself into position on the stairwell. She teetered[5] there, weapon slung across her back, looking up at us. She had tied her hair back and it made the lines of her face seem tight and drawn. Was this the moment when we were supposed to stop her? To come up with some other plan? If so, none of us had the nerve.

With a strange smirk[6], almost as if judging us, the surveyor descended until we could only see her face framed in the gloom below, and then not even that. She left an empty space that was shocking to me, as if the reverse had actually happened: as if a face had suddenly floated into view out of the darkness. I gasped, which drew a stare from the psychologist. The anthropologist was too busy staring down into the stairwell to notice any of it.

"Is everything okay?" the psychologist called out to the surveyor. Everything had been fine just a second before. Why would anything be different now?

The surveyor made a sharp grunt in answer, as if agreeing with me. For a few moments more, we could still hear the surveyor struggling on those short steps. Then came silence, and then another movement, at a different rhythm, which for a terrifying moment seemed like it might come from a second source.

But then the surveyor called up to us. "Clear to this level!" This level. Something within me thrilled to the fact that my vision of a tower was not yet disproven.

That was the signal for me to descend with the anthropologist, while the psychologist stood watch. "Time to go," the psychologist said, as perfunctorily as if we were in school and a class was letting out.

An emotion that I could not quite identify surged through me, and for a moment I saw dark spots in my field of vision. I followed the anthropologist so eagerly down through the remains of webs and the embalmed husks of insects into the cool brackishness of that place that I almost tripped her. My last view of the world above: the psychologist peering down at me with a slight frown, and behind her the trees, the blue of the sky almost blinding against the darkness of the sides of the stairwell.

Below, shadows spread across the walls. The temperature dropped and sound became muffled, the soft steps absorbing our tread. Approximately twenty feet beneath the surface, the structure opened out into a lower level. The ceiling was about eight feet high, which meant a good twelve feet of stone lay above us. The flashlight of the surveyor's assault rifle illuminated the space, but she was faced away from us, surveying the walls, which were an off-white and devoid of any adornment. A few cracks indicated either the passage of time or some sudden stressor. The level appeared to be the same circumference as the exposed top, which again supported the idea of a single solid structure buried in the earth.

"It goes farther," the surveyor said, and pointed with her rifle to the far corner, directly opposite the opening where we had come out onto that level. A rounded archway stood there, and a darkness that suggested downward steps. A tower, which made this level not so much a floor as a landing or part of the turret. She started to walk toward the archway while I was still engrossed in examining the walls with my flashlight. Their very blankness mesmerized[7] me. I tried to imagine the builder of this place but could not.

I thought again of the silhouette of the lighthouse, as I had seen it during the late afternoon of our first day at base camp. We assumed that the structure in question was a lighthouse because the map showed a lighthouse at that location and becauseeveryone immediately recognized what a lighthouse *should* look like. In fact, the surveyor and anthropologist had both expressed a kind of *relief* when they had seen the lighthouse. Its appearance on both the map and in reality reassured them, anchored them. Being familiar with its function further reassured them.

With the tower, we knew none of these things. We could not intuit its full outline. We had no sense of its purpose. And now that we had begun to descend into it, the tower*still* failed to reveal any hint of these things. The psychologist might recite the measurements of the "top" of the tower, but those numbers meant nothing, had no wider context. Without context, clinging to those numbers was a form of madness.

"There is a regularity to the circle, seen from the inside walls, that suggests precision in the creation of the building," the anthropologist said. *The building*. Already she had begun to abandon the idea of it being a tunnel.

All of my thoughts came spilling out of my mouth, some final discharge from the state that had overtaken me above. "But what is its *purpose*? And is it believable that it would not be on the maps? Could one of the prior expeditions have built it and hidden it?" I asked all of this and more, not expecting an answer. Even though no threat had revealed itself, it seemed important to eliminate any possible moment of silence. As if somehow the blankness of the walls fed off of silence, and that something might appear in the spaces between our words if we were not careful. Had I expressed this anxiety to the psychologist, she would have been worried, I know. But I was more attuned to solitude than any of us, and I would have characterized that place in that moment of our exploration as watchful.

A gasp from the surveyor cut me off in mid-question, no doubt much to the anthropologist's relief.

"Look!" the surveyor said, trailing her flashlight down into the archway. We hurried over and stared past her, adding our own illumination.

A stairway did indeed lead down, this time at a gentle curve with much broader steps, but still made of the same materials. At about shoulder height, perhaps five feet high, clinging to the inner wall of the tower, I saw what I first took to be dimly sparkling green vines progressing down into the darkness. I had a sudden absurd memory of the floral wallpaper treatment that had lined the bathroom of my house when I had shared it with my husband. Then, as I stared, the "vines" resolved further, and I saw that they were words, in cursive, the letters raised about six inches off the wall.

"Hold the light," I said, and pushed past them down the first few steps. Blood was rushing through my head again, a roaring confusion in my ears. It was an act of supreme control to walk those few paces. I couldn't tell you what impulse drove me, except that I was the biologist and this looked oddly organic. If the linguist had been there, perhaps I would have deferred to her.

"Don't touch it, whatever it is," the anthropologist warned.

I nodded, but I was too enthralled with the discovery. If I'd had the impulse to touch the words on the wall, I would not have been able to stop myself.

As I came close, did it surprise me that I could understand the language the words were written in? Yes. Did it fill me with a kind of elation and dread intertwined? Yes. I tried to suppress the thousand new questions rising up inside of me. In as calm a voice as I could manage, aware of the importance of that moment, I read from the beginning, aloud: *"Where lies the strangling fruit that came from the hand of the sinner I shall bring forth the seeds of the dead to share with the worms that..."*

Then the darkness took it.

"Words? Words?" the anthropologist said.

Yes, words.

"What are they made of?" the surveyor asked. Did they need to be made of anything?

The illumination cast on the continuing sentence quavered and shook. *Where lies the strangling fruit* became bathed in shadow and in light, as if a battle raged for its meaning.

"Give me a moment. I need to get closer." Did I? Yes, I needed to get closer.

What are they made of?

I hadn't even thought of this, though I should have; I was still trying to parse the lingual meaning, had not transitioned to the idea of taking a physical sample. But what relief at the question! Because it helped me fight the compulsion to keep reading, to descend into the greater darkness and keep descending until I had read all there was to read. Already those initial phrases were infiltrating my mind in unexpected ways, finding fertile ground.

So I stepped closer, peered at *Where lies the strangling fruit*. I saw that the letters, connected by their cursive script, were made from what would have looked to the layperson like rich green fernlike moss but in fact was probably a type of fungi or other eukaryotic organism. The curling filaments[8] were all packed very close together and rising out from the wall. A loamy[9] smell came from the words along with an underlying hint of rotting honey. This miniature forest *swayed*, almost imperceptibly, like sea grass in a gentle ocean current.

Other things existed in this miniature ecosystem. Half-hidden by the green filaments, most of these creatures were translucent and shaped like tiny hands embedded by the base of the palm. Golden nodules capped the fingers on these "hands." I leaned in closer, like a fool, like someone who had not had months of survival training or ever studied biology. Someone tricked into thinking that words should be read.

I was unlucky—or was I lucky? Triggered by a disturbance in the flow of air, a nodule in the W chose that moment to burst open and a tiny spray of golden spores[10] spewed out. I pulled back, but I thought I had felt something enter my nose, experienced a pinprick[11] of escalation in the smell of rotting honey.

Unnerved, I stepped back even farther, borrowing some of the surveyor's best curses, but only in my head. My natural instinct was always for concealment. Already I was imagining the psychologist's reaction to my contamination, if revealed to the group.

"Some sort of fungi," I said finally, taking a deep breath so I could control my voice. "The letters are made from fruiting bodies." Who knew if it were actually true? It was just the closest thing to an answer.

My voice must have seemed calmer than my actual thoughts because there was no hesitation in their response. No hint in their tone of having seen the spores erupt into my face. I had been so close. The spores had been so tiny, so insignificant. *I shall bring forth the seeds of the dead.*

"Words? Made of fungi?" the surveyor said, stupidly echoing me.

"There is no recorded human language that uses this method of writing," the anthropologist said. "Is there any animal that communicates in this way?"

I had to laugh. "No, there is no animal that communicates in this way." Or, if there were, I could not recall its name, and never did later, either.

"Are you joking? This is a joke, right?" the surveyor said. She looked poised to come down and prove me wrong, but didn't move from her position.

"Fruiting bodies," I replied, almost as if in a trance. "Forming words."

A calm had settled over me. A competing sensation, as if I couldn't breathe, or didn't want to, was clearly psychological not physiological. I had noticed no physicalchanges, and on some level it didn't matter. I knew it was unlikely we had an antidote to something so unknown waiting back at the camp.

More than anything, the information I was trying to process immobilized me. The words were composed of symbiotic fruiting bodies from a species unknown to me. Second, the dusting of spores on the words meant that the farther down into the tower we explored, the more the air would be full of potential contaminants. Was there any reason to relay this information to the others when it would only alarm them? No, I decided, perhaps selfishly. It was more important to make sure they were not directly exposed until we could come back with the proper equipment. Any other evaluation depended on environmental and biological factors about which I was increasingly convinced I had inadequate data.

I came back up the stairs to the landing. The surveyor and the anthropologist looked expectant, as if I could tell them more. The anthropologist in particular was on edge; her gaze couldn't alight on any one thing but kept moving and moving. Perhaps I could have fabricated information that would have stopped that incessant search. But what could I tell them about the words on the wall except that they were either impossible or insane, or both? I would have preferred the words be written in an *unknown* language; this would have presented less of a mystery for us to solve, in a way.

"We should go back up," I said. It was not that I recommended this as the best course of action but because I wanted to limit their exposure to the spores until I could see what long-term effects they might have on me. I also knew if I stayed there much longer I might experience a compulsion to go back down the stairs to continue reading the words, and they would have to physically restrain me, and I did not know what I would do then.

There was no argument from the other two. But as we climbed back up, I had a moment of vertigo[12] despite being in such an enclosed space, a kind of panic for a moment, in which the walls suddenly had a fleshy aspect to them, as if we traveled inside of the gullet[13] of a beast.

注释

1. douse:浇灭(火);熄(灯);往……上泼水。
2. dapple:使(某物)有斑点。
3. archipelagos:群岛,列岛;群岛周围的海。
4. canopy:天篷,遮篷,罩盖。
5. teeter:摇晃;摇摇欲坠;踉跄。
6. smirk:假笑;傻笑,得意的笑。
7. mesmerize:迷住;吸引。
8. filament:(电灯泡的)灯丝;细丝;丝状物。
9. loamy:(含丰富植物腐质、沙土或黏土量适宜的)壤土的;肥沃的。
10. spore:孢子。
11. pinprick:(光等的)点;小孔,针孔;烦心的小事。
12. vertigo:眩晕;(从高处俯视时感到的)头晕目眩。
13. gullet:食管,食道。

作品导读

选读部分讲述了生物学家、人类学家、勘测员和心理学家出发去 X 区域,他们是两年多来第一支前往那里的探险队。这个小组的成员都是女性,心理学家是队长。在 X 区域的第四天,研究小组发现了生物学家称之为"塔"的东西。塔的直径约为 60 英尺,从地面升起仅约 8 英寸。塔的最北端有处入口,露出一个向下的螺旋楼梯,蜿蜒而入地下的黑暗中。

发现塔后的第二天早上,小组成员很早就起床了。勘测员给了她们每人一把手枪,她自己则拿着突击步枪。拿着枪,生物学家感到一种新的紧张。第二支探险队的成员自杀了,第三支探险队成员相互开枪。他们是第 12 支探险队。她们检查了塔楼的结构。心理学家评论了这座塔的不同尺寸:高度、直径和建筑材料等。她想知道是否有一场暴风雨把入口掀开了,这就是为什么之前它没有出现在地图上。生物学家重申,她认为这座建筑应是一座塔,而不是隧道,其他人勉强接受她的观点。勘测员下去查看,在短台阶上挣扎。生物学家和人类学家跟着勘测员,心理学家站在最上面观看。楼梯间阴凉、多尘、微湿。在地面以下 20 英尺处,这座建筑向较低的一层敞开,有一个 8 英尺高的天花板和一堵灰白色墙壁。

勘探中,生物学家对周围异常的"寂静"感到很不舒服,她询问了很多关于塔的潜在起源和用途等问题,希望能避开这种寂静。在第二个楼梯处,生物学家观察沿着左墙发光的绿色藤蔓。藤蔓实际上看起来像绿苔藓或真菌,紧密地拥挤在一起,藤蔓上写着一段话。当生物学家靠近时,藤蔓上的一个瘤节吐出了金色的孢子,这些孢子进入了生物学家的鼻孔里。生物学家试图保持冷静,但她担心自己可能感染了什么。她还意识到,她探索得越远,空气中潜在的污染物就越多。她决定不告诉其他人任何事情,并解释说她们应该回去,希望防止她们也感染上这种东西。当她们都爬上楼梯时,生物学家有点惊慌失措,认为墙壁有了"肉质的"一面,就像他们在"野兽的喉咙"里爬行一样。

该小说的叙述者是一位生物学家,她将神秘的 X 区域描述为"原始荒野"。相比之下,人类居住的世界(X 区域边界外)已经被破坏了。这位生物学家的工作和生活经历告诉她,大自然实际上比人类更强大,X 区域不断向外扩张,这似乎是人类的不祥征兆。就在她们探测塔楼时,生物学家吸入了孢子,这些孢子开始影响她的大脑和身体,增强了她的感官,使她对催眠有了免疫力。这就确定了 X 区域的大自然是拥有着强大的力量来改变人类的。X 区域也在试图侵占人类居住的领土,因为其边界正在向外扩展,也似乎并不打算与人类共存,因为它的环境对人类入侵有很多防御。

熟知了这些,生物学家认为,在 X 区域生存下来的唯一方法不是击败它,而是成为它的一部分。以前的许多探险队都依赖灯塔(人类文明的象征)来确保安全,但这是一种"幻觉",人类文明无法保障任何人的安全。从这一点上看,为了在 X 区域生存,必须融入其中。换句话说,为了生存,生物学家必须成为 X 区域的一部分。孢子继续生长,并占据了生物学家身体的其余部分,她称之为在她体内蔓延的"光亮"。小说结尾,生物学家没有选择回家,而是留在了野外,成为了 X 区域的一部分。作为探险队中唯一能在 X 区域幸存下来的人,生物学家清楚知道:只有那些服从大自然的人才能在那里幸存下来,与大自然的力量相比,人类更加缺乏控制力,也更加脆弱。小说在消解人类中心地位的同时,传递了宇宙万物相互依存、混溶共生的生态理念,进而强化了 21 世纪人与自然生命共同体的核心内涵。

1. As far as "New Weird" is concerned, what are the most impressive features of this writing genre after your reading?

2. How do you understand this sentence, "the walls suddenly had a fleshy aspect to them, as if we traveled inside of the gullet of a beast"?

3. How does the narrative style, told from the perspective of the biologist, serve to augment the novel's effectiveness?

推荐阅读

Clapp, Jeffrey Michael. "Jeff VanderMeer, or the novel trapped in the open world." *Critique: Studies in Contemporary Fiction*, 2020(4).

Clark, Timothy. *The Value of Ecocriticism*. Cambridge University Press, 2019.

Ghosh, Amitav. *The Great Derangement*. University of Chicago Press, 2016.

Lafontaine, Tania. *Science Fiction Theory and Ecocriticism: Environments and Nature in Eco-dystopian and Post-apocalyptic Novels*. Lap Lambert Academic Publishing, 2016.

Morton, Timothy. *Being Ecological*. The MIT Press, 2018.

Prendergast, Finola Anne. "Revising Nonhuman Ethics in Jeff VanderMeer's *Annihilation*." *Contemporary Literature*, 2017(3).

Robertson, Benjamin. *None of This Is Normal: The Fiction of Jeff VanderMeer*. University of Minnesota Press, 2018.

VanderMeer, Jeff. *Annihilation*. Farrar, Straus and Giroux, 2014.

杰夫·范德米尔:《遗落的南境 1:湮灭》,胡绍晏译,天地出版社,2015。

张鲁宁、韩启群:《美国南方'新怪谭'小说〈湮灭〉的后自然书写》,《山东外语教学》,2021(06)。

张鲁宁:《作为环境危机叙事典范的"新怪谭"科幻小说——以〈湮灭〉为例》,《西安外国语大学学报》,2022(03)。

科马克·麦卡锡(Cormac McCarthy)

【作者简介】

科马克·麦卡锡(1933—2023)是当代美国最有声望的小说家和剧作家之一。文学评论家哈罗德·布鲁姆把他和托马斯·品钦、唐·德里罗、菲利普·罗斯一起列为美国当代最重要的四大小说家。麦卡锡是一位多产作家,也是各大文学奖项的宠儿。小说《血色子午线》(Blood Meridian or The Evening Redness in the West, 1985)被《时代》杂志列为1923年至2005年间出版的100本最佳书籍之一,被《纽约时报》评为美国过去25年出版的最佳小说;小说《天下骏马》(All the Pretty Horses, 1992)荣获1992年"美国国家图书奖"和"美国评论界图书奖"两大奖项;小说《路》(The Road, 2006)获得2007年的"普利策文学奖"。他的另一部小说《老无所依》(No Country for Old Men, 2005)于2007年被改编成同名电影,在不同类别中共获得4项奥斯卡奖。他的其他几部小说也被改编成电影,受到广泛好评。

麦卡锡的小说创作大致可分为三个阶段。第一阶段是"南方小说",分别是《看果园的人》(The Orchard Keeper, 1965)、《外部黑暗》(Outer Dark, 1968)、《上帝之子》(Child of God, 1974)和《萨特里》(Suttree, 1979)。这一阶段的小说题材惊悚,语言晦涩,带有浓重的地方色彩。20世纪80年代,麦卡锡把视线转移到了美国西南部边境,以《血色子午线》为始又创作了"边境三部曲",包括《天下骏马》《穿越》(The Crossing, 1994)和《平原上的城市》(Cities of the Plain, 1998)。2005年,麦卡锡再次以美国西部边境为背景,创作了《老无所依》。2006年出版的《路》是他创作的另一次成功转型,该小说属于创作的第三阶段,即"后启示录小说"阶段。

麦卡锡的小说以复杂的风格而闻名,受到但丁、马克·吐温、威廉·福克纳、约瑟夫·康拉德、塞缪尔·贝克特、拉尔夫·沃尔多·爱默生、沃尔特·惠特曼、詹姆斯·乔伊斯、赫尔曼·梅尔维尔、约翰·斯坦贝克等著名作家的影响。麦卡锡的小说较少乐观的主题,仿佛不愿用对好事的宣扬掩盖被迫面对人性之恶的深刻。他的小说中有很多对穷人、无家可归者、被剥夺权利的人、罪犯、堕落和被抛弃者的刻画。但即便是在最坏的情况下,其人物刻画也仍有人性的光辉。

小说《路》是麦卡锡最受欢迎的作品之一,被称为有史以来最伟大的气候变化作品之一。小说的主人公是一对父子,但作品从来没有给出具体名字。情节始于刚刚遭遇过浩劫的一片废墟。所有的生命在大火中化为灰烬,就连阳光也被遮蔽。为了找寻更好的栖居地,父子俩沿着美国东南部海岸继续向南,仅有两个背包和一把手枪。他们在黑暗中艰难跋涉,穿过了山脉、暴风雪、种植园、防空洞,在频繁遭遇寒冷、危险和饥饿威胁之后,终于到达了目的地,却失望地发现这里一样的灰暗和死气沉沉。更糟的是,他们所有的用品在外出探索时被盗。当他们打算离开，再次出发向南时，男人被箭射中，在重伤中继续跋行，直至身亡。男孩与父亲的尸体呆了三天后继续独自出发，路上偶遇一家"好人"——一男一女、一个小男孩和一个小女孩。男孩接受邀请，加入了他们的家庭，一起继续出发。小说以抒情的方式回忆曾经生活中的山间溪流和溪鳟结尾。

作为对当今不断发生的气候危机的回应，该小说以想象的方式描述了人类失去社会、伦理和物质支持时的生活，以及在此生存条件下人类道德的沦丧与国家秩序的崩溃，凸显了气候变化对人类生活的影响，批判了人类在环境恶化时的价值判断，并发出了警示：如果人类不惜一切代价追求技术进步，无视地球正在发生的气候变化，继续现有道路，未来将会不堪重负。

The Road (excerpt)

When he woke in the woods in the dark and the cold of thenight he'd reach out to touch the child sleeping beside him. Nights dark beyond darkness and the days more gray each one than what had gone before. Like the onset of some cold glaucoma[1] dimming away the world. His hand rose and fell softly with each precious breath. He pushed away the plastic tarpaulin and raised himself in the stinking[2] robes and blankets and looked toward the east for any light but there was none. In the dream from which he'd wakened he had wandered in a cave where the child led him by the hand. Their light playing over the wet flowstone walls. Like pilgrims in a fable swallowed up and lost among the inward parts of some granitic beast. Deep stone flues where the water dripped and sang. Tolling in the silence the minutes of the earth and the hours and the days of it and the years without cease. Until they stood in a great stone room where lay a black and ancient lake. And on the far shore a creature that raised its dripping mouth from the rimstone pool and stared into the light with eyes dead white and sightless as the eggs of spiders. It swung its head low over the water as if to take the scent of what it could not see. Crouching there pale and naked and translucent[3], its alabaster bones cast up in shadow on the rocks behind it. Its bowels, its beating heart. The brain that pulsed in a dull glass bell. It swung its head from side to side and then gave out a low moan and turned and lurched away and loped soundlessly into the dark.

With the first gray light he rose and left the boy sleeping and walked out to the road and squatted and studied the country to the south. Barren, silent, godless. He thought the month was October but he wasn't sure. He hadn't kept a calendar for years. They were moving south. There'd be no surviving another winter here.

When it was light enough to use thebinoculars he glassed the valley below. Everything paling away into the murk. The soft ash blowing in loose swirls over the blacktop. He studied what he could see. The segments of road down there among the dead trees. Looking for anything of color. Any movement. Any trace of standing smoke. He lowered the glasses and pulled down the cotton mask from his face and wiped his nose on the back of his wrist and then glassed the country again. Then he just sat there holding the binoculars and watching the ashen daylight congeal[4] over the land. He knew only that the child was his warrant. He said: If he is not the word of God God never spoke.

When he got back the boy was still asleep. He pulled the blue plastic tarp off of him and folded it and carried it out to the grocery cart and packed it and came back with their plates and some cornmeal cakes in a plastic bag and a plastic bottle of syrup. He spread the small tarp they used for a table on the ground and laid everything out and he took the pistol from his belt and laid it on the cloth and then he just sat watching the boy sleep. He'd pulled away his mask in the night and it was buried somewhere in the blankets. He watched the boy and he looked out through the trees toward the road. This was not a safe place. They could be seen from the road now it was day. The boy turned in the blankets. Then he opened his eyes. Hi, Papa, he said.

I'm right here.

I know.

An hour later they were on the road. He pushed the cart and both he and the boy carried knapsacks. In the knapsacks were essential things. In case they had to abandon the cart and make a run for it. Clamped[5] to the handle of the cart was a chrome motorcycle mirror that he used to watch the road behind them. He shifted the pack higher on his shoulders and looked out over the wasted country. The road was empty. Below in the little valley the still gray serpentine of a river. Motionless and precise. Along the shore a burden of dead reeds. Are you okay? he said. The boy nodded. Then they set out along the blacktop in the gun-metal light, shuffling[6] through the ash, each the other's world entire.

They crossed the river by an old concrete bridge and a few miles on they came upon a roadside gas station. They stood in the road and studied it. I think we should check it out, the man said. Take a look. The weeds they forded[7] fell to dust about them. They crossed the broken asphalt apron and found the tank for the pumps. The cap was gone and the man dropped to his elbows to smell the pipe but the odor of gas was only a rumor, faint and stale. He stood and looked over the building. The pumps standing with their hoses oddly still in place. The windows intact. The door to the service bay was open and he went in. A standing metal toolbox against one wall. He went through the drawers but there was nothing there that he could use. Good half-inch drive sockets. A ratchet. He stood looking around the garage. A metal barrel full of trash. He went into the office. Dust and ash everywhere. The boy stood in the door. A metal desk, a cashregister. Some old automotive manuals, swollen and sodden. The linoleum was stained and curling from the leaking roof. He crossed to the desk and stood there. Then he picked up the phone and dialed the number of his father's house in that long ago. The boy watched him. What are you doing? he said.

A quarter mile down the road he stopped and looked back. We're not thinking, he said. We have to go back. He pushed the cart off the road and tilted it over where it could not be seen and they left their packs and went back to the station. In the service bay he dragged out the steeltrashdrum and tipped it over and pawed out all the quart plastic oilbottles. Then they sat in the floor decanting[8] them of their dregs one by one, leaving the bottles to stand upside down draining into a pan until at the end they had almost a half quart of motor oil. He screwed down the plastic cap and wiped the bottle off with a rag and hefted it in his hand. Oil for their little slutlamp to light the long gray dusks, the long gray dawns. You can read me a story, the boy said. Cant you, Papa? Yes, he said. I can.

On the far side of the river valley the road passed through a stark black burn[9]. Charred[10] and limbless trunks of trees stretching away on every side. Ash moving over the road and the sagging hands of blind wire strung from the blackened lightpoles whining[11] thinly in the wind. A burned house in a clearing and beyond that a reach of meadow-lands stark and gray and a raw red mudbank where a roadworks lay abandoned. Farther along were billboards advertising motels. Everything as it once had been save[12] faded and weathered. At the top of the hill they stood in the cold and the wind, getting their breath. He looked at the boy. I'm all right, the boy said. The man put his hand on his shoulder and nodded toward the open country below them. He got the binoculars out of the cart and stood in the road and glassed the plain down there where the shape of a city stood in the grayness like a charcoal drawing sketched across the waste. Nothing to see. No smoke. Can I see? the boy said. Yes. Of course you can. The boy leaned on the cart and adjusted the wheel. What do you see? the man said. Nothing. He lowered the glasses. It's raining. Yes, the man said. I know.

They left the cart in a gully covered with the tarp and made their way up the slope through the dark poles of the standing trees to where he'd seen a running ledge of rock and they sat under the rock overhang and watched the gray sheets of rain blow across the valley. It was very cold. They sat huddled together wrapped each in a blanket over their coats and after a while the rain stopped and there was just the dripping in the woods.

When it had cleared they went down to the cart and pulled away the tarp and got their blankets and the things they would need for the night. They went back up the hill and made their camp in the dry dirt under the rocks and the man sat with his arms around the boy trying to warm him. Wrapped in the blankets, watching the nameless dark come to enshroud[13] them. The gray shape of the city vanished in the night's onset like an apparition and he lit the little lamp and set it back out of the wind. Then they walked out to the road and he took the boy's hand and they went to the top of the hill where the road crested and where they could see out over the darkening country to the south, standing there in the wind, wrapped in their blankets, watching for any sign of a fire or a lamp. There was nothing. The lamp in the rocks on the side of the hill was little more than a mote of light and after a while they walked back. Everything too wet to make a fire. They ate their poor meal cold and lay down in their bedding with the lamp between them. He'd brought the boy's book but the boy was too tired for reading. Can we leave the lamp on till I'm asleep? he said. Yes. Of course we can.

 注释

1. glaucoma：青光眼（导致视力下降的眼睛疾病）。
2. stinking：臭的，发恶臭的。
3. translucent：半透明的。
4. congeal：变稠；凝结。
5. clamp：夹紧，(用夹具)夹住；紧紧抓住。
6. shuffle：拖着脚走；(笨拙或尴尬地)把脚动来动去；坐立不安。
7. ford：涉过，驶过（浅水）。
8. decant：(把液体)）倒入，注入。
9. burn：小河，溪流。
10. char：烧焦；(使)烧黑。
11. whine：哭哭啼啼；哀鸣，惨叫。
12. save：除了，除……外。
13. enshroud：掩盖；遮蔽；笼罩。

 作品导读

　　该小说始于一片树林，一个已被毁灭的、毫无未来和希望的世界：大自然遭到毁灭，几乎没有其他生命存活。当男人和男孩沿着道路向南行进时，危险一直伴随。每天醒来，男人第一眼看到的一切均被笼罩在黑暗与灰色之中。在回忆中，男人想起自己曾梦见一只野兽，"眼瞳惨白如蜘蛛卵"。在这个无情的世界里，父子两人必须保持异常的谨慎。男人用双筒望远镜环顾四周，而他最常发现的风景却是："万物向晦暗隐没，轻柔的烟尘在柏油路上飘扬成松散的漩涡。他审视自己所见的一切。下方的大路被倒枯的树木隔得七零八落。试图寻找带色彩的事物、移动的事物、飘升的烟迹。"事实上，到处充满着沙土与烟尘，什么也看不到，什么也看不了，就连太阳也消失了，天空本身都似乎被抹去了意义。

　　从麦卡锡所描述的景观可以看出，旧的世界实际上已经失去，留下的只有褪色的记忆。这个后启示录似的新世界被证明是一个恐怖的故事，一个哥特式的噩梦。幽暗而凄凉的背景下，小说没有解释是什么烧毁了一切，是什么摧毁了文明。在这个严酷、孤独的世界里，男人和男孩只是沿着路向南旅行，试图逃避即将到来的冬天。小说开始时，整个背景死气沉沉、空空荡荡，而男人和男孩也只有彼此。慢慢地，小说揭示了更多细节——大多数生命实际上在几年前就被摧毁，男人和男孩为了生存已经被简化成一种极其原始的存在形式。男人拨打了他父亲(可能已经去世)的电话号码，但是他没有任何期待，只是沉迷于回忆更美好的过去。作为彼此"世界"的一部分，男人和男孩之间的信任程度非常高，这种艰难的处境使他们比正常的父子关系更加紧密。小说开始部分凸显的一个主题是"黑暗"。男人与男孩沿路旅行，在各种废弃建筑中探索。世界末日的火灾仍然在肆虐，一切都非常沉闷。小说家运用"像青光眼病发"这样夸张的比喻捕捉到黑暗的本质，男人在凄凉、死亡的包围中为了生存而努力。在森林中醒来的男人并不是出于与大自然交流的愿望，而是因为警惕可能的威胁。

小说从一开始就表现出碎片化的叙事方式,这呼应了他们旅途中所经历的各种没落、萧条与荒凉。麦卡锡在对话中不使用引号,对于一些缩略词也省略了撇号,而对标点符号等元素的省略也构成了一种独特的表达方式。在这个新的世界末日故事里,旧世界的残余不再存在,或者它们的数量非常有限,这是对资源稀缺性的隐喻,也是对生命能力有限性的隐喻,更衬托了男人与男孩生存希望的渺茫。由此,小说成功强化了读者对人类所造成的环境危机的关注力,并激起情感共鸣,唤起环保意识,以远离这样的未来的困境(警示人类规避未来环境风险)。

1. How is McCarthy able to make the postapocalyptic world of *The Road* seem so real and utterly terrifying? Which descriptive passages are especially vivid and visceral in their depiction of this blasted landscape?

2. Why do you think McCarthy has chosen not to give his characters names? How do the generic labels of "the man" and "the boy" affect the way in which readers relate to them?

3. Why is McCarthy's *The Road* the most important environmental book ever written?

推荐阅读

von Mossner, Alexa Weik. *Affective Ecologies: Empathy, Emotion, and Environmental Narrative*. Ohio State University Press, 2017.

Guillemin, Georg. *The Pastoral Vision of Cormac McCarthy*. Texas A & M University Press, 2004.

Hicks, Heather J. *The Post-Apocalyptic Novel in the Twenty-First Century*. Palgrave Macmillan, 2016.

McCarthy, Cormac. *The Road*. Vintage, 2006.

Frye, Steven. *The Cambridge Companion to Cormac McCarthy*. Cambridge University Press, 2013.

Edwards, Tim. "The end of the road: Pastoralism and the post-apocalyptic waste land of Cormac McCarthy's *The Road*." *The Cormac McCarthy Journal*, 2008(6).

Sanborn Ⅲ, Wallis R. *Animals in the Fiction of Cormac McCarthy*. McFarland, 2006.

陈爱华:"科马克·麦卡锡国内外研究评析",《山东外语教学》,2011(01)。

江宁康:"当代小说的叙事美学与经典建构——论 C.麦卡锡小说的审美特征及银幕再现",《当代外国文学》,2010(02)。

露易丝·格丽克(Louise Glück)

【作者简介】

露易丝·格丽克(1943—2023)是美国现代诗歌界最有才华、最有成就的诗人之一。2020 年,"因为她那无可辩驳的诗意般声音,用朴素之美使个人的存在变得普遍",格丽克被授予诺贝尔文学奖,成为第 16 位获此殊荣的女性作家。她也是美国主要文学奖的获得者,如普利策奖(*Pulitzer Prize*)、国家图书奖(*National Book Award*)等,并于 2003 年至 2004 年成为美国桂冠诗人。

格丽克是位多产的作家,已出版的诗集有:《头生子》(*Firstborn*,1968)、《沼泽地上的房屋》(*The House on Marshland*,1975)、《下降的形象》(*Descending Figure*,1980)、《阿喀琉斯的胜利》(*The Triumph of Achilles*,1985)、《阿勒山》(*Ararat*,1990)、《野鸢尾》(*The Wild Iris*,1992),合订本《最早的四本诗集》(*The First Four Books of Poems*,1995)、《草场》(*Meadow Lands*,1996)、《新生》(*Vita Nova*,1999)、《七个时期》(*The Seven Ages*,2001)、《阿弗尔诺》(*Averno*,2006)、《乡村生活》(*A Village Life*,2009),合订本《诗 1962—2012》(*Poems 1962—2012*,2012)、《忠贞而善良之晚》(*Faithful and Virtuous Night*,2014)。另外,还出版有两部诗歌随笔集:《证据和理论:关于诗的散文》(*Proofs and Theories: Essays on Poetry*,1994)和《美国原创:诗歌笔记》(*American Originality: Essays on Poetry*,2018)。

格丽克的诗歌经常利用神话、历史或自然作为主题和探索的视角,集中阐释创伤、欲望和自然与人的关系。诗人在敏锐观察的基础上,以自我的成长经历为出发点,深刻反思现代人的生存状态。她对身体、花朵等自然界中的意象甚是痴迷。在她的诗中,花朵长有嘴巴,风景见证人类的绝望,溪水歌唱永恒的失落,百合颂扬短暂的激情。当然,格丽克的诗歌最引人注目的特点是对死亡的恒久的意识。她常常用自然意象来证明结束就是开始,反之亦然,死亡也是一种重塑与再生。走进格丽克的诗歌世界,"悲伤"似乎扑面而来,然而,仅以"悲伤"定义她的诗歌是极为片面的,因为她的叙述者总是传递着这样信息:苦难不应使人类陷入绝望状态,人类面临的困境都是可以战胜的,隧道的尽头一定会有光明。

The Wild Iris[1]

At the end of my suffering
there was a door.

Hear me out: that which you call death
I remember.

Overhead, noises, branches of the pine shifting.
Then nothing. The weak sun

Flickered[2] over the dry surface.

It is terrible to survive
as consciousness
buried in the dark earth.

Then it was over: that which you fear, being
a soul and unable
to speak, ending abruptly[3], the stiff earth
bending a little. And what I took to be
birds darting[4] in low shrubs.

You who do not remember
passage from the other world
I tell you I could speak again: whatever
returns from oblivion[5] returns
to find a voice:

from the center of my life came
a great fountain, deep blue
shadows on azure[6] seawater.

 注释

1. iris：鸢尾属植物。
2. flicker：闪烁；忽隐忽现；摇曳。
3. abruptly：突然，忽然间。
4. dart：猛冲，突进。
5. oblivion：神志不清；湮没；遗忘；沉睡。
6. azure：天蓝色的，蔚蓝色的。

Snowdrops[1]

Do you know what I was, how I lived? You know
what despair is; then
winter should have meaning for you.

I did not expect to survive,
earth suppressing[2] me. I didn't expect
to waken again, to feel

in damp earth my body
able to respond again, remembering
after so long how to open again
in the cold light
of earliest spring—

afraid, yes, but among you again
crying yes risk joy

in the raw[3] wind of the new world.

注释

1. snowdrops:雪莲(一种初春开放的小白花)。
2. suppress:镇压,平定;压制。
3. raw:未经加工的;原始的;未煮的;自然状态的
。

作品导读

《野鸢尾》(*The Wild Iris*)是格丽克1992年出版的诗集,获得1993年普利策诗歌奖。这是一部由一个人、一朵花和一位神三位叙述者探讨他们矛盾思想和情感的诗集。在54个诗篇中,有18篇以花卉或以开花植物命名。野鸢尾是一种开着美丽花朵的植物,它在人类和自然界之间产生了一系列象征性的联系。野生鸢尾茁壮生长,逐渐枯萎,又重新播种,再开出美丽的花朵。拟人化的野生鸢尾叙述者似乎在解决死亡恐惧的问题。最终,它明白了死亡并不是生命的终结,因为它将在春天重新播种,并再次生长,死亡只会迎来新的生命。该诗集中剖析情感体验、身体反应和苦难历程的基础上,表现出一种终极的乐观,认为尽管面临种种苦难与挑战,人类还是有办法走出沼泽困境,迎来明媚曙光。以上节选的两首诗都是来自该诗集。

第一首诗《野鸢尾》是格丽克同名诗集的标题诗。诗中,她以精确的细节描写了逼真的自然场景,包括鸟儿在低矮的灌木丛中飞来飞去和埋在黑暗土地中的植物等。通过自然镜头的过滤,格丽克叙述了一朵花的死亡和复活:"当知觉/埋在黑暗的泥土里,/幸存也令人恐惧。"她写道:"你,如今不记得/从另一个世界到来的跋涉,/我告诉你我又能讲话了:一切/从遗忘中返回的,返回/去发现一个声音。"从一朵花的自我诉说,诗歌探讨了人类灵魂、重生、不朽以及地球上所有生命形式之间的相互关联等。尽管谈论的是一朵花,但诗歌对人类以及人类灵魂有着明显的暗示:我们注定要成为什么?生命是一个不断再生的循环吗?我们是天生美丽的吗?该诗描绘的是精神或情感上的重生,而不是肉体上的重生。

在第二首诗《雪莲》中,雪莲花讲述了它的生存状态:"我不期望存生,/大地抑制我。"它"害怕,是,但在你们当中再/喊是冒着喜悦的风险。"句中看似不连贯的语法反映了雪莲花纯

粹而丰富的情感;它不得不突破它的存在。地球可能很是荒凉,但雪莲花依然顽强存在。在诗的结尾,读者在新春中感受到了"新世界的原始的风"。在黑暗和寒冷的冬季之后,人们都需要早春。花儿开始在土壤中伸出它们的小脑袋,树木也开始苏醒过来。大自然迎接春天,庆祝季节的新能量,宣布冬天的结束,而雪莲花是最受欢迎的春花之一,也是季节变化的真正象征。该诗中,格丽克一开始带领读者走上了一条令人沮丧的"死亡"道路,但却在诗歌的终端重新连接了"生命"的希望。她用冬天后春天的到来表现死后生命的重生,记录了冬天后生命奇迹般的回归。

总的来看,在诗集《野鸢尾》中,通过对生与死的哲思,格丽克将人类与自然紧密相连,因为它们有着同样的生命结构与规律。这在自然生命的哲学意义上,宣扬了人与自然生命的相似性。其实,本质上来看,物质世界是在不断循环的,自然也从来不是一个固定的状态,而总是从一种东西变成另一种东西。世间万物都将经历从美好的盛放,到苦难的摧残,最终经历衰败,走向凋零。没有什么悲伤是巨大的,也没有什么行动是永恒的。然而,通过不同主体的视角转换,整个诗集强调了结束就是开始,死亡即走向重生,由此引导读者思考在生态视域下人与自然、人与人等之间多重相联的关系。

思考题

1. Why does Glück choose the wild iris as the speaker of *The Wild Iris*?
2. From the wild iris's experience, what can we learn about the process of life in the universe?
3. How do you understand the symbolic significance of a snowdrop flower in *Snowdrops*?
4. Rachel Carson says, "In nature, nothing exists alone." Based on your understanding of these two poems, what can nature teach us?

推荐阅读

Diehl, Joanne Feit. "An Interview with Louise Glück." *On Louise Glück: Change What You See*. Ed. Joanne Feit Diehl. University of Michigan Press, 2005.

Glück, Louise. *Poems 1962—2012*. Farrar, Straus and Giroux, 2012.

Gosmann, Uta. *Poetic Memory: The Forgotten Self in Plath, Howe, Hinsey, and Glück*. Fairleigh Dickinson University Press, 2012.

Harrison, DeSales. *The End of the Mind: The Edge of the Intelligible in Hardy, Stevens, Larking, Plath, and Glück*. Routledge, 2005.

Morris, Daniel. *The Poetry of Louise Glück: A Thematic Introduction*. University of Missouri Press, 2006.

Ryan, John Charles. *Plants in Contemporary Poetry: Ecocriticism and the Botanical Imagination*. Routledge, 2018.

包慧怡:"格丽克诗歌中的多声部'花园'叙事",《外国文学研究》,2021(01)。

柳向阳:"露易丝·格丽克的疼痛之诗",《世界文学》,2014(04)。

露易丝·格丽克:《月光的合金》,柳向阳译,上海人民出版社,2016年。

露易丝·格丽克:《直到世界反映了灵魂最深层的需要》,柳向阳、范静哗译,上海人民出版社,2016年。

熊辉:"露易丝·格丽克在中国的翻译与接受",《当代作家评论》,2021(03)。

第一版后记

这本《文学里的生态——英美生态文学赏读》从酝酿到成书历经近五年。在这些年中，2010年北京林业大学外语学院英语专业被教育部批准为"国家级特色专业建设点"，生态文学教学和研究被提上重要日程；2011年外语学院新增"生态文学"专业选修课；2012年英语系为全校开设"西方生态文学"选修课；2013年英语专业得到北京市支持中央在京高校共建项目的资助。这一切既为林大英语专业的发展提供了一个新的台阶，也为我们这本书的出现提供了契机。

在这些年之中，我们得到了很多的帮助。首先要感谢北京林业大学外语学院院长史宝辉教授。如果没有他的策划，本书不可能成形；如果没有他的鼎力支持，本书便没有编写和出版的资金来源。按照史宝辉教授自己的说法，他是位"杂家"。正是因为这个"杂"，他是我认识的学者中最开明的，虽然身为语言学领域的专家，但是他对文学的兴趣和对文学批评的敏锐感觉一直是与时俱进的。他不但是语言学领域的专家，而且对文学卓有兴趣，对文学批评有着敏锐的感觉。在全国大部分院校的英语专业都在削减文学课的形势下，他逆流而动，带领北京林业大学外语学院落实素质教育，不仅增加了英国文学、美国文学等必修课的课时，而且为学生新增了很多文学类选修课，其中就包括生态文学。也正是在他的倡议和鼓励下，我们的生态文学研究团队才得以成立。团队从这本书的选题开始，就经常跟史教授讨论，从最初的迷糊犹豫到后来的条理清晰，从确定选篇到联系出版社，我们的每一步都有他的支持，可以毫不夸张地说，正是他灵感的火花点亮了我们努力前行的小径。

感谢美国爱达荷大学（University of Idaho）文学与环境领域的专家斯科特·斯洛维克（Scott Slovic）教授。斯洛维克教授是生态文学领域成果卓著的研究者之一，是国际"文学与环境研究会"（The Association for the Study of Literature and Environment，简称 ASLE）创会会长，《文学与环境跨学科研究》的主编，也是中国学者和学生熟悉和喜欢的生态批评领域的学者之一。笔者在本书轮廓刚刚形成之际，很冒昧地给他发邮件，希望得到他的建议，很快便得到他热忱的答复。他发来自己计划出版的书稿目录供我们参考，为我们的选篇提出合理化建议，使我们少走了很多弯路。在本书即将完成之际，他欣然提笔为本书作序，是对这本书，也是对我们在生态文学领域进行研究的有力支持。

感谢北京林业大学科技处、教务处、中央高校基本科研业务费专项资金项目、教育部"国家级特色专业建设点"项目和北京市支持中央在京高校共建项目（英语专业建设项目）的资助，为本书的立项、研究、编写和出版提供了资金上的支持。北京林业大学是在生态文明、生态建设领域进行科学研究的领军高校之一。虽然学校的重点学科是林学、水土保持学、生物学、环境学等自然科学，但是学校对人文领域的研究一直给予了学术重视和资金支持，这是本书得以完成的坚实后盾。同时，学校在生态文明领域的其他成果也为我们对生态文学的研究提供了良好的支撑平台。

感谢本书选篇的各位原作者。虽然其中相当一部分作者已经作古，但是他们为我们在生态文学领域的研究所留下的丰厚遗产是永不磨灭的；还有一些作者是当代研究自然书写和环境、生态文学的新锐,他们的写作为我们打开了很多研究人与自然关系的新窗口,开拓了人类在研究与自然关系的基础上理解自身位置的新思路。我们联系到了大部分原作者或代理人,他们都欣然同意我们节选他们的作品供中国的学者和学生赏读,但是由于种种原因,有的作者实在未能取得联系,我们也希望借此机会让看到这本书的原作者能与我们尽早联系,以便商讨版权使用事宜。

感谢在生态文学领域进行研究的前辈和同仁。近几十年来,国内外生态研究风生水起,本书正是在借鉴了大量已有研究的基础上才得以完成的,但即便如此,也难免挂一漏万。笔者也借此机会希望学界同仁和使用本书的师生、读者不吝赐教,使我们在本领域的研究更上层楼。

感谢北大出版社的李颖女士,她对本书投入了极大的热情和精力,如果没有她的努力和付出,本书无法得以如期出版。

南宫梅芳

2015 年 3 月

于北京林业大学